# Point of Failure

*British Army Brigadiers in The British Expeditionary Force and North Western Expeditionary Force, 1940*

*A Study of Advancement and Promotion*

---

Wolverhampton Military Studies No.43

Philip McCarty

Helion & Company

Helion & Company Limited
Unit 8 Amherst Business Centre
Budbrooke Road
Warwick
CV34 5WE
England
Tel. 01926 499619
Email: info@helion.co.uk
Website: www.helion.co.uk
X (formerly Twitter): @Helionbooks
Facebook: @HelionBooks
Visit our blog at https://helionbooks.wordpress.com/

Published by Helion & Company 2024
Designed and typeset by Mach 3 Solutions (www.mach3solutions.co.uk)
Cover designed by Paul Hewitt, Battlefield Design (www.battlefield-design.co.uk)


ISBN: 978-1-804514-27-6

British Library Cataloguing-in-Publication Data.
A catalogue record for this book is available from the British Library.



For details of other military history titles published by Helion & Company Limited, contact the above address, or visit our website: http://www.helion.co.uk

We always welcome receiving book proposals from prospective authors.

This work is dedicated to three people who did not live to see it finished: my dear parents, John and Betty, and my maternal uncle, Ronald Cotton.

My parents taught me to read before I went to school and they and Ron, an autodidact, never made me feel that to have my head in a book was anything to be disdained. The arrival in the post, over 20 years after he had earned it, of Dad's medal for his service in Palestine after the Second World War, and Ron's service in Tunisia and Italy (where he was seriously wounded) lit the spark in me to study military history seriously. I can only hope that I have repaid the faith all the above had in me and this project.

# Contents

# List of Charts and Tables

## Charts



## Tables

# Acknowledgements

The volume in front of you did not emerge perfectly and fully formed in a single step; its progress to the page has been a lengthy one over many years. The germ of the idea originally occurred to me as a small personal project in the early 1990s, in those days when the internet was a niche activity for the technically minded and biographical research required many long hours in libraries and archives. As life, work and two Gulf Wars and other wars intervened, albeit from safely behind a desk in Whitehall, like Schubert's 8th Symphony, the project was put away in a drawer, but in this case a mental one. Perhaps it would also have remained unfinished, had I not been encouraged to leave the Civil Service and undertake the PhD 'You know you have always wanted to do' in the words of the person who spurred me to.

Therefore, the core of this work is the doctoral thesis I undertook at the University of Wolverhampton between 2012 and 2021, but its completion was hindered in its later stages by the various COVID-19 lockdowns. At the beginning of the process, my supervisor passed on a piece of wisdom that he had received from his – that a doctorate is 'an itch you simply have to scratch.' So it proved. Writing a thesis, and a book, can be a solitary undertaking, but not a completely lonely one.

This book would not have been possible without the support and assistance of a large number of people. My doctoral supervisory team of Professor John Buckley and Professor Stephen Badsey were hugely helpful, patient, wise and present. Their consistent faith in me got me there. Dr Phylomena Badsey also deserves more thanks in this regard than simple words. Professor Niall Barr of the Joint Services Command and Staff College was generous with his time and advice at a key moment. My friends in the Postgraduate Research Society at the University of Wolverhampton, Dr Edda Nicholson, Dr Peter Ringuet, Dr Chris Martin, Dr Rachel Worthington and Dr Madison Miller provided good humour, company and encouragement in those days dominated by Teams and Zoom. My thanks too to my editor at Helion, Stephen Ede-Borrett, who has proved immensely helpful.

These have been difficult times for museums and archives, with funding difficulties ever-present. The usual sources for the military historian, the Imperial War Museum in Lambeth, the National Army Museum in Chelsea, the National Archives at Kew and the Liddle Hart Centre at King's College London have been of great help. Regimental museums across the country have been under greater pressure after the withdrawal of

Ministry of Defence funding in 2017, forcing many to charge for assistance. Several curators were understanding and helpful in this regard, but their existence is still precarious, and museums deserve support.

I am particularly grateful to Mr Mike Taylor who not only allowed me access to his collection of Second World War British Army unit histories but spent considerable time copying and collating sections I needed. I also record my thanks to the late and very missed Professor Keith Jeffrey, who provided not only good-humoured encouragement, but gave me one piece of advice from his own work on the official history of the Secret Intelligence Service which unlocked a fruitful avenue of enquiry. Dr John Spencer's advice on drafting, general encouragement and friendship was and remains invaluable. To my late and greatly missed civil service colleague and friend, David Bradley, whose interest in the project while working on his own projects on the Polish Army in North-West Europe, and judicious questions kept me on track, posthumous but sincere thanks.

The deepest gratitude must go to my partner Helen, for her selfless support for this effort, from supporting my decision to leave full time employment to follow it, altering her own plans as a result, to keeping my body and soul together.

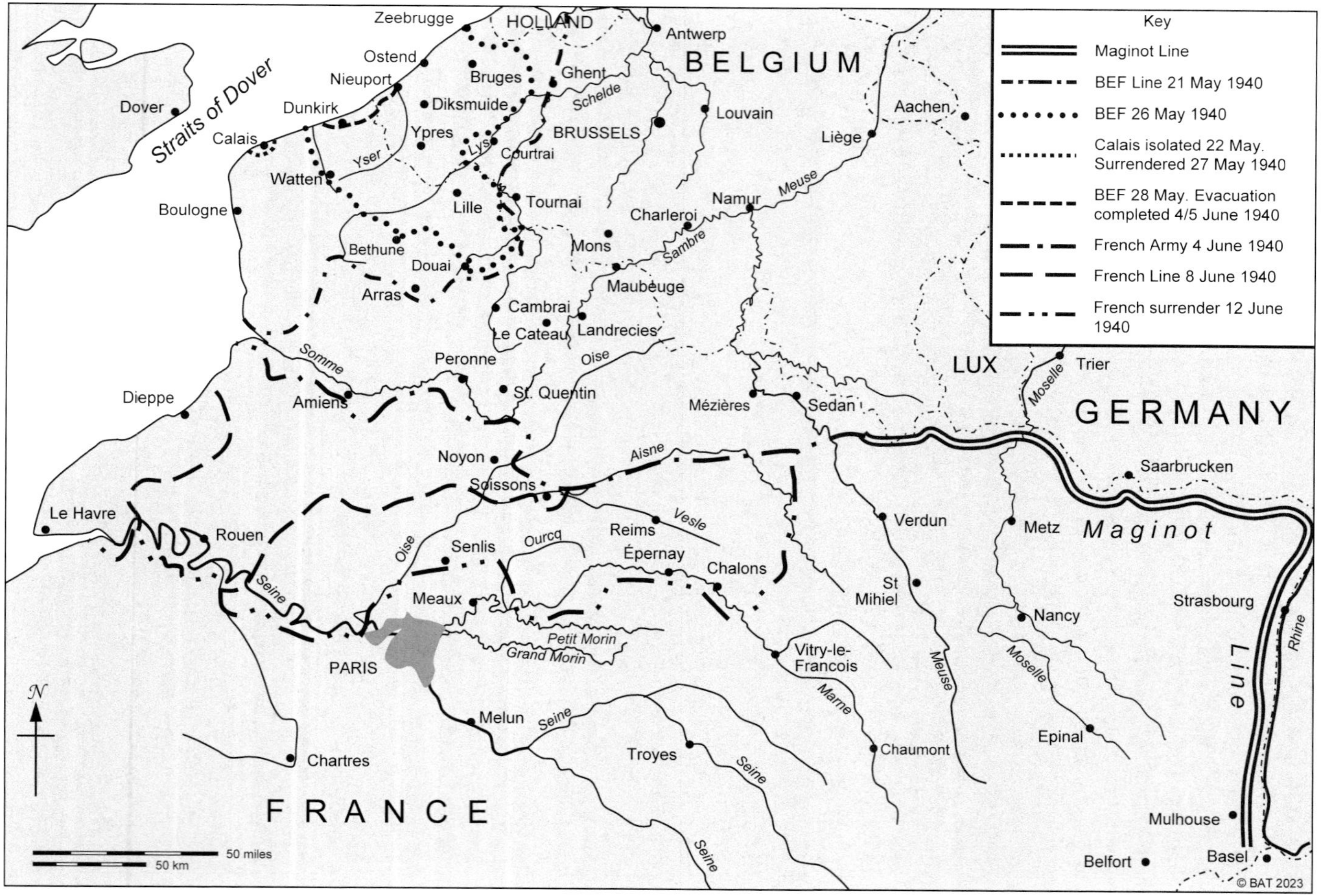
Key
Maginot Line
BEF Line 21 May 1940
BEF 26 May 1940
Calais isolated 22 May. Surrendered 27 May 1940
BEF 28 May. Evacuation completed 4/5 June 1940
French Army 4 June 1940
French Line 8 June 1940
French surrender 12 June 1940
BELGIUM
HOLLAND
LUX
GERMANY
FRANCE
Straits of Dover
Maginot Line
Dover
Zeebrugge
Ostend
Nieuport
Dunkirk
Calais
Boulogne
Watten
Bruges
Ghent
Diksmuide
Ypres
Lille
Courtrai
Tournai
BRUSSELS
Antwerp
Louvain
Liège
Aachen
Namur
Charleroi
Mons
Maubeuge
Bethune
Douai
Arras
Cambrai
Le Cateau
Landrecies
Peronne
St. Quentin
Dieppe
Amiens
Mézières
Sedan
Trier
Noyon
Soissons
Le Havre
Rouen
Senlis
Reims
Épernay
Chalons
Meaux
PARIS
Melun
Troyes
Chartres
Vitry-le-Francois
Chaumont
Verdun
St Mihiel
Metz
Nancy
Epinal
Saarbrucken
Strasbourg
Mulhouse
Belfort
Basel
Scheldt
Yser
Lys
Meuse
Sambre
Somme
Oise
Aisne
Vesle
Ourcq
Seine
Petit Morin
Grand Morin
Marne
Moselle
Rhine
N
50 miles
50 km
© BAT 2023

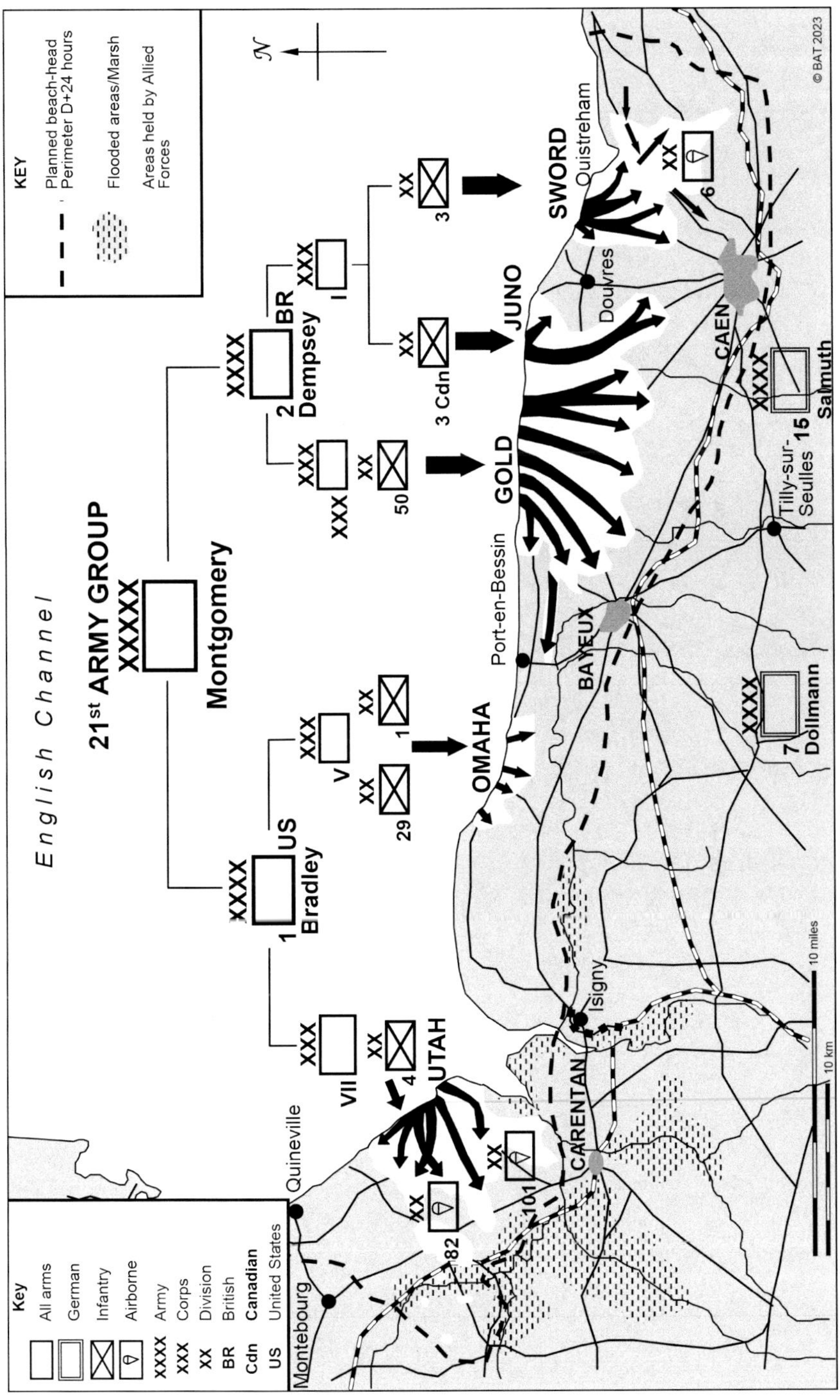
English Channel
21st ARMY GROUP
XXXXX
Montgomery
XXXX
1 US
Bradley
XXXX
2 BR
Dempsey
XXX
VII
XXX
V
XXX
I
XXX
XXX
XX
4
XX
29
XX
1
XX
50
XX
3 Cdn
XX
3
XX
82
XX
101
XX
6
UTAH
OMAHA
GOLD
JUNO
SWORD
Quineville
Montebourg
CARENTAN
Isigny
Port-en-Bessin
BAYEUX
Tilly-sur-Seulles
CAEN
Douvres
Ouistreham
XXXX
7
Dollmann
XXXX
15
Salmuth
10 miles
10 km
KEY
Planned beach-head Perimeter D+24 hours
Flooded areas/Marsh
Areas held by Allied Forces
Key
All arms
German
Infantry
Airborne
XXXX Army
XXX Corps
XX Division
BR British
Cdn Canadian
US United States
© BAT 2023

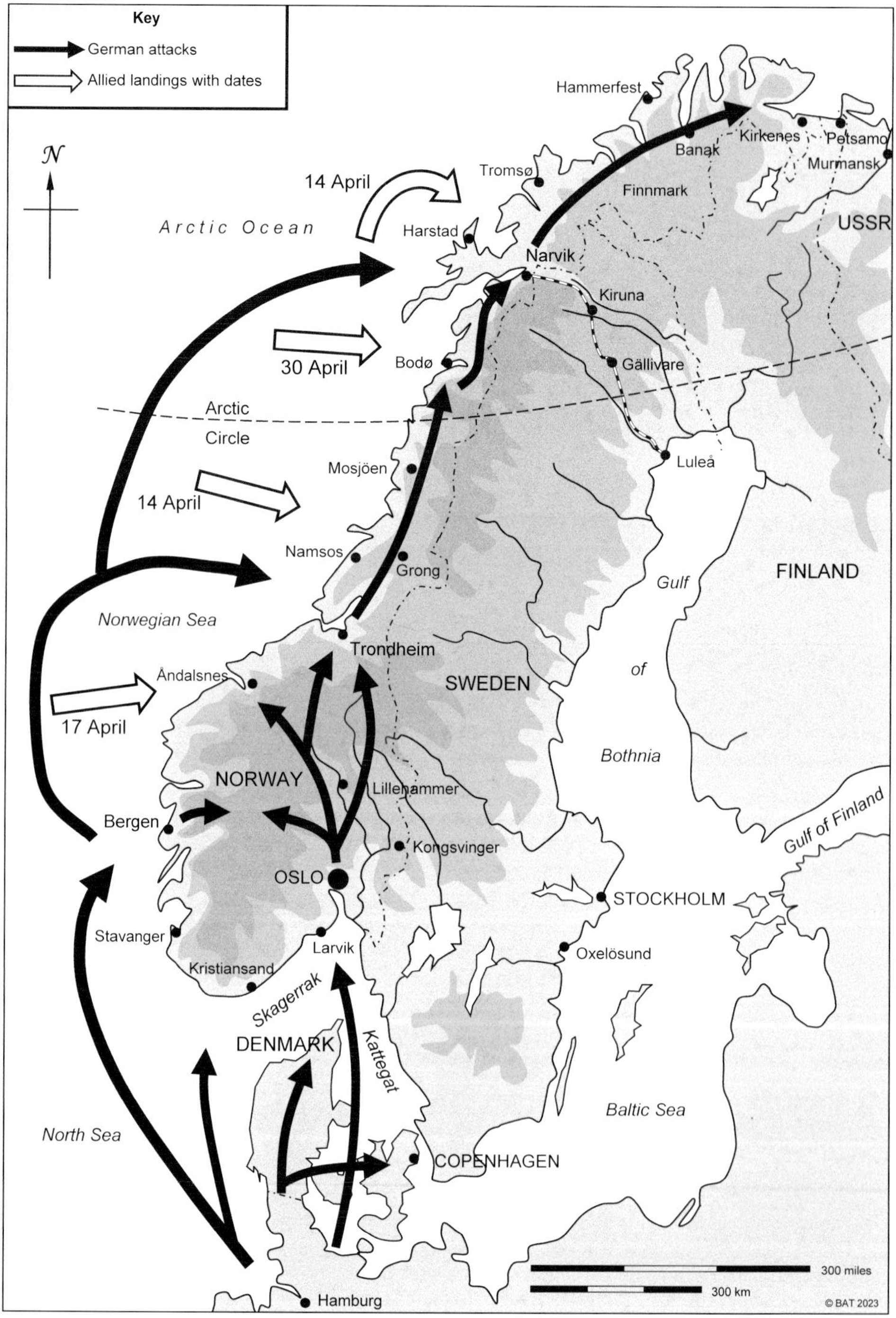

Key
German attacks
Allied landings with dates
N
Arctic Ocean
14 April
30 April
14 April
17 April
Arctic Circle
Norwegian Sea
North Sea
Skagerrak
Kattegat
Baltic Sea
Gulf of Bothnia
Gulf of Finland
Hammerfest
Banak
Kirkenes
Petsamo
Murmansk
Tromsø
Finnmark
Harstad
USSR
Narvik
Kiruna
Bodø
Gällivare
Luleå
Mosjöen
Namsos
Grong
FINLAND
Trondheim
Åndalsnes
SWEDEN
NORWAY
Lillehammer
Bergen
Kongsvinger
OSLO
STOCKHOLM
Stavanger
Larvik
Oxelösund
Kristiansand
DENMARK
COPENHAGEN
Hamburg
300 miles
300 km
© BAT 2023

# 1

# Introduction

> Amateurism, class hierarchy, snobbery, cowardice, looting, betrayal, and almost endlessly incompetent leadership characterised the whole business.[1]
>
> Nigel Hamilton, review of Christopher Nolan's 2007 film *Dunkirk*

By the early summer of 1940, the British Army had suffered two simultaneous operational failures in Europe: The Battle of France from May to June, involving the British Expeditionary Force, and the landing of forces in Norway and operations there from April to May, the North-West Expeditionary Force. Some officers involved in these operations progressed professionally after 1940; some did not. After such strategic defeats the pressure on an army to change, be it political, internal or even popular can be acute.

This book considers a defined set of British Army officers, specifically brigadiers, who served in these operations. Both campaigns ended in strategic defeat and the intention here is to determine how much an officer's subsequent professional fate was influenced through membership of, or access to, either networks within the army, outside of it, or a combination of both.

At this early stage, it is perhaps useful to outline what this book is *not*. It is neither a study of perceived combat effectiveness of the formations commanded by each officer in the respective campaigns, nor is it a campaign narrative. This is both for reasons of space and to prevent repetition of operational histories which are well known elsewhere. (The overall historiography of both campaigns is discussed later in this chapter). It cannot be denied, however, that certain brigadiers' performance in France brought them to the notice of certain senior officers, which further challenges one of the contentions which inspired this research, as is described below. It will consider issues such as award of decorations for operational service, and whether divisional commanders who had been successful 'carried' their subordinate brigadiers with them as they themselves were promoted. Such factors could reflect their operational performance in 1940.

1 Nigel Hamilton, review of Simon Sebag-Montefiore, *Dunkirk: Fight to The Last Man* in *Journal of Military History*, vol. 71 issue 2, April 2007, pp.557–559.

While formations existed in 1940 which were designated brigades, such as infantry and armoured brigades, and the officers commanding them were labelled 'brigadiers', technically this was, and had been since the eighteenth century, an appointment rather than a substantive rank, and held by the officer as long as he was needed in the particular role. There is no order of seniority within the Army List of the period for brigadiers. The Gradation List (part of the Army List which indicates officers by seniority within their rank) moves from full colonels to major generals.

The aim of this work is to examine a specific set of British Army officers who served in these roughly simultaneous operations in Europe in 1940. Both campaigns resulted in operational and strategic defeat. The core group is of officers who held the rank of brigadier, either substantively or temporarily, in each expeditionary force during the relevant period of operations. It will examine factors which may have contributed to the advancement of certain officers, as well as those which may have been presumed to do so, but which this work shows were either ineffectual or less influential than such presumptions and even instinct may suggest or imply. It will also examine certain prevailing presumptions arising from the modern literature concerning the British Army in the Second World War, such as the influence of patronage by senior officers, most notably Bernard Montgomery and Alan Brooke.

By its nature, this work draws considerably on secondary sources, such as campaign narratives, biographies and biographical sources. Primary sources, such as war diaries, personal papers, and autobiographies are used but are subject to the limitations which are discussed below. The main primary source which would be profoundly informative on a personal level, namely officers' annual confidential reports throughout their careers, remains closed and inaccessible to researchers.

It should also be stressed that this book does not seek to offer a general paradigm for the mechanics of advancement among all, and particularly senior, officers across the British Army in the Second World War; this would require a much broader work encompassing other theatres of operations and a much larger, even unwieldy, sample of officers. However, the methodology used does lend itself to wider application across such groups and will be employed in subsequent works.

The inspiration for this project was triggered by a series of separate assertions made several years apart. The first was an informal discussion in the margins of a military history conference in the early 1990s. One participant asserted that any senior officer's career was effectively finished by their participation in the failure at Dunkirk. Another participant agreed and asserted confidently that all officers above the rank of colonel who returned from France in 1940 found their careers abruptly terminated. He continued by saying that the reason was association with a major failure, as a 'new broom' approach was required to facilitate the necessary reform and reconstruction of the army in the face of strategic defeat. Another, equally confidently, dismissed this declaration as far too generalised, and identified a number of officers whose progress upwards seemed unimpeded by their service in France. These included Alan Brooke, who was en route to become Chief of the Imperial General Staff (CIGS) for the remainder of the war; Harold Alexander, later Supreme Allied Commander in the Mediterranean; Ronald Adam, who would become the Army's Adjutant General in 1941 and implement major reforms in personnel policy. Finally, there was a then relatively obscure, at least to the public, divisional commander named Bernard Montgomery. Three of these – Brooke, Alexander and Montgomery – would become field marshals, the army's highest rank.

He could have added officers such as Richard McCreery, a successful commander of armour and the last commander of the Eighth Army, and John Crocker, a colonel in 1939 who ended the war as a corps commander in North-West Europe and gained Montgomery's confidence sufficiently to be his preferred, if unsuccessful, choice after the war to succeed him as CIGS. Both McCreery and Crocker had taken over command of armoured brigades in the field in France in 1940. Montagu 'Monty' Stopford, a highly successful corps commander in the Far East later in the war, performed well in France commanding an infantry brigade. Brian Horrocks had left his post as Chief Instructor at the Staff College, Camberley on its temporary closure at the outbreak of war in September 1939. He commanded a battalion of his parent regiment, the Middlesex Regiment, in France but at the end of the campaign briefly took command of his brigade to bring it successfully within the Dunkirk evacuation perimeter. By 1944, he too was a lieutenant general and a corps commander. Kenneth Anderson, promoted to take over Montgomery's 3rd Division when the latter took over Brooke's II Corps in France, would command an Army in North Africa. There are other examples which could be cited to refute a simplistic zero-sum analysis that service in France or Norway was enough on its own to inhibit or end a professional soldier's career.

The second trigger was a casual suggestion concerning Lieutenant General Neil Ritchie, as he then was, when in command of the Eighth Army in the Middle East in the early summer of 1942. Ritchie, who served as the Brigadier, General Staff (BGS) of II Corps in France in 1940, had been appointed to command of Eighth Army in November 1941 by the General Officer Commanding-in-Chief Middle East, Sir Claude Auchinleck (Auchinleck had commanded the force in Norway in its later stages). Ritchie was comparatively junior, at the time lacked experience for such an important command, and did not perform well when seriously tested. Ritchie had not commanded any unit in the field since the First World War. In 1938 he was a lieutenant colonel commanding a battalion of the King's Own Regiment in Palestine; all his service in the Second World War to this point was in senior staff positions, but he had favourably impressed influential supporters.[2] Following the Eighth Army's defeat at the Battle of Gazala and its headlong retreat to the El Alamein line in May and June 1942, Auchinleck was forced to dismiss Ritchie and send him home to the United Kingdom. Most of the later opprobrium for the failure of the Eighth Army fell on Auchinleck for his poor selection of

2 In his diary for 15 July 1942, Alan Brooke wrote, in the context of Ritchie's dismissal from Eighth Army, 'Neil Ritchie had done me so wonderfully well in the fighting leading to Dunkirk and I had grown so fond of him.' A. Danchev and D. Todman (eds), *War Diaries 1939–1945: Field Marshal Lord Alanbrooke* (London: Weidenfeld and Nicholson, 2001), p.280.

subordinates rather than their actual performance. Ritchie's professional survival may have been through his supposed connections to the Royal Family via his wife, who, it was said, was a lady-in-waiting to the Royal Family. Indeed, when Ritchie landed back in the UK from the desert after his sacking, his first meeting was an audience with King George VI at Buckingham Palace. It was suggested that Ritchie's social connections had saved his career. Subsequent research showed this claim of spousal influence via royal connections is unsustainable. Catherine Minnes, later Lady Ritchie, had only married him in 1937 (when he was merely a lieutenant colonel) and had no connections to the Royal Household at the time.

Ritchie's professional survival and advancement after his failure in the desert was more attributable to his having impressed Alan Brooke when serving as his BGS at II Corps in 1940 and also encountering Montgomery when the latter briefly assumed command of the Corps from Brooke in France later in the year.[3] In addition, his being informally considered the head of a so-called 'Highlander faction' within the army, the senior officer among those in and from the Highland infantry regiments, possibly bore more weight and influence.

This example is telling, in that the power of hearsay and rumour, often unattributed, cannot be put aside when examining biographical detail such as this, even if not fully sourced or supported by documentary evidence. There is a risk in that the effect of such statements can be amplified by repetition, even without confirmation. This does not automatically bar them from consideration, evaluation or examination. Although the original inference concerning Ritchie proved to be untrue, it remained valid as a launching point for the examination of factors possibly contributing to advancement. He was from a well-to-do family background; was educated at a public school and was originally commissioned into a 'smart' regiment of social standing, the Black Watch. He was a graduate of the Staff College and attracted the attention and potential patronage of an influential officer.

After most of the BEF had returned from France there was a pressing need to identify the lessons to be learned from the catastrophe on the European mainland.[4] The urgency was enhanced in the face of a possible German invasion of the UK from across the English Channel. A Committee, chaired by General Sir William Bartholomew, was convened in mid-June 1940 to report on the lessons learned from the defeat in France and to suggest vital reforms of the army which could rapidly be carried out. Bartholomew had recently retired from active service as the General Officer Commanding-in-Chief, Northern Command and had previously served as the Director Military Operations and Intelligence at the War Office and as Chief of the General Staff (India); the Committee

3 A. Danchev and D. Todman (eds), *War Diaries 1939–1945: Field Marshal Lord Alanbrooke* (London: Weidenfeld and Nicholson, 2001), p.280.

4 The Committee formed, and took evidence, while around 100,000 troops were still in France south of the River Somme and were gradually evacuated during Operations CYCLE and ARIEL from Cherbourg, Le Havre and other smaller Channel ports between 15–25 June. The 51st (Highland) Division surrendered at St Valery during this period.

convened while troops were still fighting.[5] The final report did not censure individuals, which would surely have been deleterious or even terminal for their career prospects, but neither did it distribute specific or individual praise. The final document did, however, have a list appended commending certain officers in a general sense. While the report was being circulated concerns were expressed by senior officers that if it were released publicly, it could damage the reputation of, and confidence in, the army in general. As such, few individuals were singled out in the deliberations by name or by post held.

Only one brigadier was interviewed by the Committee. This was Sir Oliver Leese Bt, who had served as the BGS to Lieutenant General Sir Ronald Adam, the latter having originally been sent to France to establish and command a new III Corps but who was instead forced by circumstances to organise and maintain the defence of the Dunkirk evacuation perimeter. As the threat of invasion diminished, the report became bogged down in the army's bureaucracy as senior officers debated its findings and recommendations. These were watered down in the face of considerable opposition from within the Army Council, the Army's highest decision-making body, and beyond. The sole surviving copy of the draft circulated for comment which survives in the National Archives at Kew contains multiple angry marginalia; the author is not named but the handwriting matches that of Lieutenant General Sir William Lindsell, the BEF's Quartermaster General. A major proposal in the report – that the brigade become the primary operational building block of the army in preference to the division – was not adopted.

The defeat in France was not the only strategic failure in the spring of 1940. In April, a month before the German attack in the West, Hitler invaded Norway, violating its neutrality. An Allied expeditionary force failed both to stem the German advance from Oslo in the south and, in cooperation with the French, to deny the northern Norwegian ports, particularly Narvik, to the invaders. The aim of the latter was to prevent the export of vital materials, predominantly Swedish iron ore, to Germany. The Anglo-French joint operation was hastily mounted, poorly planned and badly equipped. It was ending in failure and evacuation just as the German attack on the Low Countries and France was beginning on 10 May 1940. However, of the 13 officers holding brigadier's postings in the NWEF, seven proceeded to the rank of major general or beyond during the war. Although the secondary literature on the Norwegian campaign focuses on its negative aspects, with titles of books carrying variations on 'catastrophe', 'fiasco' and 'disaster',[6] involvement at this level of command was not inherently as career limiting as has been supposed, and as such terms imply. Although the failure of the Norwegian expedition resulted in a fierce parliamentary debate, a division to vote, and the ultimate fall of the Chamberlain administration, the incoming War Cabinet led by Churchill did not press for an equivalent of the Bartholomew Committee.

5 TNA CAB 106/220 (1940) 'Final report of the Bartholomew Committee on lessons to be learned from the operations in Flanders.'

6 For example, J. Kiszeley, Anatomy of a Campaign: The British Fiasco in Norway, 1940 (Cambridge: CUP, 2017).

The charge that participation in either the Battle of France or the Norwegian Campaign in 1940 was the automatic end of an officer's career is therefore readily refuted. The question arises, however, whether those who survived and advanced professionally, or those who did not, was either because of their participation in the campaigns, or their connections both within and outside the army.

The key question is to what extent participation in these campaigns, or an officer's connections (in and outside the army), influenced their subsequent career.

## Some Notes on Methodology

This work is based on a qualitative analysis of the dataset of officers as compiled. The methodology drew inspiration from aspects of the area of academic enquiry known as social network analysis. The discipline can and has been typified by highly technical and mathematical language which may exclude those from less technical backgrounds seeking to make practical use of the tools offered. An attempt to bridge this divide is outlined by Professor John Scott in *Social Network Analysis: A Handbook*.[7] Professor Scott, a sociologist, has sought across three editions of his work to simplify the mathematical constructs to allow non-mathematicians to apply social network analysis methodologies to derive information through data handling of large data sets. Scott warns that care must be taken against applying social network analysis terminology in an overly general manner – a specific example being of the term 'clique' – stating that the context of the issue being examined is vital; the selection of appropriate tools and the use of informed judgement being of particular importance.[8] Use of social network theory in an historical context remains comparatively young as a discipline, only developing over the last 20 years or so, and typified in the work of historians such as Charles Wetherell, and Niall Ferguson.[9] Wetherell notes that the basis of the social network approach is founded on four principles:

> Firstly, actors in social systems are interdependent rather than independent.
> Secondly, linkages between actors in a system channel knowledge and other resources.
> Thirdly, the structure of those relations can both constrain or facilitate action.
> Finally, patterns between the actors can define economic, political and social structures.[10]

7 J. Scott, *Social Network Analysis: A Handbook* (London: Sage Publications Ltd, 3rd edition 2012).
8 J. Scott, *Social Network Analysis: A Handbook* (London: Sage Publications Ltd, 3rd edition 2012), p.2.
9 In particular, in his article: C. Wetherell, 'Historical Social Network Analysis' in *International Review of Social History*, 43 (1998), pp.125–44. N. Ferguson, *The Square and the Tower: Networks, Hierarchies and the Struggle for Global Power* (London, Allen Lane, 2017).
10 C. Wetherell, 'Historical Social Network Analysis' in *International Review of Social History*, 43 (1998), p.126; in this case Wetherell referred to his case study of European peasantry.

Wetherell states that social network analysis demands evidence of social interaction among all members of a social system for a variety of behaviours, and thus necessitates a broad range of high-quality records for the place, time and activities being studied; where the historical record is incomplete, or the understanding of past social relations is imperfect, social network analysis remains an inherently problematic enterprise. In this example, a rigid interpretation of 'social' interaction may be of less application than a 'professional' viewpoint.

Charles Kadushin in *Introduction to Social Network Theory*[11] offers accessible definitions for the non-specialist. A network is a set of relationships; a simple network contains two 'nodes' and one relationship that links them; however even this can be symmetrical or non-directional (e.g. A likes B; B likes A). Yet a third party, C can be connected to B, and although non-reciprocal, is connected to A via B. As such relationships expand, regardless of the scale of the issue being addressed, it is the set of conditions which will make it more or less likely that paths will exist between these nodes and whether they are reciprocally or mutually related. Kadushin goes on to note that social science defines three types of networks:

Egocentric: Connected by a single node or individual, such as a group of friends or companies which all do business with a single company. However, to be a proper network there must be an information set available about the connections between the nodes, or there is no network. (An example may be, for example, officers favoured by Montgomery for advancement under his command in, and after, 8th Army)

Socio-centric networks are closed, i.e. within defined boundaries such as children in a classroom or the board of a company. (For example, commonality of regiment, or being contemporaries at Staff College)

Open system networks are not confined to a box or exist in a state where boundaries are not clear or difficult to define.

For the purposes of this work, it was presumed that the group is predominantly sociocentric, although elements of the egocentric are certainly present.

In his 2017 work *The Square and The Tower*,[12] Niall Ferguson presented examples to illustrate the influence of networks and hierarchies throughout history. He contends that the impact of these structures has been significant, although at times at a lower level than has been supposed, namely, below the level of 'great men' and their like. Ferguson adds that networks, by virtue of being more widespread, can have a greater influence than hierarchies. He adds, to underline this, that hierarchies can also be

11 Provided as a free download: C. Kadushin, http://communityanalytics.staging.r2integrated.com/portals/0/resource_library/social%20network%20theory_kadushin.pdf. accessed May 2012.

12 N. Ferguson, *The Square and The Tower* (London: Allen Lane 2017), Chapter 3 'Networks, Networks Everywhere', pp.14–20 and Chapter 4 'Why Hierarchies', pp.21–24

horizontal and broad, by comparison with narrow, straight up and down, hierarchies. The latter assertion, of horizontal and broad hierarchies, is the most applicable to the analysis in this work.

The data set from which this work was compiled used a series of spreadsheets branched out from a master sheet containing criteria including age, school and university attended, regiment of first commissioning, whether or not each officer was a Staff College graduate, post occupied in 1940, whether the individual had deposited papers (or other materials) in repositories such as the Liddell Hart Centre, the Imperial War Museum and the National Army Museum. A checklist was also added to see if individual officers featured in certain senior officers' diaries and accounts, as a launching point for further investigation. As a starting point, these were the published diaries of Alan Brooke and Henry Pownall (Chief of Staff of the BEF) and the memoirs of Bernard Montgomery.

This master sheet was subsequently broken down into subsets both to allow direct sorting of the data, and to break out information derived in the biographical area, such as awards of decorations and interwar active service, which were compiled into the tables contained later in this work.

In the original academic thesis from which the present work is derived, the key questions identified were:

1. What social networks existed in the British Army in the period 1919–1939?
2. What impact did service in the First World War have on officers' careers in the period 1918–39?
3. To what extent did attendance at Staff College between the wars influence an officer's career?
4. Did interwar active service generate any connected networks among officers?
5. What proportion of officers in the group proceeded to higher rank after the conclusion of operations in France and Norway after June 1940?

Follow-on, or secondary questions for consideration included:

If such networks were present, to what extent were these formal, informal, or perceived.

Whether influencing networks external to the army were present, including, but not limited to, family and connections, and whether they had an effect on an officer's progression.

The influence, or patronage of senior officers towards former subordinates, or in the case of education – particularly at the Staff College level.

If service on the staff as a junior officer in the First World War (whether or not an officer later proceeded to graduate from the Staff College) provided an advantage for their later progression or generated a talent pool for promotion or selection.

Whether the possession of decorations for gallantry and/or distinguished service in the First World War made an officer more likely to be selected for advanced education or promotion before and after 1940.

If awards made for service in 1940 played any part in whether an officer advanced in rank after the campaigns in France and Norway.

Officers who attended Staff College from 1919 on the first post-war course, where admission criteria were relaxed by comparison, until the early 1930s (after which officers would have been too junior to reach brigadier by 1940) are also examined to determine whether attendance on the course generated networks between the students and between students and instructors and whether these were inherent or durable. Conversely, if an officer did not succeed in gaining a place at Staff College did this inhibit his advancement or prove a block to it, whether or not this restricted access to patronage or networks.

## Why Choose Brigadiers?

The selection of this level of rank was driven by the following factors.

Until 1922, the rank had been that of brigadier general, and holders of it were considered general officers. Following the First World War the rank was reduced from General officer status to that of 'Colonel Commandant' or 'Colonel on the Staff' depending on what specific type of post the individual was serving in, reducing its status from that of general officer to that of field officer. The move proved unpopular and the rank of brigadier – minus its previous suffix of general – was reinstated in 1928 and new rank insignia introduced of a crown above three stars, removing the sword and baton, and reinforcing the distinction between general and field officers. A brigadier's posting did not suggest the holding of an operational level command per se, as the fundamental operational unit of the British Army remained the division, a major general's command. The rank of brigadier was not to become a substantive rank until 1947.

The post of brigadier was regarded, until the late 1930s at least, as a form of extension of a full colonel's posting to fulfil a temporary or particular need. This was comparable to the Royal Naval rank of commodore; until the late twentieth century a holding position for senior captains, ahead of advancement to flag rank.[13] As late as the January 1942 HYAL there was no separate listing for brigadiers; after the gradation (seniority) list for major generals, the next category below was for full colonels, some of whom occupied temporary or acting brigadier rank.

13 Commodore only became a substantive rank in the Royal Navy in 1997. Prior to this, it continued to be an appointment conferred on senior captains holding certain positions. For example, the senior commander of destroyers within a fleet in the Royal Navy could carry the title of 'Commodore (D)', while the fleet's senior commander of submarines could carry the title of 'Commodore (S)', although in both cases as an appointment rather than a rank. Source: 'Debrett's' Forms of Address' https://archive.is/20120729172653/http://www.debretts.co.uk/forms-of-address/professions/armed-forces/royal-navy/commodore-and-captain.aspx. accessed 30 October 2012.

An officer holding a brigadier's position in 1940 is most likely to have been a pre-war, professional Regular Army officer. As such, he will have left a detailed paper trail in official and unofficial, primary and secondary records. This eases the assembly of the data required to create both a comprehensive sample and a picture of an individual's personal and professional activities and social standing in comparison to officers of more junior rank, such as lieutenant colonels. Aside from command of a brigade, or brigade level, formation, brigadiers held senior staff appointments; for example, the senior staff officer at corps level was a BGS. The chief artillery officer in a division was also a brigadier – the brigadier, Royal Artillery (BRA) or in some accounts commander, Royal Artillery (CRA). In the BEF of 1939–1940, there were several supporting service arms posts held by brigadiers, such as the Director of Labour, the Director of Works, the Command Paymaster and so on. Such positions were included in the group.

In the BEF, some Territorial Army (TA) brigades were commanded, even if only temporarily, by TA officers – but such command could not be taken as granted. In Norway for example, despite a preponderance of TA troops in the NWEF and the forming of local, ad hoc 'Forces' rather than a system based on a formal brigade structure, all the brigadiers there were Regular Army officers. In general, Territorial officers can be more challenging to research as they did not leave as many traces in sources such as newspapers, and Territorial officers were not included in the biographical sections of the Half Yearly Army List in the interwar and early war periods. Also, very few were included, unless they rose to eminence in their civilian occupation, in biographical directories such as *Who's Who*[14] or *Debrett's*.[15] The short biographies included in the HYAL list dates of birth, commissioning, key appointments and decorations. With officers of the TA these must be reconstructed from source material such as the *London Gazette* and the monthly Army List. Also, until the late 1930s, there were no vacancies put aside for Territorials on the course at the Army Staff College at Camberley, also denying them an opportunity to form networks there.

There is also anecdotal evidence which suggests that TA officers commanding their TA battalions were removed from their command on the outbreak of war and replaced by regular officers. Many were transferred to staff posts. Colonel Donald Dean, who had been awarded a Victoria Cross in 1918 while serving with the Royal West Kent Regiment and remained with the regiment as a Territorial between the wars, eventually taking command of his battalion, made such a claim in his personal diaries.[16] Although such action could be justified by the fact that Territorials, lacking Staff College experience, were not qualified for these levels of operational command, it is also possible that

14 *Who's Who* (various editions 1849 to 2024) '…the definitive directory of everyone who's anyone in Britain, and beyond, today', published by Baily Brothers Ltd, London, from 1849 to 1897 and subsequently AC Black Ltd, London from 1897 to date.

15 The Peerage of the United Kingdom of Great Britain and Ireland (London, John Debrett Ltd. Various editions 1812–2024).

16 See T. Crowdy and S. Bavin (eds), *Donald Dean VC* (Barnsley: Pen & Sword), p.65.

with the outbreak of war Regular Army officers would not wish to face increased competition for such a scarce commodity as brigade and divisional command.

However, this did not prevent officers from Territorial backgrounds from being promoted to the rank of brigadier, however temporarily, in 1940 (albeit from necessity rather than merit) nor of holding operational commands later in the war. Major General Harry Willans, who was Director General of Army Welfare and Education at the War Office from 1940–1942, was a Territorial officer, having been a senior executive of J. Lyons Ltd, the catering company. He once expressed frustration at the obstacles to the advancement of Territorial officers to a group of members of the Army Council thus: 'We know that you dislike us [Territorial officers] but we are going on soldiering whether you like us, or not.'[17]

The Monthly Army List for May 1940 lists 1,027 brigadiers in the British and Indian Armies. The latter includes officers of the British Army in India, and of the Indian Army (1903–1947). However, except for Honorary Officers, no native Indians, or 'Viceroy Commissioned Officers' reached the level of brigadier. Of all these officers, 45 were brigadier generals, indicating that they had not seen active service since 1922 and remained on the Army List by virtue of holding honorary positions such as equerries to the Royal Household or representative Colonels Commandant of regiments, a ceremonial rank. One of this group was listed in the obituaries column, which reduces the total to 982; there are 146 honorary brigadiers. These officers cannot be automatically excluded as several were serving colonels in staff posts in home commands, made honorary brigadiers as a mark of distinction for previous service.

## Why 1940 and 1944?

In order to test the findings of the study of 1940 brigadiers, a comparison was made with another group of brigadiers in the British Army later in the war in order to compare and contrast any changes in the advancement and promotion of officers at this level. As described above, 1940 was chosen – above and beyond the trigger of a casual remark – as a point where a major global power suffered simultaneous strategic defeats. Its officer corps, certainly at this level, predominantly consisted of veterans of the First World War, who received their further professional education (if at all) around the mid-1920s. In this period, such training was in flux as changes were made to the syllabus and demand greatly outstripped supply. Furthermore, a shortage of qualified officers in 1939–1940

17 Willans in a letter to Sir Basil Liddell Hart, 23 May 1963, cited in D. French, 'Colonel Blimp and the British Army: British Divisional Commanders in the War against Germany, 1939–1945' in *The English Historical Review*, vol. 111, no.444 (November 1996), pp.1182–1201. Willans was a rarity in that he had commanded a Territorial Army division before the war; he was killed in an air crash in the Middle East in February 1943 http://www.kzwp.com/lyons.pensioners/obitary2W.htm (accessed 15 October 2017).

necessitated the recall of older, sometimes retired, officers to fill skill gaps, particularly in rear echelon posts.

D-Day, 6 June 1944, was chosen in preference to any other key point, such as the war in the Western Desert, in the Mediterranean from 1943 on and the war in the Far East for the following reasons. The formations landing on D-Day were led by a mixture of officers with varying degrees of battlefield experience prior to 1944, with some who had fought in France in 1940 in more junior ranks and subsequently in other theatres of operations. Some had remained in the United Kingdom after 1940 in training and administrative posts and would therefore be completely new to active service at such levels, even if they had seen active service in 1940. This was considered to be a level starting point from which to conduct a comparison of the type of officer who had risen to such rank where, arguably, the brigade had increased in operational importance.

Another point of investigation was also to determine whether there had been a level of rejuvenation – with younger officers attaining the rank – in the intervening years by comparison with four years before. Also, the necessity to address officers from Empire and Commonwealth backgrounds, with differing traditions of selection, training and advancement was deemed to overcomplicate an already well-populated sample. In theatres such as the Middle and Far East, an additional factor would have been the necessity to take account of officers from the Indian Army (this is also why Canadian officers in Canadian formations were omitted from both the 1940 and 1944 analysis). Lastly, as noted elsewhere, it was to begin from a basis of an army which had been comprehensively defeated to one on the threshold of final victory.

The aim here is to examine factors from before 1940 which could, aside from operational performance in France or Norway, have influenced the professional survival of officers from the primary group. Therefore, the use of a comparative group in 1944 was to examine if such factors had a remaining prevalence by then, rather than to attempt a wide-ranging review of reform of officer selection and promotion in the course of the war, which merits its own study. Such changes as occurred, driven by first by the Hore-Belisha reforms in 1938 to clear promotion log jams and improve possibilities for advancement, and Sir Ronald Adam's further reshaping of officer selection after 1941, were as noted here likely to have little impact on the 1940 group and arguably less on the brigade level of command by 1944 than it did on more junior officers thereafter.

The final influence and trigger for this research was a large graphic posted in the Ministry of Defence after 2001 which undertook to establish linkages between insurgent commanders in South-West Asia. This illustration used a combination of social network analysis methods and classified intelligence. Combining this with the ideas generated in the discussions at the conference in the 1990s sparked a curiosity as to whether other officers who were perceived to have underperformed in action may have evaded career ruin or termination through their connections. The intelligence-led example of insurgent commanders indicated that there may be methodologies to determine and discover such linkages in the proposed sample, and perhaps indicate others less apparent from a visual or cursory sifting of the evidence. The current United States Army Field Manual *Insurgencies and Countering Insurgencies* states that social network analysis is an essential tool in modern warfare; while this is couched predominantly in terms of 'attack the network' operations, it also states:

> A social network analysis allows analysts to identify and portray the details of a network structure. It shows how …. [an insurgency's] networked organisation behaves and how that connectivity affects its behaviour. A social network analysis allows analysts to assess the network's design, how its members may or may not act autonomously, where leadership resides, how leadership is distributed across the network and how hierarchical dynamics may mix or not mix with network dynamics.[18]

## Assembling the Group

The first tier was the most straightforward; the officers commanding brigade level formations, predominantly infantry brigades, both in France and Norway. These officers are clearly identified in the respective volumes of the *Official History of the Second World War*[19] in the appendices which list forces engaged. Ellis' official history of the war in France and Flanders also occasionally lists brigadiers who held temporary command of divisions in the absence of the major general commanding. However, neither source lists officers in staff posts in their appendices, although there are occasional passing references in the body of the narrative. Joslen's two-volume *Orders of Battle*, part of the *Official History*, was also used to cross check post holders and temporary commanders of formations.

The second tier in assembling the group was via reference to higher command level War Diaries at the National Archives at Kew. The Corps War Diaries in WO 167[20] of the three corps in France (including the proposed III Corps under Sir Ronald Adam, which became instead the operational headquarters for the defence of the Dunkirk evacuation perimeter) contain staff returns of the operational commanders and some senior support arm commanders who were brigadiers, such as the Commander (also 'Brigadier') Royal Artillery (CRA) at Divisional level; and the posts of Chief Engineer (CRE) and the Deputy Adjutant & Quartermaster General (DA&QMG) at Corps level. Operational orders contained within this series also identified some officers in staff postings moved between units during the period of the so-called Phoney War from October 1939 to May

18 US Army Field Manual FM 3-24/MCWP 3-33.5 (Washington DC, Department of the Army) cleared for public release on unlimited distribution 2 June 2014.

19 T. K. Derry, *The Campaign in Norway*. History of the Second World War, United Kingdom Military Series (London: HMSO, 1952) and Major L. F. Ellis, *The Campaign in France and Flanders, 1939–40*, History of the Second World War, United Kingdom Military Series (London: HMSO, 1953); Lieutenant Colonel H. F. Joslen, *Orders of Battle*, vols 1 & 2, History of the Second World War, United Kingdom Military Series (London: HMSO, 1960).

20 TNA WO167/124 – I Corps; WO167/148 – II Corps; WO167/168 – III Corps. UK National Archives

1940.[21] A shadow series in WO 166[22] is more concerned with general administrative details but occasionally illuminates or corroborates the presence of officers appropriate to the group.

The war diaries for the Norwegian campaign in the WO 198 series[23] are less illuminating and in one specific case, due to a lack of detail and an administrative error, required many further attempts to ascertain the correct information to identify the individual officer concerned. Derry's volume of the *Of Hist* refers to very few brigadiers beyond field commanders at this level. Ellis' volume is slightly better in this regard for the period before 10 May 1940 and for the Battle of France thereafter but still omits many brigadiers in key staff positions who would play a significant part in operations.[24] The files of the Cabinet Office Historical Section used in the preparation of Derry's volume include correspondence with key figures which provided some more insight, but not markedly so.[25]

The complete group comprises 156 officers. Completion and corroboration of the group, and expansion of their biographical records was achieved through the following sources:

**The Half Yearly Army List.** This official publication contained the Gradation List of the British Army, which listed all officers of the Regular Army by rank and according to their seniority, the date on which they were appointed to that rank. Up to January 1940 it also contained an outline synopsis of a Regular Army officer's career. It does not give an officer's postings in precise detail, presumably for reasons of operational security.

**The Operational Honours Lists** for France and Norway published in the governmental newspaper, *The London Gazette*. These lists have specific headlines indicating the theatre of operations. The first list for France was published in the *Gazette* on 11 July 1940, being an extension (or supplement) of the list for the King's Birthday Honours published on 9 July.[26] A second list published on 26 July 1940[27] was of awards for performance of duty in the period up to 31 March 1940. Some awards made for France were announced on 10 August 1940 and the last list was published on 20 January 1941, this latter

21 An illustrative example of such moves is that of Brigadier C. Le Bas Goldney, Director Royal Army Service Corps, who was held on strength of I Corps on 15 February 1940 but was transferred to III Corps at some point before 6 May 1940.

22 TNA WO166/169 – I Corps; WO166/186 – II Corps; WO166/204 – III Corps.

23 TNA WO198/1-5; 6–7, 9-11; 16-17.

24 For example, Brigadier Sir Oliver Leese Bt (later General Sir Oliver, GOC Eighth Army) who's posting to be BGS of III Corps in May 1940 was reversed as a result of the German attack and he spent the rest of the campaign at GHQ BEF. Leese was a key witness to the Bartholomew Committee on lessons learned from the Battle of France in June 1940.

25 In the series TNA CAB 106/1154-1178 in particular.

26 *The London Gazette (Supplement)*, 9 July 1940. pp.4243–4269. The list had been delayed from its usual publication date in June because of the change of government on 10 May 1940.

27 *The London Gazette* (3rd Supplement to the edition of 23 July 1940), 26 July 1940, pp.4579–4586.

one being predominantly of Mentions in Dispatches. Two main lists for operations in Norway were published on 6 August and 27 September 1940.

**Biographical Directories.** The main source was *Who's Who*.[28] All personal detail contained in entries was at the discretion of the individual and therefore varies considerably in the amount of detail provided. It is perhaps the best single source for personal information aside from the Army List. Family connections were traced via sources such as *Debrett's Peerage & Baronetage*,[29] *Burke's Peerage* and *Burke's Landed Gentry*.[30]

**Online Biographical Resources.** The co-location of archive sources via genealogy websites and gateways is a dynamic and expanding resource. In this case, the primary source used on a personal subscription was *Find My Past*[31]; its main rival *Ancestry* has been accessed via public libraries and at the National Archives at Kew. A third party website, *The Peerage*[32] proved useful in discerning family linkages but this was treated with caution due to its third party nature and amalgamation from other sources which were sometimes unattributed.

**Obituaries.** Many of the officers in the group were sufficiently eminent to merit obituary notes in broadsheet newspapers. The most readily accessible archive is that of *The Times* (London). A secondary result which was of value is the notification of memorial services; the list of attendees can prove useful in the extrapolation of military and personal connections through representation.[33]

**Newspapers.** Broadsheet newspaper indices and their online resources proved of value in identifying postings, awards and the careers of many officers in the group. Again, the online archive of *The Times* was the most valuable single resource in this regard. This latter source was also of value in tracking participation in sport and highlighting potential connections in this area. However, the British Newspaper Archive, both in physical form at the British Library and in its subscription based online presence, also proved of value. This was because military news in the pre-war period would often be announced in a wider range of newspapers than may be assumed to be the case, sometimes reflecting the geographic background of regiments or officers serving in them. For example, if a regiment which had its depot in Yorkshire deployed to Aldershot, it would appear in newspapers for both areas, and sometimes individual officers would be mentioned similarly.[34]

28 *Who's Who and Who Was Who* (London, AC Black Ltd, various annual directories 1914–1990).
29 (London: Debrett's, various annual directories 1914–50).
30 (London: Burke's Ltd, various annual directories 1914–50).
31 www.findmypast.co.uk; accessed on multiple dates.
32 www.thepeerage.com/; accessed on multiple dates.
33 I am indebted to the late Professor Keith Jeffrey of Queen's University Belfast for suggesting this source, which he noted proved extremely useful in the writing of his history of the Secret Intelligence Service – *MI6: The History of the Secret Intelligence Service* (London: Bloomsbury, 2010).
34 https://www.britishnewspaperarchive.co.uk/ accessed on multiple dates.

**Personal Papers.** Very few sets of complete personal papers have been located for the majority of the group. The single most significant repository is the Liddell Hart Centre for Military Archives at King's College London, although even here in the main there are few detailed accounts of operations in 1940. The Archive's *Survey of the Papers of Senior UK Defence Personnel, 1900–1975* includes very few officers in the group of 156 who have deposited personal papers with national repositories. A cross check with the holdings of the Imperial War Museum and the National Army Museum confirmed this or highlighted fragmentary sets of papers which did not specifically further this research. This was cross-referenced again against the *Culture Grid UK* website, a search engine from the Collections Trust intended to locate assets in national collections.[35] A difficulty with personal papers, which was reflected in those used in the research for this study, is a reticence to be critical of senior commanders and not to mention issues such as patronage as the subject may not have been aware of it.

One modern account of operations[36] by the covering force of rear echelon troops draws on an account from one Brigadier, John Gawthorpe, held in the regimental archives of his original regiment, the West Yorkshire Regiment.[37] Also in this category are published and/or edited personal diaries. At present the three most useful examples of this have been the edited diaries of Viscount Alanbrooke, Lord Ironside and Sir Henry Pownall. The first has also been of value in the study of officers post-Dunkirk after his assumption of the post of Chief of the Imperial General Staff.[38]

Within the literature on the British Army in the Second World War, detailed studies of the brigade level of command in the early period of the war are nonexistent; individual brigade histories exist, but these focus predominantly on the campaign in North-West Europe and are narrative rather than analytical.[39] In one aspect at least, academic analysis agrees as to the root causes of the defeat in 1940, which apply generally to France

35 *http://www.culturegrid.org.uk/* accessed on 20 February 2013: Searches conducted on 'Private Papers', 'Dunkirk' and 'Norway'.

36 Lynch, T. (2010) '*Dunkirk 1940: Whereabouts Unknown*' (Stroud; The History Press).

37 Gawthorpe commanded 137 Brigade in 46th Division, a Territorial formation originally assigned to labour and training duties in France. The account was published in *Ca Ira, The Journal of the West Yorkshire Regiment*, in 1948. He was National President of the Dunkirk Veterans' Association in 1975–76.

38 Danchev and Todman, (eds.), *War Diaries 1939–1945: Field Marshal Lord Alanbrooke* (London: Weidenfeld & Nicholson, 2002); Colonel R. McCleod and D. Kelly, *Time Unguarded: The Ironside Diaries 1937–1940* (London: Constable, 1962); B. Bond, *Chief of Staff: The Diaries of Lieutenant General Sir Henry Pownall. Volume 1: 1937–40* (London: Leo Cooper, 1974).

39 A rare example is A. Horton, *56th Infantry Brigade and D-Day: An Independent Infantry Brigade and the Campaign in North-West Europe 1944–1945* (London: Bloomsbury, 2010) based on the author's 2009 PhD thesis from the University of Plymouth

and Norway. The common threads, from Brian Bond's *France and Belgium 1939–40*[40] in 1975 to Edward Smalley's *The British Expeditionary Force*[41] in 2015, agree that the combination of an habitually under-resourced army, with its officers inappropriately trained at Staff Colleges, linked to an awareness of the emergent doctrine of infantry-armour cooperation but the lack of a coherent method to implement or propagate it were equally at fault.

Both Smalley and David French in *Raising Churchill's Army*[42] indicate that the speed of British defeat was not due purely to the inflicting of heavy casualties upon the BEF by the Germans, but the latter's focus on the rapid disruption of the means of command and control, within a hierarchical system which was insufficiently flexible at this stage – and further into the war – to allow effective delegation to subordinate officers and units, notwithstanding the direction in the 1935 *Field Service Regulations* that the local commander should be trusted to make decisions based on immediate knowledge of the actual situation, on his own initiative.

Interest in the Army as an institution in the interwar period has attracted more study since Brian Bond's *British Military Policy Between The Wars* was published in 1980.[43] Bond focuses on those institutional challenges facing a much-reduced post-First World War Army and the demands of modernisation in the face of financial constraint and the concomitant pressures of Imperial policing and peacekeeping. Studies of British generalship in the Second World War began to emerge in the 1960s and 1970s, such as Corelli Barnett's *The Desert Generals*,[44] which sought to correct the excessive credit given, in the author's view, to Montgomery for success in the desert while overlooking the part played by Auchinleck and his subordinates, not least due to Montgomery's portrayal of his predecessor in his own writings. Sir John Smyth's *Leadership in War 1939–45: British Generalship in Victory and Defeat* from 1974 was a general survey from a veteran of France in 1940, but his more sympathetic analysis is weakened by an overly broad approach and an over-emphasis on officers he himself had encountered in his career.

Jeremy Crang's study *The British Army and the People's War* from 2000[45] and David French, in *Raising Churchill's Army* observe that in the 1930s there was a system in place which appeared to ensure that selection for promotion and advancement to higher ranks in the Army was, if not fully transparent, at least fair on its use of the system of confidential reporting and recommendation, in its turn requiring the approval of the Military Secretary and the agreement of the Army Council. However, both agree, in a point also noted by Bond, that this system was not immune to being influenced by the views of senior commanders such as the CIGS, or indirectly by the social background of

40 B. Bond, *Britain, France & Belgium 1939–1945* (London: Brassey's, 2nd edition 1990).
41 E. Smalley, *The British Expeditionary Force 1939–40* (London: Palgrave Macmillan, 2015).
42 D. French, *Raising Churchill's Army – The British Army & the War Against Germany 1919–45* (Oxford: OUP, 2000).
43 B. Bond, *British Military Policy Between the Two World Wars* (Oxford: Clarendon, 1980).
44 C. Barnett, *The Desert Generals* (London, William Kimber, 1960).
45 J. Crang, *The British Army and People's War* (Manchester: Manchester University Press, 2000).

an individual officer. However, French adds in his *Military Identities* that the hold of the upper classes on the senior ranks of the British Army was weakened by the First World War and continued to do so past the Second World War.[46] Such analysis is in step with the findings of the sociologist CB Otley, who traced the weakening of the connection of the upper classes to officer ranks to the abolition of purchase in the 1870s.

Although there is already a body of study on divisional command in the British Army in the Second World War, there is little which examines brigade level operations specifically and in 1940 in particular. This is not entirely surprising as the brigade was not considered to be an independent, self-sustaining formation until the Bartholomew Committee recommended this to be the way forward in its findings in June 1940. From this point it is therefore arguable that brigadiers became more significant as field commanders than they had been in the interwar period and would briefly be allowed greater levels of operational and command autonomy. Histories of individual British Army brigades exist, but there is a dearth of analytical work on brigade level operations in France, with most (based on a survey of the holdings of the Imperial War Museum and of the National Army Museum other than War Diaries held at the National Archives) covering the later period of the war and focussed particularly on operations in the Mediterranean and North-West Europe. A rare example of closer focus on brigade operations in 1940 is Charles More's *The Road to Dunkirk*,[47] a re-evaluation of the BEF's 5th Division and its battle on the Ypres-Comines Canal from 26–28 May. However, this is a detailed study of a divisional battle in a limited time period and has the benefit of space to examine brigade level operations in more detail.

Many of the popular accounts of 1940 operations published in the 1960s, 1970s and 1980s proved of little value in determining any possible omissions in the group as they are focussed, understandably, on combat operations and those of divisions and above in particular. Those from the 1950s and 1960s were also disadvantaged by the lack of public access to the official records, which remained closed into the 1970s. With regard to the Battle of France, accounts often slant into the politico-strategic examination of high command tensions between Gort and the French Supreme Command. These are typified in Sir Edward Spears' *Assignment to Catastrophe*, his two-volume account of his time with the BEF, particularly in the first of them, *Prelude to Dunkirk*.[48] Spears, arguably, inclines too much towards wishing to emphasise his championing of General De Gaulle in his writings but has the benefit of actual presence at several key meetings as the situation deteriorated.

Alistair Horne's *To Lose A Battle*,[49] otherwise a standard account of the Battle of France, almost never ventures below divisional level and even here is very selective

46 D. French, Military Identities: The Regimental System. The British Army and The British People (Oxford: OUP, 2005), pp.169–170.
47 C. More, The Road to Dunkirk: The British Expeditionary Force and the Battle of the Ypres-Comines Canal, May 1940 (Barnsley: Frontline Books, 2013).
48 Sir Edward Spears (1955) *Assignment to Catastrophe. Volume 1: Prelude to Dunkirk* (New York: AA Wyn, 1955).
49 A. Horne, *To Lose A Battle: France 1940* (London, Macmillan, 1969).

rather than comprehensive. Gregory Blaxland's *Destination Dunkirk*[50] goes into more detail on British operations as its subtitle, *The Story of Gort's Army*, suggests. It is one of the most useful sources in terms of identifying brigadiers engaged. Blaxland consulted regimental sources extensively in terms of published histories, personal accounts and regimental records, and his presence in France as an officer of 2nd Battalion, The Buffs also informed his writing at a period when most of the official records were still closed to public access. He is also perceptive on the state of officer promotion in the interwar army, remarking that:

> Speed of promotion differed from Corps to Corps .... the fact that Major General Harold Alexander, GOC 1 Division, belonged to the Irish Guards may have helped him gain promotion at the age of 45 .... the Divisional commanders of II Corps came from the infantry of the line and were older men .... A Divisional commander under the age of fifty was likely to be younger than his brigade commanders.[51]

Two modern works which are more helpful, but again both mainly focus on operations above brigade level, are Simon Sebag-Montefiore's *Dunkirk: The Fight to the last Man*[52] and Julian Thompson's *Dunkirk: Retreat to Victory.*[53] Thompson, a retired major general of the Royal Marines, writes with a soldier's eye for operational details, leavened with personal stories. He mentions, however briefly, more brigadiers by name than any other account save that of Blaxland.

Nick Smart's *British Strategy and Politics During The Phony War*[54] takes a more sympathetic view of the ability of the BEF to fight a modern war on the Continent, including its leadership, even if the opportunity of the Phoney War between September 1939 and May 1940 to equip and train further was not fully exploited. Smart's contention that had units been better equipped (such as Major General Roger Evans' 1st Armoured Division) the outcome could have been affected differently is somewhat overstated. However, his assertion that the shock effect of the breakthrough at Sedan unravelled French planning is sound.

Accounts of the Norwegian campaign are even less illuminating in terms of individual brigadiers than those for France. Of 14 brigadiers identified as serving in Norway, only five are referred to by name, and of these five only three merit more than passing notice in either Derry's *OH* volume or the majority of secondary accounts.[55] Kiszely's *Anatomy*

50 G. Blaxland, *Destination Dunkirk: The Story of Gort's Army* (London: William Kimber, 1973).
51 Blaxland, *Destination Dunkirk*, p.15.
52 S. Sebag-Montefiore, *Dunkirk: Fight to the Last Man* (London: Viking, 1996).
53 J. Thompson, *Dunkirk: Retreat to Victory* (London: Sidgwick and Jackson, 2008).
54 N. Smart, *British Strategy and Politics During the Phony War* (Westwood: Praeger, 2003).
55 These are Brigadier The Honourable William Fraser, of 24 Guards Brigade; Brigadier Colin Gubbins of 'Scissorforce' and Brigadier Douglas Hogg, Commander Base Area Adalsnes. Derry (1952) refers.

*of a Campaign*[56] is the most insightful and considered analysis of the battle for Norway, covering actual operations with a more analytical eye than many other accounts.

The concept of the army as an organisation within which officers could be part of a network, be it formal or informal, by virtue of their professional connections as their careers developed and enjoying the patronage of senior officers for whom they had worked is not new. As one example there were the competing, so-called 'rings' which developed around Field Marshals Lord Wolseley and Lord Roberts in the second half of the nineteenth century. These two Field Marshals actively sought to appoint officers who had served on campaign with them in Africa and India respectively, and such patronage is identified and well established in the literature.[57] Authors such as David French, Brian Bond and Timothy Harrison-Place have identified General Officers of the Second World War who actively encouraged the careers of those they had encountered earlier. This was either when they were their commanding officers or when they instructed them in officer training establishments such as the Staff Colleges at Camberley or Quetta.

In his edited diaries it is apparent that once appointed CIGS, Sir Alan Brooke had his favourites and protégés – not least Bernard Montgomery. Montgomery had built a solid reputation as a trainer, particularly of officers, when on the directing staff at the Army Staff College, Camberley while still in his twenties and later as Chief Instructor at the Staff College at Quetta in India.[58] (British Army officers serving in India were not excluded from attending Camberley, but if serving in India at the time were preferred to attend the latter). His elevation to divisional command at the age of 51 did not necessarily indicate his being singularly ahead of his contemporaries, some of whom, such as Bernard Freyberg and Harold Alexander, achieved it while still in their mid-forties. In this regard, Montgomery was not a particularly 'networked' officer and he stands almost atypically to the thesis of interconnected officers prior to the outbreak of the Second World War. Brooke's promotion after Dunkirk opened the door for Montgomery's advancement after his creditable performance in command of the 3rd Division in France. Montgomery was also ready to advance the careers of those officers who had gained his approval before, during and later in the war. He was, however, equally ready to dispose of those who either did not live up to his standards or represented a different command regime to his, however successful.[59] For example, when in command in North-West Europe, Montgomery did not employ officers who

56 J. Kiszeley, *Anatomy of a Campaign: The British Fiasco in Norway, 1940* (Cambridge, CUP, 2017).

57 Examples include E. Spiers, *The Army and Society 1815–1914* (London: Longman, 1980); Christopher Brice, *The Thinking Man's Soldier: The Life and Career of Sir Henry Brackenbury 1837–1914* (Solihull: Helion & Co, 2012) examines the impact of such patronage on one of Wolseley's acolytes for both good and for ill when the former was perceived to have slighted the latter in his later career.

58 A. Danchev and D. Todman (eds), *War Diaries 1939–1945: Field Marshal Lord Alanbrooke* (London: Weidenfeld and Nicholson, 2001).

59 A. Danchev and D. Todman (eds), *War Diaries 1939–1945: Field Marshal Lord Alanbrooke* (London: Weidenfeld and Nicholson, 2001), p.78.

had performed successfully in Tunisia with Kenneth Anderson's First Army, such as Dick McCreery and Anderson himself, even though they had both performed well in France in 1940. Brooke's patronage could also be curtailed if someone who had previously come to his attention in favourable terms no longer performed successfully in the field. A rare exception was Neil Ritchie, towards whom Brooke remained well disposed even after his failure in the Western Desert.

This account broadens the basis of this analysis to go beyond key factors identified in other studies, such as regimental connections, officer education and shared active service. Works such as *Regimental Identities* by David French[60] and his paper on divisional commanders in the British Army of the Second World War, *An Extensive Use of Weedkiller*[61] and studies on the Victorian and Edwardian Army (whose influence would endure) by authors such as Edward Spiers in *The Army and Society 1815–1914*[62] and Ian Beckett in *A British Profession of Arms*[63] are examples of this approach. This work examines these areas, and others such as social and family connections, military sport and so on. Until now these areas have not been the subject of detailed research.

Mark Frost's unpublished 2017 PhD on the senior commanders of British Second Army,[64] also looked at higher level command, such as those at division or corps. He considered these officers with respect to age, Staff College attendance and father's profession but not at the level of detail in this volume or consolidated across as many databases as used in this work. It is, however, a very useful addition to the literature.

The end result of this book, using information sets previously unexamined or used only in passing, is an examination of the careers of a representative set of professional officers from the interwar period to the critical point of 1940 and after. Going beyond traditional military and institutional factors, it looks at the interwar army as a connected body and social entity to show how such networking influenced either advancement or professional survival after two major operational failures.

Although charges of nepotism in senior appointments can be rebuffed in the twentieth century, with increased checks and balances such as the requirement for appointments to be approved by the Army Council, the army's senior decision-making body, it would be impossible completely to eradicate all traces of patronage. The distinction should be made, however, between patronage, which could be backed by objective appreciation of ability, and favouritism. French identified that Brooke and Montgomery used patronage

60 David French, *Military Identities – The Regimental System, the British Army & the British People c. 1870–2000* (Oxford: Oxford UP, 2005).

61 D. French, "An extensive use of weedkiller': patterns of promotion in the senior ranks of the British Army 1919–1939' in D. French and B. Holden Reid (eds), *The British General Staff: Reform and Innovation, 1890–1939* (London: Frank Cass, 2002), pp.159–174.

62 E. M. Spiers, '*The Army and Society, 1815–1914*' (London, Prentice Hall 1980) and '*The Late Victorian Army, 1868–1902*' (Manchester, Manchester UP, 1992).

63 I. F. W. Beckett, *A British Profession of Arms: The Politics of Command in the Late Victorian Army* (Oklahoma, Oklahoma UP, 2018).

64 M. R. Frost, 'Preparation is Key: The effect of the pre-war years on Senior Command in the British Army, 1944–45' (Unpublished PhD thesis, King's College London, 2017).

'assiduously' to promote merit and professionalism among those they had taught when instructors at the Staff College and after, but equally appreciated that use of it had to be judicious or it could reflect back to the patron to their own disadvantage.[65] Personal knowledge of an officer selected for advancement can smooth the process, as in any other form of official service. This book aims to determine the interconnections on various levels and indicate their extent, both known and previously unknown.

## Social Composition of the Army and the Group of Brigadiers in Particular

The social composition of the army between the wars has been covered in the literature to some extent, most notably in Brian Bond's *British Military Policy Between The Two World Wars*[66] which addresses the problems of an army re-establishing itself as a professional force after a period of massive expansion and transformation into a citizen army in less than five years, and its equally rapid contraction from the early 1920s – leaving a surfeit of young, comparatively senior officers. Bond describes the immediate period after the war as one of 'contraction, fragmentation and uncertainty'.[67]

Notwithstanding such a state of affairs, some pre-war regulars considered that a return to a regular force focussed on Imperial policing would restore normal, pre-war soldiering. Many officers reverted to their substantive rank and spent several years climbing back up the seniority system before they regained their wartime standing of 10 or 15 years before. An illustrative case is that of Brigadier Archibald Beauman. He had ended the First World War aged 29 and in command of an infantry brigade as an acting brigadier general. He had also been decorated twice. On his appointment to the first post-war Staff College course at Camberley in 1919 he had to revert to his substantive pre-war rank of captain. It would take until 1932 for him to regain the rank of colonel; he would retire briefly in 1938 and be granted only the honorary rank of brigadier – he would be recalled in 1939 as a temporary brigadier.[68]

According to Bond in *British Military Policy Between The Two World Wars*,[69] a major problem for those seeking advancement was that retirement ages for senior officers were set too high. This created demoralising logjams at the top, leading promising officers to retire prematurely at the lack of promotion prospects.[70] Many officers also spent periods languishing on half pay when there were no appointments for them to fill, with no incentive to retire as doing so from half pay would lead to a reduced pension.

65 D. French, 'Colonel Blimp and the British Army: British Divisional Commanders in the War against Germany, 1939–1945' in *The English Historical Review*, vol. 111, no.444, November 1996, pp.1182–1201.

66 B. Bond, *British Military Policy Between the Two World Wars* (Oxford: Clarendon Press, 1980).

67 B. Bond, *British Military Policy Between the Two World Wars* (Oxford: Clarendon Press, 1980). p.2.

68 A. B. Beauman, *Then A Soldier: A Memoir* (London: Macmillan. 1960).

69 B. Bond, *British Military Policy Between the Two World Wars* (Oxford: Clarendon Press, 1980).

70 Bond, *British Military Policy…*, p.53.

In 1937, the new Secretary of State for War, Leslie Hore-Belisha, attempted to initiate reforms, firstly by dismissing the entire Army Council and by both reducing the mandatory retirement ages for general officers and setting tenure limits for their posts. However, those below general officer rank were not affected by these changes and reviewing them in retrospect with regard to preparations for the outbreak of war, the reform would prove to be too little too late.[71]

Although Bond does to some extent examine the social makeup of the interwar army, it is not to the extent of Spiers' work on the Victorian and pre-war army,[72] or of Bowman and Connelly's for the period 1902–1914.[73] Regular officers at the outbreak of war in 1939 would not be atypical compared to their forbears of 1914, being predominantly products of the major and lesser public schools. A further minority within the overall 1940 group were those officers who had attended public school and university. This latter sub-group was dominated by the universities of Oxford and Cambridge. Bowman and Connelly contend that it is 'difficult to define a uniquely Edwardian officer corps'[74] as its senior officers had begun their careers in the 1870s; even battalion commanders at the outbreak of the First World War were officers of the 1880s and 1890s, and veterans of the Second Boer War, 1899–1902. The brigadiers of the 1940 group, who were interwar regular soldiers, were either products of the pre-First World War era or commissioned, mainly, during the early period of the war itself.

David French argues that even before the First World War a commission in the army could not be viewed as the refuge for the dissolute sons of the landed gentry, a trend he notes as declining while at the same time, what he terms the 'self-replication' of sons following fathers into the army was increasing. The latter trend, he suggests, would accelerate through the 1930s, but the primary source for potential officers would remain the public schools.[75] A point of agreement in Bond and in French is that the interwar army was a dubious choice for a fulfilling and constant career. Promotion log jams, a lack of active service and opportunities to show worth, which would invite accelerated promotion, caused difficulties which were not easily overcome in the 1920s and 1930s,

French's conclusions are also in harmony with the work of the sociologist C. B. Otley, who examined the social backgrounds of British Army officers in a series of works in the 1970s. Otley's findings indicated that the influence of the upper classes was eroded by the abolition of the system of purchase of commissions in the 1870s but endured, albeit reduced, due to the dominance of the products of the public schools in the body of officers.

71 Bond, *British Military Policy…*, p.46.
72 E. M. Spiers, *The Army and Society 1815–1914* (London: Longman, Themes in British Social History Series, 1980).
73 T. Bowman and M. Connelly, *The Edwardian Army: Recruiting, Training and Deploying the British Army 1902–1914* (Oxford; OUP, 2012).
74 Bowman and Connelly, *The Edwardian Army…*, p.7.
75 D. French, *Raising Churchill's Army: The British Army and the War Against Germany 1919–45* (Oxford: OUP, 2000), p.51.

Choice of regiment could also influence one's rate of progress up the promotions ladder, with Royal Artillery officers suffering the worst and Guards officers coming off best (as shown in Blaxland's remark concerning Harold Alexander's advancement to major general at the relatively youthful age of 45 in 1940 being attributed to his being a Guards officer). Gunner officers could remain subalterns for as long as 17 years, whereas Guards officers could, in the same period, rise to command their battalions, or be serving elsewhere in a lieutenant colonel's post.

## Professional Education of Officers

The main avenues for higher professional education of officers beyond that conducted within their battalions and equivalents were the Senior Officers' School at Sheerness; the Staff Colleges at Camberley and Quetta in India (in 1940 a wartime outstation of the Staff College was also established at Haifa in Palestine but it ran short wartime courses which did not award a p.s.c. qualification), and from 1927 the Imperial Defence College at Seaford House in London. It is well established that Camberley in particular was a source of 'talent spotting' for future commanders and David French[76] specifically notes Alan Brooke's tenure as an instructor at Camberley in 1924–1925 and how he would later advance the careers of his most promising students.

Wider studies of patronage networks at the Staff College in the interwar period are made more difficult by the fact that many records, by the Staff College's own admission, were destroyed following an 'administrative decision' in 1940.[77] The Staff College Archives are maintained by the Joint Command and Staff College Library at Shrivenham. The staff list of the Staff College was known as 'The Camberley Pink' and the Joint Command and Staff College provided a listing for the interwar period from their database. In the interwar period, the instructors and students at Camberley and Quetta were laid out in the Army List, but for the Senior Officers' School only the directing staff is listed. No list of the graduates of the Senior Officers' School exists as a single, consolidated entity.

It has been possible to reconstruct and fill some gaps from the annual publication of lists of graduates from the College which were published in *The Times*. These usually appeared in February or March of the year following the end of the course the previous December, but there are gaps which break continuity, for example in 1924 reflecting the graduates of 1923 (this was reconstructed using the Staff College's internal annual journal, *Owl Pie*, held at the British Library); for Quetta, complete lists for 1926, 1927 and 1928 did not appear, although shorter notes headed 'among those graduating' were published for 1926 and 1927.

76 D. French, *Raising Churchill's Army* (Oxford: Oxford University Press, 2000).
77 'Staff College, Camberley' entry in 'Archives in London and the M25 Area' (AIM25) site: www.aim25.ac.uk/cgi-bin/vcdf/detail?coll_id=19233&inst_id=117&nv1=search&nv2=

Of two studies published on the history of the Staff College in the twentieth century, the first, Godwin-Austen's 1927 work *The Staff and the Staff College*, while illuminating as to the evolution of the college when it reopened after the First World War, is rather colloquial and lacks identification of many attendees.[78] It does, however, underline the importance of the Staff College Drag (the College hunt) as a social body, referring to the rivalry between officers to occupy committee positions in it. Gregory Kennedy contends that there was also a practical function to the Drag; it allowed the directing staff to assess which students were able to remain mentally alert while physically tired, vital in an efficient staff officer.[79] Hunting and polo were also considered advantageous in this regard. One wonders whether such skills may have been more successfully achieved in field exercises, of which there were few on the syllabus.

A recent biography of General Sir Richard McCreery highlights the struggle between the then Captain McCreery and Captain Claude Nicholson when fellow students at Camberley for the post of Secretary of the Drag.[80] A generation earlier, in 1896, Douglas Haig and Edmund Allenby, both of whom rose to be Field Marshals and be ennobled, had also been rivals for the same position. Allenby prevailed because 'nobody wanted D. H.'[81] In the 1920s, Nicholson prevailed, but both officers remained on friendly terms. During the Second World War, McCreery would command, first, an armoured brigade in France in 1940 and later the Eighth Army in the Mediterranean. Nicholson was captured in command of 30 Brigade defending Calais in May 1940 and died in captivity in 1943.

The second account of the Staff College, published by the College's Librarian to mark the centenary of its founding in 1958, is a collection of short accounts in a small volume by various authors.[82] Of most immediate use to this research is the third part of the chapter 'Four Generations of Staff College Students – 1930' by Brigadier C. N. Barclay, himself an author of Second World War regimental and divisional histories.[83] Barclay admits that he found attendance at Camberley '...to be a great advantage in later life. In whatever part of the world one later served, and in whatever capacity, there was certain to be a few 'old boys' of Camberley days.'[84]

78 Major A. R. Godwin-Austen Bt, *The Staff and the Staff College* (London; Constable and Company, 1927).
79 D. French, 'Officer Training in the British Army 1919–1939' in G. Kennedy and K. Neilson (eds.) *Military Education and Training Past. Present and Future* (New Haven: Praeger, 2002), pp.105–29.
80 R. Mead, *The Last Great Cavalryman: The Life and Career of Sir Richard McCreery* (Bradford; Pen and Sword, 2012).
81 Sir James Edmonds to Lord Wavell, 27 August 1936, Allenby Papers 6/III cited in G. De Groot, 'The Pre-War Life and Early Military Career of Douglas Haig' (unpublished PhD thesis, University of Edinburgh, 1983), p.135.
82 Lieutenant Colonel F. W. Young, *The Story of the Staff College 1858-1958* (Aldershot: Published for the Staff College by Gale and Polden Ltd, 1958).
83 Young, *The Story...*, pp.25–28.
84 Brigadier C. N. Barclay in Young, *The Story...*, p.26.

French further points out in his 2002 essay on senior officers' promotion patterns, 1919–1939 published in the collection *The British General Staff: Reform and Innovation*,[85] that a Staff College qualification (be it from Camberley or Quetta) became a prerequisite for advancement from the mid-1920s to the mid-1930s as former Staff College graduates, instructors and commandants sought out those similarly qualified or to 'talent spot' those they had taught. Indeed, *all* senior appointments made by Field Marshal Sir Cyril Deverell during his tenure as CIGS in 1936–37 were Staff College graduates.[86] The expansion programme of the army from 1938 meant that demand soon exceeded supply. As a result, several brigadiers in the group, including several in fighting commands, were not graduates of either Camberley or Quetta.[87]

As noted above, the Senior Officers' School is less well documented. It was established originally in Aldershot in 1915 as a temporary wartime expedient but was put on a permanent footing in 1920 and eventually relocated to Sheerness. Its function was to prepare senior majors for battalion command, but throughout the 1920s its curriculum expanded to include non-military subjects to further a wider geopolitical and technical view amongst its students. It was also, in modern terms, a joint service establishment, with the Royal Navy sending lieutenant commanders and the Royal Air Force sending squadron leaders, to take part in the course. The School was unpopular with some senior officers, who felt that the professional development of junior officers was the role of their local commanders – an increasingly outdated view as officer training developed along more professional lines and also attempted to instil a coherent and uniform doctrine throughout the Army. The lack of comprehensive records on the school in the National Archives or elsewhere has rendered it impossible to achieve a complete listing of staff and students at Sheerness, although as noted above the directing staff were named in the Army List. Some of the officers in the group served as instructors at the School and are listed later in this work.

There are some articles in the *Journal of the Royal United Services Institution* of the interwar period which suggest that the School's existence was controversial and its training was thought inadequate by some.[88] Nonetheless, it had powerful supporters such as the then CIGS, Field Marshal Sir George Milne (CIGS 1928–1933), who felt that while local commanders lacked the time to perform such training (his belief was that they should devote one day a week to the training of their officers) the School was essential.[89] The next educational step, for the select few, was attendance at the Imperial

85 D. French, "An extensive use of weedkiller': patterns of promotion in the senior ranks of the British Army 1919–1939' in D. French and B. Holden Reid (eds), *The British General Staff: Reform and Innovation, 1890–1939* (London, Frank Cass, 2002).
86 French in French & Holden Reid, *The British General Staff*, p.168.
87 'Fighting' commands in this context suggests officers commanding infantry or armoured brigades, and officers holding the position of 'Commander, Royal Artillery' at divisional level.
88 For example, Colonel H. R. Sandilands, 'The Case for the Senior Officers' School' in *Journal of the Royal United Services Institution*, vol. 73 issue 490, May 1928, pp.235–238. Sandilands was a senior instructor at the School.
89 D. French, "An extensive use of weedkiller': patterns of promotion in the senior ranks of the British Army 1919–1939' in D. French and B. Holden Reid (eds), *The British General Staff: Reform and Innovation, 1890–1939* (London, Frank Cass, 2002).

Defence College, founded in 1927[90] and intended to prepare officers of the British and Imperial armed forces, with some senior civil servants, for higher posts in the military and government. The syllabus was intended to go beyond purely military subjects and encourage greater strategic thought and vision. The College closed on the outbreak of war; of the group of 156 officers in this work, 9 attended, mostly in the early 1930s. All advanced beyond brigadier during the Second World War (as discussed in Chapter 4).

## Notes on the Structure of This Book

This book has six main chapters. After this introduction, the second chapter considers the educational and family backgrounds of the officers in the group and the regiments into which they were originally commissioned. It examines the trends or groupings which may have developed among the attendees of schools and through service with regiments. The third chapter covers the period 1919–1939, and considers, firstly, the further professional education and training of the officers in the group. Examined next is the possible influence and impact on their careers of overseas postings, particularly those in garrison, staff or operational roles, in a period when opportunities for active service were scarce. Chapter 4 is a closer examination of those officers in the group who advanced in rank between 1940–1945, looking to determine further trends and traits which may have contributed to their professional success after 1940.

Chapter 5 employs the methodology used to examine the 1940 group, but in a slightly reduced format (to employ the full methodology would lead to a product worthy of a standalone work) to look at brigadiers serving in fighting formations which landed in France on, and for a period immediately following, D-Day, 6 June 1944. The intention of this chapter is to determine how, or if, the criteria for advancement to brigadier had altered after four further years of active service, if the notional profile of a typical brigadier had changed and if so, to compare them. The final chapter draws together the findings and conclusions.

Although the officer cadres of the British Army of the World Wars, and to a lesser extent of the period 1919–1939 has been extensively studied in the literature, no previous work has looked into the social and professional backgrounds of its officers in such detail, and doubly so for officers at this level. Studies of future senior commanders exist in the literature (including some officers included in this group) but they have not compared those who progressed against those who did not in pursuit of potential characteristics and connections to explain success, or its absence. The addition of the Normandy chapter also seeks to identify whether the requirements for officers in a fighting command by the later part of the Second World War had evolved in the intervening years; from an army which had suffered two simultaneous strategic defeats, to one moving towards final victory over the enemy responsible for them.

90 Since 1970, the Royal College of Defence Studies.

# 2

# Education, Regiment and Family

The Army knows the debt it owes to the Public Schools.[1]
General Sir William Robertson, Chief of the Imperial General Staff, Address at Bradfield College, November 1916

The intention of this chapter is, firstly, to examine the educational backgrounds of all the officers in the 1940 group to determine the impact of their schooling on their subsequent advancement, or lack thereof, after 1940. It will also investigate whether certain schools were prevalent in the production and supply of officers serving in 1940. From this, it will consider whether groupings of former pupils from those schools were significant over other institutions for advancement, for example if Old Etonians were singularly significant over those from other schools. Secondly, there is an examination of the regiments into which officers were originally commissioned, both to determine whether certain schools directed their pupils to certain regiments, or that belonging to particular regiments was advantageous for promotion. Finally, this chapter will examine the family backgrounds of the officers in the group, looking at how many were the sons of military officers or other eminent persons, in order to examine the social composition of the group. The combination of education and family background is assessed to determine certain presumptions as to the prevailing social status of those officers who formed the 1940 group.

## Initial Education

Initial bonds between individuals can be formed during the period when they are in education undergoing long periods of teaching and sports. In the case of boarders at public schools, communal living in school dormitories can promote enduring connections between those who shared the experience simultaneously. It has been possible to

1 Quoted in J. Blackie, *Bradfield 1850–1975* (Bradfield: Bradfield College, 1976), p.44.

confirm the educational background of all but two of the officers in the group studied. Six did not fit the traditional pattern of education,[2] by far the majority, 84 percent, were taught at British public schools.[3]

Authors such as Spiers,[4] Simpson[5] and Sheffield[6] have shown that, certainly in the early period of the First World War up to late 1915, the selection and recruitment of officers sought to replicate the social foundations of the pre-war army. An officer would preferably be public school educated and from the upper tiers of society, ideally from a wealthy family who could provide a private income to their son to supplement the army salary. The latter, especially in regiments deemed 'fashionable' or of high social standing such as the Guards, cavalry regiments or infantry regiments which did not recruit from county areas,[7] was often inadequate to meet the considerable costs of life as an army officer. In the period 1914–1916 professional competence took second place to social acceptability and an ability to fit into an officers' mess, regardless of whether a candidate had been a member of the Officer Training Corps (OTC) at public school or university or received any previous form of military education. However, nearly half of the overall group, some 74 officers, had left their schools before the OTC system was fully embodied under the Haldane Reforms of 1908.[8] The OTC had two divisions, the junior division established in the school system, and the senior division established in universities. Prior to 1908, some, although not all, public schools possessed school contingents of the Rifle Volunteer Corps.

As the war progressed, casualty rates increased and the army continued to expand, the demand for officers would outstrip the ability of the traditional routes of supply – such as the public schools, the scions of the gentry, the clergy, the land-owning classes, and the sons and younger relatives of officers – to fulfil this need. The class-based bar would lower as more officers were promoted from the ranks on the basis of practical and battle experience. An officer could no longer be considered automatically to be 'a gentleman' on the basis of their birth and upbringing – and almost all[9]

2 For example, Crocker was home schooled; two officers were from Grammar Schools and one was educated in Australia.

3 For the purposes of this chapter, schools which were members of the Clarendon Group and/or the Headmasters' Conference are considered to be public schools.

4 E. M. Spiers, 'The Regular Army' in Beckett and Simpson (eds), *A Nation in Arms*, (Manchester: Manchester UP, 1985), pp.36–61.

5 K. Simpson, 'The Officers' in Beckett and Simpson (eds), *A Nation in Arms*, (Manchester: Manchester UP, 1985), pp.85–86.

6 G. Sheffield, Leadership in the Trenches: Officer-Man Relations on the Western Front (London, Macmillan, 2000).

7 In particular, the King's Royal Rifle Corps and the Rifle Brigade in England and the Royal Irish Rifles in Ireland.

8 The OTC system was incorporated as a contingent of the new Territorial Force in October 1908, in accordance with Army Order 160 of July 1908, which itself was a result of the Territorial and Reserve Forces Act 1907 (7 Edw. 7, c.9).

9 Officers promoted from the ranks to fill specialist posts such as quartermasters, riding and musketry instructors were not expected to be of similar social standing.

army officers were expected to have the social standing of 'gentlemen', a tradition which could trace its origins back beyond the Napoleonic Wars. Laurence James argues that its basis lies in the warrior elite which controlled British society after the Romans left, and whose[10] political and territorial authority was founded on their success on the battlefield. [11] The Duke of Wellington noted that the necessary 'character' of an officer was 'Due to the officer exclusively, the man of education, manners, honesty, and other qualities required by education which English gentlemen receive...'[12] Character was the trait that most clearly defined a gentleman, even more than wealth or birth, and it was character that was the most desirable trait in a potential officer. Anthony Clayton notes that social norms were upheld in the interwar period, citing as an example that 'at least ninety percent' of officers serving in the (amalgamated post-1924) Royal Artillery had received a public school education at the 'better known' schools.[13]

Yet this gentlemanly ideal, which army officers were deemed to embody, was predominantly transmitted from generation to generation via Britain's public schools. It was from such institutions that the majority of officers, and specifically among the group studied here, were drawn. Rupert Wilkinson's characterisation of the public school gentleman underlines the importance of officers as being gentlemen:

> It is .... true that a prime characteristic of the public school gentleman ideal was to attach great importance to a dignified bearing and aura of command. Such leadership qualities were readily identified with character – a confusion of manners with the morals they were means to symbolise.[14]

By the middle of 1916, as officer recruitment shifted more towards selection on grounds of experience and ability, all prospective officers were expected to have spent some time in the ranks and to have been trained in an Officer Cadet Battalion. These later entrants were unofficially labelled 'temporary gentlemen', indicating that the bearer was an officer only for the duration of hostilities. It was worn half mockingly as a badge of honour by those deemed so to be, even though some, especially soldier-poets such as Siegfried Sassoon and Robert Graves detested the term.[15] The origins of the term are unclear, but

10 A. Clayton, *The British Officer* (London: Longman Pearson, 2006) p.156; Clayton cites '*The History of the Royal Artillery 1918–1938*' (Woolwich, Royal Artillery Institution 1978) p.15.
11 L. James, *Warrior Race: The British Experience of War from Roman Times to the Present* (London: Little, Brown, 2001), pp.288–90.
12 Cited in Richard Blanco, 'Reform and Wellington's Post Waterloo Army, 1815–1854' in *Military Affairs*, vol. 29, no.3 (1965), p.130.
13 A. Clayton, *The British Officer* (London: Longman Pearson, 2006) p.156; Clayton cites '*The History of the Royal Artillery 1918–1938*' (Woolwich, Royal Artillery Institution 1978) p.15.
14 R. Wilkinson, *Gentlemanly Power: British Leadership and the Public School Tradition* (London: OUP, 1964), pp 13–14.
15 Despite this, both men held 'Permanent' commissions by virtue of their having been commissioned via the Special Reserve, a route taken by some which bypassed the military

it was in popular use in Britain by 1916, when a book of letters was published, with War Office permission, under the title a *'Temporary Gentleman' in France: Home Letters from an Officer at the Front*.[16] Its 'editor', in fact its author, Captain A. J. Dawson, a pre-war traveller and author, had been commissioned into a service battalion of the Border Regiment in 1914, but was invalided to home service in 1915. The traditional view was that if one was a gentleman, one was born and died a gentleman. The status was conferred by birth and education. But being an officer in the British Army also indicated gentlemanly status, the 'officer and gentleman,' and the connection continued despite lower class men being offered temporary and artificial elevation to it. Dawson himself – much older than the usual 'New Army' officer as he was 43 when commissioned – uses the term in gentle self-mockery as he was from humble origins and had not had the typical education of an 'officer and a gentleman'.[17]

The officers in the 1940 group studied in this book were predominantly products of the pre-war system. There was one exception; Brigadier Sidney Rice, who was a civilian put into uniform as a member of the Regular Army Reserve of Officers. This was to allow him to serve with GHQ BEF as its Chief Financial Adviser by virtue of his expertise and he was in no sense a professional soldier (and does not feature further in the analysis contained in this volume),[18] the majority of the group were products of the pre-First World War period. Five were commissioned during the reign of Queen Victoria; 62 under King Edward VII and 43 under King George V from 1911–1913 prior to the outbreak of the First World War. 1914 itself produced a spike – indeed, it produced the single highest annual number of commissions among the group – but the advent and outbreak of war is the reason for this. Only 39 officers of the 156 in the group gained their commissions after 1913, with two brigadiers, exceptionally young in 1940 terms, being commissioned in the 1920s. The majority, therefore, were products of the Victorian/Edwardian officer selection and training process – and the social norms which applied to it. Thus, an officer who reached brigadier rank in 1940 would have had over 20 years' experience in uniform, even if he had retired but was recalled in 1939–1940.

academies. See Laura Root, *Temporary Gentlemen' on the Western Front: Class Consciousness and the British Army Officer, 1914–1918*, all volumes (2001–2008). *72.https://digitalcommons.unf.edu/ojiivolumes/72.*

16 Captain A. J. Dawson, *'Temporary Gentleman' in France: Home Letters form an Officer at the Front* (London; George Putnam's, 1916).

17 Laura Root, *'Temporary Gentlemen' on the Western Front: Class Consciousness and the British Army Officer*, 1914–1918, all volumes (2001–2008). https://digitalcommons.unf.edu/ojiivolumes/72 Root (2006), p.2.

18 Rice ended the war as the Chief Accountant of the War Office (HYAL Jan 1945). Sidney Noel Rice, who served as the Chief Financial Adviser to GHQ BEF as a brigadier but was appointed CBE (Civil Division) in the New Year's Honours List as 'Chief Accountant, War Office' *London Gazette*, 1 January 1941, p.14.

**Chart 1 1940 Brigadiers by Year of First Commissioning**

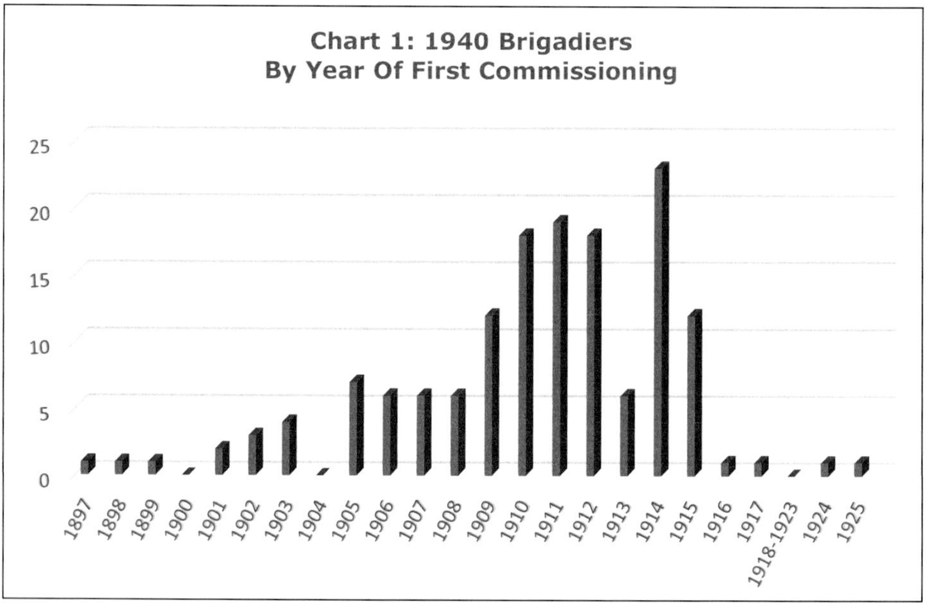


Among the six officers in the group who were identified as not educated via the public school system, and therefore represent the sole significant deviation from the norm, notable were: John Crocker, who home schooled both due to a respiratory ailment which precluded him attending conventional school and to the premature death of his father, leaving his mother to cope with his four other siblings.[19] Gordon Gill, commander of the BEF's Nantes Sub-Area was a grammar school pupil among the 1940 group, although he later attended the University of Cambridge.[20] Tommy Clifton, who commanded 2nd Light Reconnaissance Brigade in the BEF spent seven years in the ranks of the Royal Field Artillery before being commissioned as an infantry officer and did not attend either public school or grammar school.

The remaining officers attended 35 different public schools at varying times. No single school absolutely dominates the group, although Eton with 12 former pupils

19 Commander, 3rd Armoured Brigade in the BEF; later a corps commander in North-West Europe and Adjutant General. See Delaney, D. (2011*) 'Corps Commanders: Five British and Canadian Generals at War, 1939–45' (Vancouver, University of British Columbia Press) pp.122–123*: and D. Delaney, *'A Quiet Man of Influence: General Sir John Crocker' in Journal of the Society for Army Historical Research, vol. 85 (Autumn 2007), pp.185–207.*

20 See J. Venn, Alumni Cantabrigienses: A Biographical List of All Known Students, Graduates and Holders of Office at the University of Cambridge, from the Earliest Times to 1900, volume 2, From 1752 to 1900 (Cambridge: CUP, 2011) p.51.

and Cheltenham, Wellington and Winchester with nine each, figure prominently. As Sheffield points out,[21] by the outbreak of war in 1914, most officers had followed the path of public school followed by initial officer training either at the Royal Military College, Sandhurst (for infantry or cavalry officers) or the Royal Military Academy, Woolwich (for artillery, engineer and technical officers). Some would circumvent this via commissions in the Militia, the Special Reserve or via service in the Officers' Training Corps at school (the junior division) or university (the senior division). The only two officers, educated at public school but not schools which were members of the Clarendon Group or Headmasters' Conference were William Ramsden (Bath College) and George Sutton (Kersal School).

A university education was much less common, as it was a minority experience across the country overall, as it still remains. The percentage of the UK population in higher education did not rise above 3 percent until the 1950s. Although 21 officers in the group of 156 were graduates, 13 percent of the total, they would remain a minority group within a minority of the population, being both army officers and graduates.[22] Oxford and Cambridge Universities predominate in this list, though no individual colleges of those universities are pre-eminent. It is noteworthy that the representation of graduates was four times the norm across society in general, coming from the social classes which produced army officers, and the ability to fund a public school education, a university education and enable their sons to afford an army career.

In the period after the First World War, the old preferences began to reassert themselves, where officers who did not 'fit in' would face varying degrees of ostracism and even pressure to leave the army. The future brigadiers considered here had already proved themselves suitable to be considered permanent officers by virtue of their active service, many having decorations for gallantry and distinguished service during the past war or between the wars, which would lend them an advantage in resisting and overcoming such pressures in comparison to contemporaries without them.[23]

The first, enlarged, post-war course at the Staff College, Camberley in 1919 was opened to officers who had particularly distinguished themselves in the past war and who might not otherwise have gained entrance via the traditional routes of competition by examination or nomination by a senior officer. Beauman notes in his memoir that his possession of a Distinguished Service Order and two Military Crosses was probably more influential than his command of a battalion, and temporarily a brigade, while still in his twenties on the Western Front. The impact on career prospects through the possession of decorations for gallantry or distinguished service is discussed separately in a forthcoming chapter. Equally, they also survived a period of retrenchment in defence

21 G. Sheffield, Leadership in the Trenches: Officer-Man Relations on the Western Front (London, Macmillan, 2000). pp.2 & 8.

22 P. Bolton, *Education: Historical Statistics*' Standard Note SN/SG/4252, 27 November 2012 (London; House of Commons Library, 2012); Table G 'Higher Education' p.13 and Table 8, 'Students Obtaining University Degrees', p.20.

23 A. B. Beauman, *Then A Soldier: A Memoir* (London: Macmillan. 1960), p.2.

spending in the 1920s and early 1930s where many other officers retired either voluntarily or forcibly. As Bond indicates,[24] the system of placing under-employed officers on half pay in the 1920s and 1930s did not encourage officers, especially those without private means or supplementary incomes, to leave the army and free up the seniority list; the effect on an officer's pension was also a factor, as described above.

Even those few in the group who entered as 'temporary gentlemen' in and after 1916 were deemed sufficiently suitable by their peers and superiors to remain in the army and convert to permanent commissions. Sheffield contends that overall, officer candidates who emerged from outside the traditional paths were quickly inculcated with the officer class ethos founded on the basis of a public school education.[25] Bond suggests that the massive expansion of the officer corps between 1914 and 1918, followed by an equally 'breakneck' demobilisation in 1919–1920, left the post-war officer corps at a similar level to that of 1913 – but in command of a much smaller army. This would exacerbate the problems of advancement; too many officers for too few placements where they might distinguish themselves for promotion.[26]

Although a public school education is sufficiently prominent among the officers to lead one to conclude that it was a prerequisite (albeit an implied rather than a mandated one) to remain in the army and build a career after the First World War, the group is not dominated by the seven 'great' public schools and the two day-schools of the Clarendon Group (CG).[27] Schools from the Headmasters' Conference (HMC) are more frequently represented, but there were more schools in the HMC than the CG.[28] Although individuals may be separated during their time at a public school by virtue of being in different school houses and different starting times, mixing only on communal activity such as

24 B. Bond, *British Military Policy Between the Two World Wars* (Oxford: Clarendon Press, 1980), p.46.

25 G. Sheffield, Leadership in the Trenches: Officer-Man Relations on the Western Front (London, Macmillan, 2000). p.2.

26 B. Bond, *British Military Policy Between the Two World Wars* (Oxford: Clarendon Press, 1980), p.44.

27 So-called after the 1861–1864 Clarendon Commission established to investigate the management of nine schools after complaints over the running of Eton College; the Public Schools Act of 1868 resulted. The schools of this group were Eton, Charterhouse, Harrow, Rugby, Shrewsbury, Westminster and Winchester; the day schools were St. Paul's and Merchant Taylors. Colin Shrosbree, *Public Schools and Private Education: The Clarendon Commission, 1861–64, and the Public Schools Acts* (Manchester: Manchester University Press, 1988), p.12.

28 The Headmasters' Conference (since 1996, The Headmasters and Headmistress' Conference) was formed in 1869, when Edward Thring, Headmaster of Uppingham, invited some 60 other headmasters to convene and form a grouping of schools and have an annual conference. Fourteen accepted, but membership expanded considerably up to the First World War and beyond. Clarendon schools are also members of the HC, for example, Eton. Membership of the HC is widely accepted to define what constitutes a 'public school' in the United Kingdom. See D. P. Leinster-Mackay, *The Educational World of Edward Thring: A Centenary Study* (London, Falmer Press, 1987), p.100.

sport, chapel or the OTC, such distinctions diminish after leaving, becoming substituted by a broader allegiance to the school as a whole – encapsulated in terms such as 'the old boys' network' or 'the old school tie'.

Therefore, it can be determined that among this group of officers who continued as professional soldiers after the First World War, regardless of their means of initial entry to the profession of army officer, products of the public school system reasserted their dominance in the interwar period. In the difficult economic times of the 1920s and early 1930s, officers deemed suitable to remain in the army may also have done so in the absence of opportunity or qualification to work elsewhere. As the army contracted following demobilisation and the retrenchment in public spending following the recommendations of the Committee on National Expenditure chaired by Sir Eric Geddes in 1921, the army would revert to recreating its social basis among those who elected or were selected to remain as regular officers with permanent commissions in the post-war army. Bond observes that many officers commissioned from the ranks, or 'ranker officers' as they were known, to further highlight their separation from the mainstream, wondered whether they could survive as the pre-war regimental system and traditions reasserted itself.[29] Furthermore, E. S. Turner wrote in his study *Gallant Gentlemen* 'men who had kept their nerve in the trenches lost it on the social front and resigned.'[30]

Seldon and Walsh[31] seek to reclaim the public school ethos from its detractors and critics, a position they contend has been prevalent in the popular conception of the British officer since the 1960s. They suggest that public schoolboys were not all the 'bluff, anti-intellectual, sporting hearties of popular image',[32] and their focus on instilling values of 'duty, service to others and personal responsibility, as well as courage and loyalty' grounded in classical philosophies stands.[33] However, this may be expected of a former headmaster and senior master of eminent public schools, as the authors are; Seldon having been Master of Wellington and Walsh, among other appointments, a master at Tonbridge.

Sheffield challenges the generally negative position adopted by Parker, suggesting that a reliance on sport, or 'the cult of athleticism', channelled aggression into cooperation and developed both self-discipline and team discipline. On entering an institution (the army) where sporting prowess was equally prized, such ability would impress the men who had spectated at games such as football. Parallels were also drawn to cricket as 'a form of stalking' and how polo developed stamina, with hunting also doing this, as well as promoting an eye for the ground and decision-making when physically tired

29 B. Bond, *British Military Policy Between the Two World Wars* (Oxford: Clarendon Press, 1980), pp.44–45.
30 E. Turner, Gallant Gentlemen: A Portrait of the British Officer, 1660–1956 (London: Joseph, 1956), p.294.
31 A. Seldon, and D. Walsh, *Public Schools and The Great War: A Generation Lost* (Bradford, Pen and Sword, 2013).
32 Seldon and Walsh, *Public Schools…*, p.5.
33 Seldon and Walsh, *Public Schools…*, p.5.

– qualities also emphasised in the Staff College Drag as mentioned above.[34] The latter was re-emphasised to officers attending the Staff College, especially at Camberley, in the interwar years.

Schoolboys were inculcated with honour codes based on ancient history and philosophy and encouraged to believe that they were born into a class intended to lead, although in the later nineteenth century, Kipling's writings had also emphasised the paternalistic, courageous and self-denying virtues of those appointed over the 'working classes' of the soldiery to lead them. Equally, these men came to expect the demonstration of such virtues.[35]

Horace Vachell's novel *The Hill*,[36] published in 1905, also gave an idealised view of the public school experience, based on his own time at Harrow in the 1870s. However, his portrayal is of a school where the titled hold sway over the sons of the rising middle classes. The latter were eager to acquire social status and therefore acquiesced in an inherent culture of random punishment, acting as servants, or 'fagging', for senior boys and the dominance of the sports field. Yet Vachell inclines to the romanticised view. Kipling's own *Stalky and Co*[37] (published as a novel in 1899, following prior magazine serialisation) predates Vachell. In contrast, it presents 'the College' as a school where there is no system of fagging. Chapel features less prominently and the classroom prevails over the sports field.

Kipling's hero, Stalky himself, was inspired by and based on Lionel Dunsterville, who retired as a major general, latterly in command of his eponymous Dunsterforce, in Persia and the Black Sea during the First World War and after. Dunsterville's command was a mixed multinational formation akin to modern special forces which both deterred a Germano-Turkish force from attacking India through the Transcaucasus and prevented the establishment there of a separate republic. In the book, Stalky, who feels he is assured a career in the army after school, pays less heed to academic subjects than of being active and dynamic, yet well read, something the college indulges.

Kipling's boys are resourceful and patriotic without jingoism (and deriding of those who seek to invoke the latter). Nevertheless, all the protagonists are shown, in adult life, as serving as Imperial administrators and soldiers. While the book, and 'the Coll' are not utterly devoid of cruelty and violence among the boys, overall, the book mocks other popular works from the Victorian schooldays canon.

These include Frederick Farrar's *Eric, or Little by Little* originally published in 1858 and in print for over 50 years. However, Kipling's 'College' in Stalky is an idealised version of his own school, the United Services College at Westward Ho! Devon, described as 'something between a traditional public school and an army crammer',[38] established

34 G. Sheffield, *Leadership in the Trenches: Officer-Man Relations on the Western Front* (London: Macmillan, 2000). pp.47–48.
35 Sheffield, *Leadership*…, p.53.
36 H. A. Vachell, *The Hill: A Romance of Friendship* (London: John Murray, 1905).
37 R. Kipling, *Stalky & Co* (London: Macmillan, 1899).
38 P. Parker, *The Old Lie: The Great War and The Public School Ethos* (London: Constable, 1987), p.59.

to educate the sons of army officers, ideally to become officers themselves or Colonial and Imperial administrators. The College, absorbed by the Imperial Service College in 1906, was not a member of the Clarendon Group or the Headmasters' Conference and despite its background would only produce one officer in this group – Cecil Haydon, who attended from 1910 to 1914.

Even Haileybury, which records on its website that a 1956 memoir of the school notes that 'the College's contribution to the British Army alone stands at one Field Marshal [Viscount Allenby], seven generals, four lieutenant generals, 32 major generals and 106 brigadiers'[39] only produced two of the officers considered here. (Haileybury would amalgamate with the United Services College under the single Haileybury banner in 1942).

Furthermore, Seldon and Walsh highlight that in the Great War public school educated officers were at risk of becoming fatalities at an inverse proportion to their number as a group within the army itself:

> Some 35,000 public schoolboys .... died in the war out of a total of 900,000 dead; just over 3% of the total and less than 2% of those who fought .... [Public schoolboys] were to die at about twice the average of those who served. While 11% of those who served overall were to die as a direct result of the fighting, the figure for public schoolboys was 18%. Those who left between 1908 and 1915 were to die at even higher rates as they were most likely to be serving in the front line as junior officers.[40]

For over 130 officers[41] of the group to have survived to the end of the First World War indicates that they were ahead, if only through good fortune, of the statistical trend. At least 55 of them left their schools during that critical time period recognised by Sheldon and Walsh. Whether the very fact that they had survived underlined and enhanced networks between these officers is difficult to prove with certainty, but subsequent commemoration of the dead within schools, universities and regiments can act as a unifying force between those with common experience, or communal connection.

Messenger[42] suggests that in the period 1914–1916, there was an institutional bias against candidates from the grammar schools presenting themselves for commissions, whether or not they had experience within the junior division of the OTC at school. He describes a system, certainly present in the autumn and winter of 1914 and into 1915, where those from the public schools or universities with experience in the senior division of the OTC, and particularly if they were in possession of a Certificate B

39 https://www.haileybury.com/explore/haileybury/heritage-archives/haileyburys-military-heritage accessed 26 September 2016.
40 A. Seldon, and D. Walsh, *Public Schools and The Great War: A Generation Lost* (Bradford, Pen and Sword, 2013), p.1.
41 Excluding the six not educated at public school, and those for whom schools could not be traced.
42 C. Messenger, *A Call to Arms: The British Army 1914–1918* (London. Cassell, 2005), p.293.

training qualification, could be commissioned instantly by the regiments to which they had presented themselves. Holding Certificate B was held by the recruiting authorities to be equivalent to six months attendance at the Royal Military College, Sandhurst.[43] (Certificate B focussed on the tactical employment of an infantry company in the field.) Those from the junior division would require the recommendation of the respective commanding officer. Furthermore, Messenger suggests a 'north-south divide' in this latter case; grammar school boys from the south of the United Kingdom generally found it harder to be commissioned quickly, whereas in the Midlands and the North, the sons of the 'managerial classes' educated at grammar schools were quickly admitted as officers, especially in the hastily and locally raised Pals Battalions of the so-called Kitchener Armies in the industrial cities.[44]

R. C. Sheriff, an infantry officer in the war and the playwright who wrote the early and defining play of the Western Front experience *Journey's End* in 1928, encountered this directly. Presenting himself to the depot of the local county regiment as a potential officer, the adjutant declined his application on the grounds 'I am sorry, but it isn't a public school.'[45] Sheriff's school was Kingston Grammar School, founded in 1567, five years before Harrow School, founded in 1572. It did not have an OTC. Sherriff would enlist in the ranks, eventually becoming an officer in a Service Battalion of the Kitchener Army's 9th Battalion, East Surrey Regiment.[46]

However, as so few of the group under examination here were products of the grammar schools and there are no common schooling connections between those who were, their influence on the group as a whole is less marked than those who attended public schools. Examination of the schools listed can be further reduced to a smaller group as those schools producing a single officer who progressed in rank after 1940, by the very definition did not produce networks based on periods of mutual attendance. The focus for this research is to examine officers who were exact contemporaries or overlapped significantly in their time spent at certain schools.

Bowman and Connelly state that the Edwardian officer corps, as difficult as it is to determine a uniquely 'Edwardian' group due to the short reign of King Edward VII, was dominated by a small group of schools:

> Reinforcing the class consciousness of the Edwardian officer corps was the small number of schools which cadets came from [to the Royal Military College,

43 E. Spiers, *University Officers' Training Corps and the First World War* (Leeds: COMEC [Council of Military Education Committees of the United Kingdom], 2012) Occasional Paper No.4, p.11.

44 C. Messenger, *A Call to Arms...* p.293.

45 Sheriff, cited in G. Panichas, *Promise of Greatness* (London, The John Day Company, 1968) and quoted in Lewis-J. Stempel, *Six Weeks: The Short and Gallant Life of the British Officer in the First World War* (London: Weidenfeld and Nicholson, 2010), p.38.

46 M. Lucas, *The Journey's End Battalion: The 9th East Surreys in the Great War* (Bradford: Pen & Sword, 2012).

> Sandhurst]. Bedford Grammar, Cheltenham, Clifton, Eton, Harrow and Marlborough provided the majority of cadets between 1902–1914. The position at the Royal Military Academy, Woolwich, was similar.[47]

The group examined in this book[48] does not completely reflect this assertion and suggests that the dominance of those schools was neither as complete or enduring as Bowman and Connelly suggest. Those six schools produced just under one-third of the group, 46 officers, or 30.06 percent of the total. Eton produced 12; Cheltenham and Wellington nine each; six went to Marlborough, five to Harrow and four to Clifton. There was a sole representative from what was then Bedford Grammar School.[49] Although officers originating from these schools commissioned in the Edwardian period were more likely to have been trained at Sandhurst or Woolwich, a smaller group of officers bypassed this route via direct commissioning based on service in Special Reserve or Militia units.

The adapted Gantt charts presented below are intended as an aid to visualisation of the narrative which follows them.

## The Clarendon Group

The boarding schools in the Group were Charterhouse, Eton, Harrow, Rugby, Shrewsbury, Westminster and Winchester. Shrewsbury and Westminster provided no officers who proceeded past the rank of brigadier. The day schools were St Paul's and Merchant Taylors', neither of which produced officers who advanced.

The schools outside the grouping identified by Bowman and Connelly which produced three or more officers were:

**Clarendon Group:**
Charterhouse, Rugby, Winchester and St Paul's
A total of 26 officers

**Headmasters' Conference:**
Dover College, Edinburgh College, Renton, Uppingham
A total of 39 officers

The schools producing two officers to the sample were:

47 T. Bowman and M. Connelly, *The Edwardian Army'* (Oxford: OUP, 2012), p.10.

48 All references to first commissioning of officers in this section are derived from either *'The HYAL* for January 1939 [for the Period Ending 31 December 1938] (London: His Majesty's Stationery Office,1939), or *HYAL* January 1940 [for the Period Ending 31 December 1939] (London: His Majesty's Stationery Office, 1940).

49 Brigadier Henry George Pyne, the Chief Engineer in IV Corps of the North Western Expeditionary Force.

## Table 2.1 Officers from Schools in the Clarendon Group (All Officers)

TABLE 2.1: OFFICERS FROM SCHOOLS IN THE CLARENDON GROUP (ALL OFFICERS)

| SCHOOL/ DATES | 1897 | 1898 | 1899 | 1900 | 1901 | 1902 | 1903 | 1904 | 1905 | 1906 | 1907 | 1908 | 1909 | 1910 | 1911 | 1912 | 1913 | 1914 | 1915 |
|---|---|---|---|---|---|---|---|---|---|---|---|---|---|---|---|---|---|---|---|
| CHARTER HOUSE | | | | | | BISSETT | | | | | | | | | | | | | |
| | | | | | | | | FRASER | | | | | | | | | | | |
| | | | | | | | | SWAYNE | | | | | | | | | | | |
| | | | | | | | | | ANDERSON | | | | | | | | | | |
| | | | | | | | | | | | JARDINE | | | | | | | | |
| | | | | | | | | | | | | | | FOX-PITT | | | | | |
| ETON[1] | | | | WILLIAMSON | | | | | | | | | | | | | | | |
| | | | | CHURCHILL | | | | | | | | | | | | | | | |
| | | | | | | | BECKWITH-SMITH | | | | | | | | | | | | |
| | | | | | | | | LAWSON | | | | | | | | | | | |
| | | | | | | | | NORMAN | | | | | | | | | | | |
| | | | | | | | | | | LAURIE | | | | | | | | | |
| | | | | | | | | | | | FITZGERALD | | | | | | | | |
| | | | | | | | | | | | LEESE | | | | | | | | |
| | | | | | | | | | | | | | WHITAKER | | | | | | |
| | | | | | | | | | | | | | | | MC CREERY (TO 1916) | | | | |
| HARROW | FINDLAY | | | | | | | | | | | | | | | | | | |
| | | DAWES | | | | | | | | | | | | | | | | | |
| | | | | | MORGAN | | | | | | | | | | | | | | |
| | | | | | | | | | MILES | | | | | | | | | | |
| | | | | | | | | | | | | | CREWDSON | | | | | | |
| RUGBY | | | | | PERCIVAL | | | | | | | | | | | | | | |
| | | | | | | EDEN | | | | | | | | | | | | | |
| | | | | | | FRANKLIN | | | | | | | | | | | | | |
| | | | | | | | WOOTTEN | | | | | | | | | | | | |
| | | | | | | | | | HAMILTON | | | | | | | | | | |
| | | | | | | | | | | BERNEY-FICKLIN | | | | | | | | | |
| | | | | | | | | | | | | REFORD | | | | | | | |
| | | | | | | | | | | | | RAITT-KERR | | | | | | | |

## Table 2.2 Officers from Schools of the Headmasters Conference (All Officers)

| TABLE 2.2 OFFICERS FROM SCHOOLS OF THE HEADMASTERS' CONFERENCE (ALL OFFICERS) | | | | | | | | | | | | | | | | | | | |
|---|---|---|---|---|---|---|---|---|---|---|---|---|---|---|---|---|---|---|---|
| SCHOOL/DATES | 1897 | 1898 | 1899 | 1900 | 1901 | 1902 | 1903 | 1904 | 1905 | 1906 | 1907 | 1908 | 1909 | 1910 | 1911 | 1912 | 1913 | 1914 | 1915 |
| **BRADFIELD** | | | | CURREY | | | | | | | | | | | | | | | |
| | | | | | | | | | MCMULLEN | | | | | | | | | | |
| **CHARTERHOUSE** | | | | | | BISSETT | | | | | | | | | | | | | |
| | | | | | | | | FRASER | | | | | | | | | | | |
| | | | | | | | | SWAYNE | | | | | | | | | | | |
| | | | | | | | | | ANDERSON | | | | | | | | | | |
| | | | | | | | | | | | JARDINE | | | | | | | | |
| | | | | | | | | | | | | | | FOX-PITT | | | | | |
| CHELTENHAM[i] | | | | ORMSBY JOHNSON | | | | | | | | | | | | | | | |
| | | | | MASSY | | | | | | | | | | | | | | | |
| | | | | | HOGG | | | | | | | | | | | | | | |
| | | | | | | | | PHIPPS | | | | | | | | | | | |
| | | | | | | | | GRANT | | | | | | | | | | | |
| | | | | | | | | | DUNCAN | | | | | | | | | | |
| | | | | | | | | | | PRATT | | | | | | | | | |
| | | | | | | | | | | | | | GUBBINS | | | | | | |
| **CLIFTON** | | | | | | | | | | | | | | LEE | | | | | |
| | | | | | | | | | | | | MORGAN | | | | | | | |
| | | | | | | | | | TOWELL | | | | | | | | | | |
| | | | WHITTY | | | | | | | | | | | | | | | | |
| **DOVER COLLEGE** | | | | | GOLDNEY | | | | | | | | | | | | | | |
| | | | | | | | | | | | PARMINTER | | | | | | | | |
| | | | | | | | | | | PRATT | | | | | | | | | |
| **EDINBURGH** | MILLIGAN | | | | | | | | | | | | | | | | | | |
| **ACADEMY** | | | | | GRAINGER-STEWART | | | | | | | | | | | | | | |
| | | | | | | | | SHEPHERD | | | | | | | | | | | |

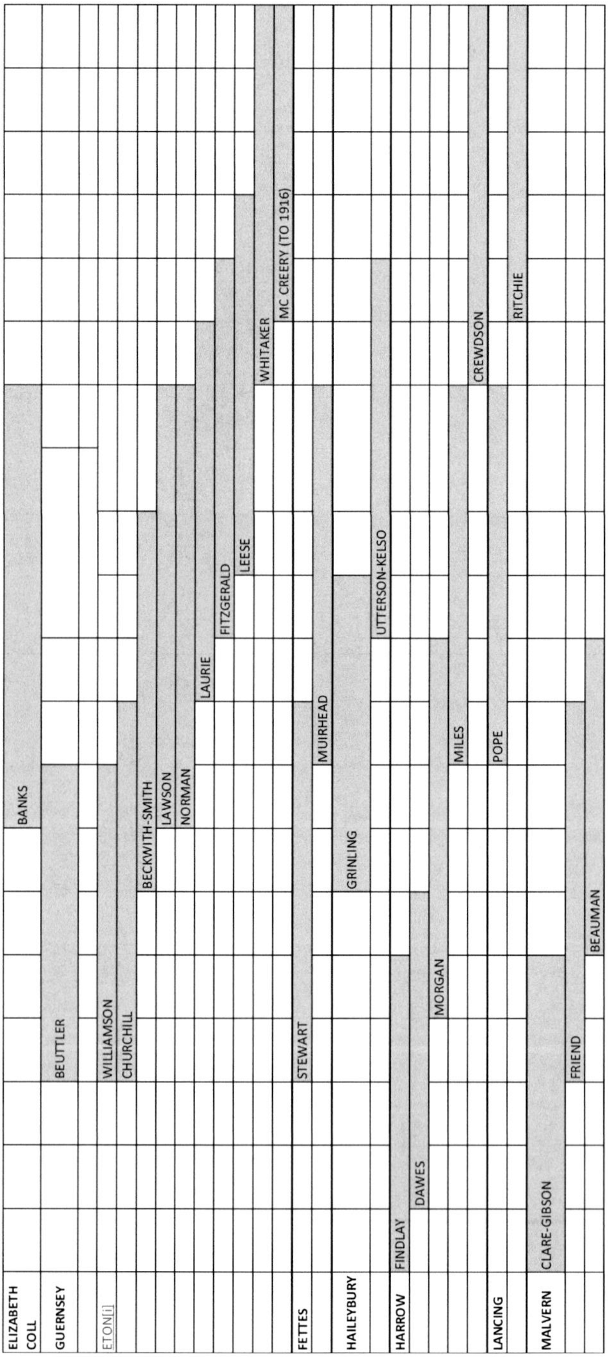
ELIZABETH COLL
BANKS
GUERNSEY
BEUTTLER
ETON[i]
WILLIAMSON
CHURCHILL
BECKWITH-SMITH
LAWSON
NORMAN
LAURIE
FITZGERALD
LEESE
WHITAKER
MC CREERY (TO 1916)
FETTES
STEWART
MUIRHEAD
HAILEYBURY
GRINLING
UTTERSON-KELSO
HARROW
FINDLAY
DAWES
MORGAN
MILES
CREWDSON
LANCING
POPE
RITCHIE
MALVERN
CLARE-GIBSON
FRIEND
BEAUMAN

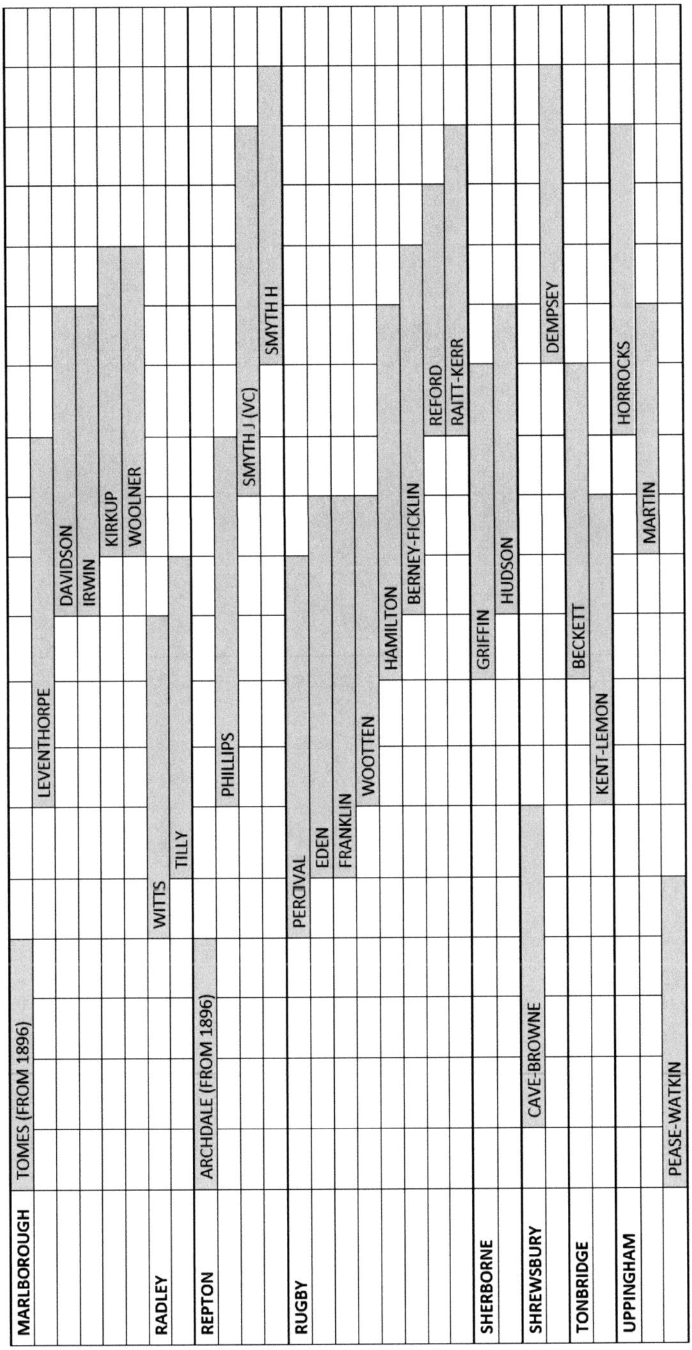
MARLBOROUGH
TOMES (FROM 1896)
LEVENTHORPE
DAVIDSON
IRWIN
KIRKUP
WOOLNER
RADLEY
WITTS
TILLY
REPTON
ARCHDALE (FROM 1896)
PHILLIPS
SMYTH J (VC)
SMYTH H
RUGBY
PERCIVAL
EDEN
FRANKLIN
WOOTTEN
HAMILTON
BERNEY-FICKLIN
REFORD
RAITT-KERR
SHERBORNE
GRIFFIN
HUDSON
SHREWSBURY
CAVE-BROWNE
DEMPSEY
TONBRIDGE
BECKETT
KENT-LEMON
UPPINGHAM
HORROCKS
MARTIN
PEASE-WATKIN

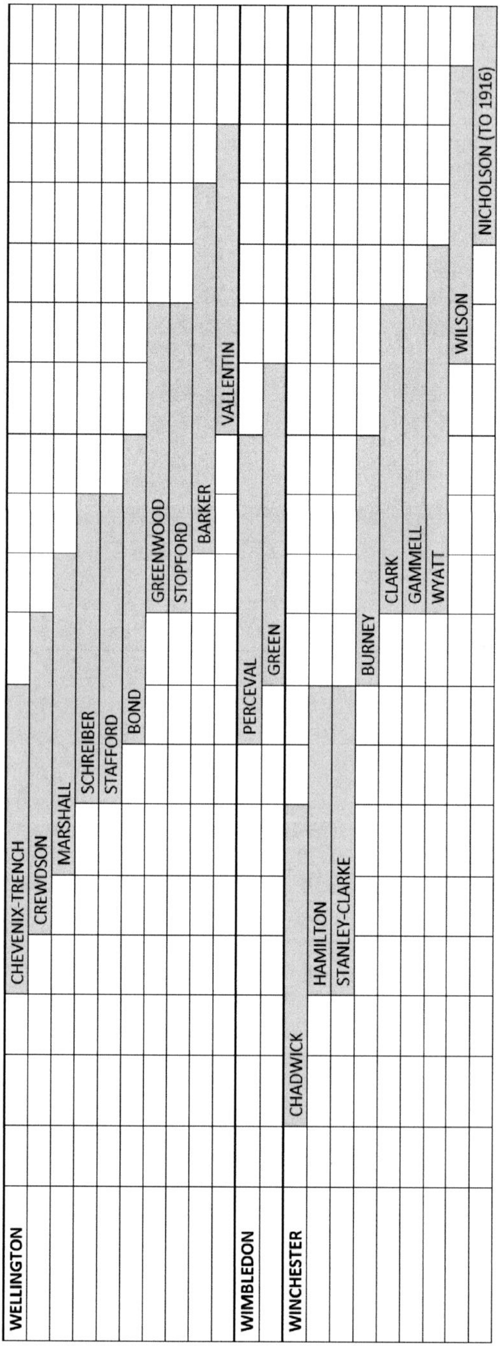
WELLINGTON
CHEVENIX-TRENCH
CREWDSON
MARSHALL
SCHREIBER
STAFFORD
BOND
GREENWOOD
STOPFORD
BARKER
VALLENTIN
WIMBLEDON
PERCEVAL
GREEN
WINCHESTER
CHADWICK
HAMILTON
STANLEY-CLARKE
BURNEY
CLARK
GAMMELL
WYATT
WILSON
NICHOLSON (TO 1916)

**Clarendon Group:**
Shrewsbury

**Headmasters' Conference:**
Bradfield, Elizabeth College Guernsey, Fettes, George Watson's, Haileybury, Lancing; Radley, Sherborne, Tonbridge and Wimbledon
A total of 20 officers.

Therefore, while the group of brigadiers overall is dominated by public schoolboys, within this set a smaller number of 15 (of 35) schools combining members of the Clarendon Group and Headmasters' Conference produced the majority of the group – 87, or 55 percent of the total. As noted at the beginning of this chapter, initial connections between individuals often begin in schooldays. Therefore, the first point of comparison used is the officers who attended these 15 schools. In performing this comparison, the core period is those who attended school between 1897 and 1914.

Three officers, although educated at schools within this group, were excluded as they stood sufficiently far apart from the core of the sample as not to be connected to other members of it. Alfred Young from Cheltenham College (who commanded 35 Brigade temporarily in France), attended from 1917–1921; and from Eton, Gervase Thorpe (Base Commandant, Cherbourg) who was at the school from 1891–1895 and Richard Dawnay, 10th Viscount Downe (commanding 69 Brigade in France), who attended Eton from 1917–1921.

Examining the Clarendon Group schools specifically, the biggest single collection of future officers was that of the 12 Old Etonians. With Thorpe and Dawnay excluded from this analysis, a group of 10 remains, with a spread of attendance from 1900 to 1909, meaning that not all the Old Etonians were contemporaneous. Huddleston 'Noel' Williamson and John 'Jack' Churchill were direct contemporaries at Eton in the period 1900–1902, although their army careers diverged with Williamson joining the Royal Artillery from RMA Woolwich in 1907 and Churchill the Durham Light Infantry from RMC Sandhurst in 1906. (Churchill remained at Eton until 1903).[50]

Merton Beckwith-Smith (1903–1908) just overlapped with Churchill, but in turn was a year ahead of the direct contemporaries The Honourable Edward Lawson and Charles Norman (1904–1909). Beckwith-Smith, after attending Oxford, was commissioned into the Coldstream Guards in 1911. Lawson joined the Royal Horse Artillery after Oxford, Norman the 9th Lancers after Cambridge.

John Laurie arrived at Eton in 1906, overlapping with Beckwith-Smith, Lawson and Norman, leaving in 1910. This made Laurie senior to, but contemporary with, John Fitzgerald (1907–1911) and Oliver Leese (1908–1912). Laurie, who would succeed to a baronetcy, was commissioned into the Seaforth Highlanders from the RMC; Fitzgerald

50 Entries in *The Eton Register Vol. VII, 1899–1909* (Eton: Spottiswoode, Ballantyne and Co., 1922), p.36.

the Irish Guards and Leese the Coldstream Guards. Arriving in 1910, John Whitaker would follow Leese to the Coldstream after leaving Eton in 1914. In turn, Whitaker was a year ahead of Richard McCreery (1911–1915) who would join the 12th Lancers in 1915.

The nine officers from Cheltenham College, known as Old Cheltonians, attended across a fourteen-year spread, from 1900 to 1914. Guy Ormsby-Johnson (1900–1904) and Charles Massy (1900–1905) did not attend university and were commissioned into the Bedfordshire Regiment[51] and the Royal Artillery respectively. Douglas Hogg (1901–1906) overlapped with both, joining the Royal Engineers in 1908. Charles Phipps (1904–1908), commissioned into the Royal Engineers in 1910, entered the school in the latter days of all three of his predecessors, but he was more directly contemporary to Ian Grant (1904–1909) and William Duncan (1905–1909), the former becoming an officer in the Cameron Highlanders, the latter in the Royal Artillery. A later arrival, Fendall Pratt (1906–1911), entered a year after Duncan, but was at the College behind Hogg, Phipps and Grant; he joined the Royal Engineers in 1912. Colin Gubbins (1909–1914) entered three years behind Pratt and was present when Phipps and Grant were ending their time at the school; Gubbins entered the Royal Artillery from the RMA in September 1914.

The officers from Wellington College, Old Wellingtonians, were again nine in number, and present across a spread of attendance from 1900–1913. Ralph Chevenix-Trench (1900–1904) and Wilson Crewdson (1901–1905) were close school contemporaries, being commissioned into the Royal Engineers and Royal Artillery out of the RMA in 1905 and 1908 respectively. Charles Marshall, who would be commissioned into the Royal Artillery via the Special Reserve in 1908 (thus bypassing the RMA) attended Wellington from 1902–1906, overlapping Chevenix-Trench and Crewdson. Edmond Schreiber and John Stafford (both 1903–1907) were direct school contemporaries and like the predecessors they overlapped, would also join the Royal Artillery and Royal Engineers respectively. Richard Bond (1904–1908), another gunner, was more contemporary to Schreiber and Stafford.

Charles Greenwood and Montagu Stopford (1906–1910) were at the school in the same period, Greenwood becoming a sapper and Stopford the first infantryman to emerge from this group, being commissioned into the Rifle Brigade in 1911. A year behind him was another 'greenjacket', Evelyn Barker (1907–1912) who joined the King's Royal Rifle Corps in 1913. Greenwood, Stopford and Barker attended at the same time, albeit two and three years behind, Marshall (except Barker), Schreiber, Stafford and Bond. The last arrival was Claude Vallentin (1909–1913), commissioned into the Royal Artillery from the RMA in September 1914, five weeks after the outbreak of war. He was therefore present in the same time bracket as Greenwood, Stopford and Barker, but was closer in time of attendance to Barker.

The Marlborough group of Old Marlburians' attendance period was more extended over time, between 1896 and 1911. Clement Tomes (1896–1900) had left the school

51 Ormsby-Johnson transferred to the Army Pay Department in 1911 and remained in it and its successor, the Royal Army Pay Corps, for the remainder of his career (*HYAL* January 1940).

in 1900 and had been a serving officer in the Royal Warwickshire Regiment for over two years before the next Marlburian, Graham Leventhorpe, arrived there in 1903; he left in 1908 for, firstly, the RMA and then the Royal Artillery. Three years behind Leventhorpe were the direct contemporaries Francis Davidson and Noel Irwin (1906–1910) both receiving their commissions in 1911, Davidson joining the Royal Engineers from the RMA and Irwin the Essex Regiment from the RMC. A year behind them were two other pupils whose time there was also contiguous, Philip Kirkup and Christopher Woolner (1907–1911), both of whom were commissioned into the Royal Engineers in 1912.[52]

The Old Harrovians were sufficiently widely spread across a time frame of arrival there (1897–1910) as to suggest that opportunities for immediate connections to form were fewer than in other schools. Charles Findlay (1897–1901) entered the Royal Artillery via the Militia in 1903, bypassing the RMA. Hugh Dawes (1898–1902) a near contemporary, also entered the army via the Militia, joining the Royal Fusiliers in 1906. Harold Morgan arrived in 1902, leaving in 1906 for Oxford University and a commission in The Buffs in 1910; he would only briefly coincide with Dawes and Eric Miles (1905–1909) before joining the King's Own Scottish Borderers in 1911. The last of the group was Henry Crewdson (1910–1915) whose time did not coincide with any of the others; he was also exceptional in that he was a Territorial infantry officer in the Sherwood Foresters, serving only part-time in most of the interwar period while working as a barrister.[53]

Clifton College, of which Douglas Haig was an old boy,[54] produced four 1940 brigadiers as Old Cliftonians, but they were mostly disconnected in terms of attendance there. This largely eliminated any network based on direct personal connection. Noel Whitty, born in Australia in 1885, was at the school from 1899–1903; he was originally commissioned into the Royal West Kent Regiment in 1906. Roland Towell (1905–1909) joined the Royal Artillery in 1911; Frederick Morgan arrived at Clifton in 1908, leaving in 1912 for the RMA and the Royal Artillery also and thus coincided briefly with Towell; Alec Lee (1910–1914) arrived halfway through Morgan's time at the school. He was commissioned into the South Staffordshire Regiment in 1915, having spent a year in the ranks of the Special Reserve.

The six Old Carthusians of Charterhouse in the group spanned an attendance bracket reaching from 1902 to 1915. Frederick Bissett (1902–1906), an officer recalled from retirement to serve in the BEF, was originally commissioned in the Duke of Cornwall's Light Infantry. He was still at the school when The Honourable William Fraser arrived

52 Both would, however, command infantry brigades in the BEF; Woolner 8 Brigade and Kirkup 70 Brigade.

53 Source: 'Henry Alistair Fergusson Crewdson' entry in http://geneagraphie.com, citing 'Genealogy of the Pease Family' (1997), accessed 12 February 2013.

54 Robin Prior and Trevor Wilson, 'Haig, Douglas, first Earl Haig (1861–1928)' in *DNB* (Oxford: OUP, 2004), online edn, January 2011. http://www.oxforddnb.com/view/article/33633, accessed 17 September 2015.

in 1904; originally an officer in the Gordon Highlanders after leaving Charterhouse in 1908, he would later transfer to the Grenadier Guards. John Swayne was a direct contemporary of his and after attending Oxford University became an officer in the Somerset Light Infantry. Kenneth Anderson (1905–1909) arrived slightly behind Fraser and Swayne and just as Bissett was leaving; he would join the Seaforth Highlanders from the RMC in 1911. Colin Jardine (1907–1910) was a Baronet who did not use his title in the army (despite its being noted in the Army List) and joined the Royal Artillery from the RMA in 1912. He was therefore in the school contemporaneously with Fraser, Swayne and Bissett. The last OC of the group was William Fox-Pitt, (1910–1914) who briefly overlapped with Jardine in his final year; he would join the Welsh Guards after six months' service in the Special Reserve in April 1915.

Of the eight former pupils of Rugby School, Old Rugbieans, who attended in a period between 1901 and 1913, the first four were closest contemporaries: Arthur Percival (1901–1906), Henry Eden (1902–1907), Geoffrey Franklyn (1902–1907) and Richard Wootten (1903–1907). Percival was not thought to be a good student except for sport and left with minimal qualifications;[55] he did not go to university or the RMC but was commissioned in the Bedfordshire Regiment in 1914 direct from civilian employment.

Eden and Franklyn (1902–1907) would also be contemporaries at the RMA, Woolwich and joined the Royal Artillery in 1909. Wootten (1903–1907) went to the RMC and passed out into the 6th (Inniskilling) Dragoons in 1909. Hugh Hamilton (1905–1910) and Horatio Berney-Ficklin (1906–1911) overlapped; the former went to the Royal Artillery from the RMA in 1912, the latter the Norfolk Regiment from the Special Reserve in 1914. Both therefore overlapped to some degree with Percival, Eden, Franklyn and Wootten. The last two Old Rugbieans, Robert Reford and Edmund Raitt-Kerr were direct contemporaries from 1909, but Reford left in 1912 with Raitt-Kerr remaining until 1913. Reford, after attending Oxford, gained his commission in the Sherwood Foresters via the Special Reserve in 1915. Raitt-Kerr went to the RMA and the Royal Engineers in 1914.

The Wykehamists of Winchester College were the most spread out of the groups of old boys; from 1898–1917, with fewer opportunities to create informal networks. Edward Chadwick (1898–1902) entered the Royal Artillery from Woolwich in 1903. James Hamilton and Arthur 'Kit' Stanley-Clarke were directly contemporary (1900–1904) and partly overlapped with Chadwick; Hamilton joined the Seaforth Highlanders at the age of 21 in 1907. Stanley-Clarke, after attending Oxford, joined the Cameronians in 1908. George Burney (1905–1908) went into the Gordon Highlanders in 1909 from the RMC.

John Clark, James Gammell and Richard Wyatt (1906–1910; Wyatt 1911) arrived at Winchester together. Clark went via the RMC to the 12th Lancers; Gammell served briefly in a Yeomanry regiment (The Scottish Horse) after leaving Cambridge University

55 C. Smith, *Singapore Burning: Heroism and Surrender in World War Two* (London: Penguin, 2006), p.24.

before joining the Royal Artillery. In 1927 he transferred to the infantry, serving with the Queen's Own Cameron Highlanders. Wyatt, after Oxford, joined the Royal Sussex Regiment. Clark, Gammell and Wyatt briefly coincided with Thomas Wilson (1910–1914) who, after the RMC, joined the King's Royal Rifle Corps in November 1914. The last of the group, Claude Nicholson, joined the school in 1912, coinciding only with Wilson; he would join the 16th Lancers from Sandhurst in 1916.

With the two officers from St Paul's School, Old Paulines, one, Arthur Clementi-Smith,[56] was the son of a Privy Councillor and colonial administrator who attended the school from 1892–1896, joining the Royal Engineers in 1897. James Whitehead, at St Paul's from 1894–1898, was originally commissioned into the Royal West Kent Regiment later transferring to the Indian Army.

Moving from the Clarendon Group to the Headmasters' Conference. Dover College's three alumni, Old Devorians, were not completely connected. Claude Goldney (1901–1905) attended in isolation before passing into the Gloucestershire Regiment via the RMC. Douglas Pratt (1906–1910) arrived the year before Reginald Parminter (1907–1911); Pratt went to the Royal Irish Regiment from the RMC in 1911 (he would later transfer to the Royal Tank Corps). Parminter also went to the infantry, joining the Manchester Regiment from the RMC in 1913.

At Edinburgh Academy, two of the three officers originating from the school, known as Edinburgh Academicals, spent their entire education there as opposed to the English pattern of an affiliated Preparatory School and then the main school. Eric Milligan (1897–1909) was commissioned into the Royal Garrison Artillery from the RMA in 1911. Thomas Grainger-Stewart (1904–1914) was commissioned into the Royal Scots, an infantry regiment, after attending Edinburgh University but served as a Territorial officer between the wars. James Shepherd (1904–1909) who was the officer who attended for his secondary education only, departed to a commission in the Royal Artillery, but like Grainger-Stewart also served in the Territorial Army in the interwar period.

The four officers from Repton, Old Reptonians, were not connected, save for two who were brothers. Arthur Archdale (1896–1900) went to the Royal Artillery from the RMA in 1901. Charles Phillips (1903–1908) went from the RMC to the West Yorkshire Regiment in 1909. John 'Jacky' Smyth (1908–1912) and Herbert Smyth (1910–1914) coincided but were already strongly 'connected' being brothers. Jacky, after a short period on the Unattached List, would transfer to the Indian Army in 1913, serving with the 15th Ludhiana Sikhs, the regiment with which he would earn a Victoria Cross in 1915. Herbert would join the Oxfordshire and Buckinghamshire Light Infantry directly in 1915.

Uppingham produced three Old Uppinghamian officers: two graduates of the RMA heading to the Royal Artillery and one infantry officer. Edward Pease-Watkin

56 C. Mosley (ed.), *Burke's Peerage, Baronetage & Knightage, 107th edition*, (Wilmington, Delaware, USA: Burke's Peerage (Genealogical Books) Ltd, 2003), entry for Sir Cecil Clementi-Smith.

(1897–1901) joined the Royal Artillery in 1903; George 'Noel' Martin (1907–1911) the Royal Field Artillery in 1912. Brian Horrocks arrived at the school in 1909, leaving in 1913; he was commissioned into the Middlesex Regiment the day before the outbreak of war in 1914. One of his biographers claimed that his performance at RMC was sufficiently poor that his very commissioning could have been far from certain, were it not for the outbreak of war.[57]

To briefly review the 10 schools which produced two officers apiece; Shrewsbury's Old Salopians, William Cave-Browne and Miles Dempsey were separated by eight years between the former's departure and the latter's arrival completely distancing them as contemporaries. At Bradfield, Old Bradfieldians Henry Currey left in 1904; Donald McMullen arrived in 1905.

The two Channel Islanders who attended Elizabeth College Guernsey, Old Elizabethans, Valentine Beuttler and Donald Banks, similarly failed to overlap in departure and arrival, Beuttler leaving in 1904 and Banks arriving later in the same year. Beuttler, after a brief period serving as a second lieutenant in the Royal Guernsey Light Infantry – a Militia unit, transferred to the Regular Army and the Northamptonshire Regiment on the mainland in 1907. Banks served during the First World War with Service Battalions of the New Army, the 10th Battalion of the Essex Regiment and the 8th Battalion, Royal Berkshire Regiment. He served as a Territorial infantry officer between the wars, commanding the 13th (Kensington) Battalion (Princess Louise's) of the London Regiment from 1927–1931 as he was a senior civil servant in the General Post Office.

Fettes, in Edinburgh, produced two Old Fettessian officers again who only coincided by departure and leaving dates and are therefore unlikely to have been directly connected at school; Herbert Stewart (1900–1905) went to the Royal Scots Fusiliers from the RMC in 1906; James Muirhead (1905–1910) joined the Seaforth Highlanders from the RMC in 1911.

Haileybury's pair of Old Haileyburians overlapped only in their last and first years there. Edward Grinling (1903–1906), whose younger brother also attended the school and was killed at Gallipoli as an officer in the Royal Marines, joined the Lincolnshire Regiment. John Utterson-Kelso (1906–1910) went to the Royal Scots Fusiliers in 1912. There was no connection, in direct school terms, between Vyvyan Pope (1905–1909) and Neil Ritchie (1911–1915) at Lancing. Pope was commissioned into the Northamptonshire Regiment via the Special Reserve in 1912; Ritchie the Black Watch in 1914. (Pope and Ritchie, Old Lancings, would both serve in the Western Desert in 1941–1942).

The pair from Radley is more likely to have known one another, if only indirectly. Old Radleians Frank Witts (1901–1905), after attending Oxford, entered the Irish Guards via the Special Reserve in 1914 and Justice (his given name) Tilley (1903–1906), who bypassed Sandhurst to a commission in the Special Reserve battalion of the West Yorkshire Regiment in 1909. He would eventually transfer to the newly formed Tank

57 P. Warner, *Horrocks: The General Who Led from The Front* (London: Hamish Hamilton), p.7.

Corps in 1917. Both officers would become fatalities during the first half of the Second World War.

John Griffin (1905–1909) attended Sherborne just ahead of Charles Hudson (1906–1910); Griffin was commissioned into the Lincolnshire Regiment in 1911. Hudson was forced to drop out of the RMC due to his father's illness; working as a tea planter in Ceylon from 1912, he returned on the outbreak of war in 1914 and was directly appointed a second lieutenant in the Sherwood Foresters. Hudson noted in a privately published memoir that he did not excel as a student and his complete aversion to physical pain led him to avoid participating actively on the football pitch, making him an atypical Old Shelburian. This made him feel 'terribly conscious of being a coward.'[58] He would be awarded a Victoria Cross in 1918[59] as a 26-year old lieutenant colonel, for rushing an enemy position in Italy while wounded by a grenade explosion.

The final pairs came from Tonbridge, Wimbledon and George Watson's College. Arthur Kent-Lemon arrived at Tonbridge in 1903, leaving in 1907. Clifford Beckett (1905–1909) was therefore in the school as a near contemporary. Kent-Lemon would join the York and Lancaster Regiment in 1913 after a year and a half's service in the Special Reserve battalion of the Royal West Kent Regiment, before his twenty-fourth birthday, comparatively late.[60] Beckett followed his father, Brigadier General Edward Beckett, to the RMA and into the Royal Artillery, in 1911. His maternal grandfather, Major General Edward Thomason, had been an Indian Army engineer in Bengal in the second half of the nineteenth century. The Wimbledon pair overlapped; Christopher Perceval (1904–1908) went to the Royal Artillery via the RMA aged 20 in 1910; Michael Green (1905–1909) took the Special Reserve route to the Gloucestershire Regiment in May 1915, aged 24. The pupils from George Watson's College in Edinburgh were William Morgan and William Robb; they were not closely contemporary due to a three-year difference in age (Morgan being born in 1891 and Robb in 1888) but would have been in the school simultaneously.

For completeness, the 28 schools which generated one 1940 brigadier each were:

| | |
|---|---|
| Aldenham | Bath College |
| Bedford | Downside |
| Eastbourne College | Emmanuel School |
| Felsted | Glenalmond |
| Imperial Service College | Kersal |

58 C. Hudson and M. Hudson, Two Lives 1892–1992. The Memoirs of Charles Edward Hudson, VC, CB, DSO, MC, and Miles Matthew Lee Hudson, also some poems by Charles Edward Hudson (Privately published by Wilton 65: York, 1992), pp.2–3.

59 *The London Gazette*, 9 July 1918, No.30790., p.8155.

60 His Army service record, held at The National Archives, reportedly covers the period 1912–1920 but is incomplete save for one page listing his promotions from 1916–1918. His intervening career has not emerged from research and he does not appear in the online transcripts of the 1911 census.

| | |
|---|---|
| King William College, Isle of Man | King's School Canterbury |
| Magdalen College School | Mercers' |
| Merchiston | Rochester Grammar |
| Rossall | Royal Belfast School |
| Royal Naval School, Eltham | Sedbergh |
| St Bees | St Lawrence Ramsgate |
| St Mark's Chelsea | Stonyhurst |
| Stubbington | Wakefield |
| Weymouth College | |

As noted, university graduates are a minority among the group, albeit represented at a significantly higher rate than in the wider population, totalling twenty-three or 15 percent of the total. One officer, unsurprisingly a senior medical officer, Brigadier Gilbert Blake, the Assistant Director Medical Services of the North-West Expeditionary Force to Norway trained at Guy's Hospital in London. Of the remaining 22, the most represented university was Oxford, with 13 graduates who started there between 1905 and 1914.[61] Five officers attended Cambridge, starting there between 1900 and 1911.[62] There were two graduates of the University of London, and one each from Queen's University Belfast and Edinburgh University.

The future brigadiers from Oxford who overlapped in their time spent there were Arthur Friend (Hertford College, 1905) Arthur Stanley-Clarke (University College, 1906) and Frank Witts (Trinity College, 1906). Harold Morgan went up to Worcester College in 1907, and three officers arrived at Oxford in 1908: James Muirhead (Oriel College), John Swayne (Trinity College) and Raleigh Chichester-Constable (Exeter College). Merton Beckwith-Smith went up to Christ Church College in 1909. His Eton contemporary The Honourable Edward Lawson went up to Balliol College the same year. Richard Wyatt followed to Christ Church College in 1911. John Hawkesworth matriculated at Queen's College in 1912 and Robert Reford went up to New College in 1914. The last of the Oxford group to attend, Henry Crewdson, went up to Magdalen College after his First World War service in 1919.

Of the five graduates from Cambridge, the overlap was less notable. Gordon Gill, as one of the older officers in the group, went up to St John's College in 1900. Hugh Scott-Barrett also went to St John's, but in 1906. Three officers were roughly contemporaries at Cambridge: Charles Norman (Trinity College, 1910) James Gammell (Pembroke College, 1911) and Horatio Berney-Ficklin (Jesus College, 1911). The two University of London graduates, Percy Clark and Archibald Hughes, although close in age (born 1886 and 1888 respectively) studied at affiliated schools of the University and were not

61 E. S. Craig and W. M. Gibson, W. M. (eds), *Oxford University Roll of Service* (Oxford, Clarendon Press, 1920), pp.various.

62 G. V. Carey (ed.), *The War Roll of the University of Cambridge* (Cambridge, The University Press, 1921).

contemporaries. Neither are represented in the University of London War List for 1914–1918, but its preface admits a difficulty in locating all external students.[63]

Seldon and Walsh[64] in their conclusions also consider the proportional casualty rates sustained by graduates of universities, if only to contend that those of the public schools were higher. They state that from the provincial, or redbrick, universities, such as Liverpool, Birmingham and Manchester, the ratio of those killed to those serving was 1:8, roughly equivalent to the national average, but that a smaller proportion of graduates from those universities was commissioned, citing Leeds, where 60 percent of graduates became officers. They assert that 97 percent of Oxford and Cambridge graduates were commissioned.

However, their main source for this data is a book published in early 1917, *British Universities and The War*. It was intended for consumption in the American market for propaganda purposes to indicate the scale and sacrifice already made by the 'brightest and the best' in Britain prior to America's entry into the war and its compilation of statistics is neither uniform nor, given its date of publication, complete for the whole period of the war.[65] The book also asserts (based purely on statistics gleaned from the award of school prizes at Eton) that the more academically gifted one was, the higher the probability of being killed, citing a quarter of King's Scholars at Eton (25 out of 100) becoming fatal casualties.[66]

To return to university graduates. A study of the First World War Memorial for Pembroke College, Cambridge analyses the proportion of casualties to year of admission; 16 percent of 1905 admissions would be lost, dropping to 10 percent for the 1906 intake, spiking at 26 percent for 1907, falling back to 10 percent for 1908. However, the trend from 1909 to 1912 is upwards, rising from 10 percent to 35 percent of the 1912 intake. Twenty-six officers admitted to Pembroke, contemporaries of James Gammell, would die in the war.[67]

Of course, one cannot draw counterfactual arguments about those who became casualties as potential connections to the officers who survived and progressed within the army, not least as it would require a large and unsafe presumption that they would have continued to serve in the army between the wars. However, it highlights that as part of an elite within a set, firstly of public schoolboys and secondly, in an even smaller group, university graduates, those officers who survived and progressed did so against not insignificant statistical odds.

63 Anonymous, University of London War List, containing names of Appointed and Recognised Teachers, Graduates and Matriculated Students who have served or who are serving in His Majesty's Armed Forces, 1914–1918 (London: University of London Press, 1918).

64 A. Seldon and D. Walsh, *Public Schools and The Great War: A Generation Lost* (Bradford, Pen and Sword, 2013), p.237

65 'A.W.M.' (ed.), British Universities and the War: A Record and Its Meaning (Boston, Houghton Mifflin Co, 1917).

66 A. Seldon, and D. Walsh, *Public Schools and The Great War: A Generation Lost* (Bradford, Pen and Sword, 2013). p.239.

67 http://www.pem.cam.ac.uk/wp-content/uploads/2014/08/Pembroke-College-Cambridge-the-dead-of-the-war-of-1914-1918-2.pdf accessed 26 September 2016.

## Schools and Regiments

At this point, the intention is to examine whether another possible layer of connection exists; that of certain schools providing officer candidates to certain regiments at first commissioning – transfers to other regiments or corps will be discussed later. This section will also examine whether certain schools were predominant in the supply of officers to the army, or whether there was a direct and particular association of certain schools to certain regiments. Although it was perfectly possible for an officer to serve in a distinct battalion of a regiment and not directly overlap with another officer in early service, for example if one battalion of a regiment was on home service and another deployed overseas, this research looks back from 1940 towards the sense of regimental 'brotherhood' and ties that a common core provides, even if very specific contemporary service in early commissioned service, such as in the same battalion, is less common. By way of an illustrative example, in 1940, the then Captain J. D. Frost of The Cameronians was detached for loan service to the Iraq Levies. Despite requests for a transfer home, as Frost was keen to be on active service, these were turned down firstly because his contract with the Levies was still running and secondly, because of his fluency in Arabic, he was told he would be of more use in the Middle East. In his subsequent memoir, he expresses regret that he did not write to another officer of his regiment elevated to senior rank for help:

> ...our armies had achieved spectacular success against the Italians in Libya under General 'Dick' O'Connor, himself a Cameronian, and I wondered if I had not made a great mistake in neglecting to have asked him to fit me in somewhere.[68]

Although this example is specific, it highlights that officers of other regiments could expect or hope for paternalistic oversight by officers of their regiment who had risen to senior rank, and to encourage and support the careers of promising junior officers in their former regiments. Brian Bond adds this could have its drawbacks; he cites that General Sir John Burnett-Stewart, formerly of the Rifle Brigade, and notwithstanding his part in mechanising the army in the 1920s and 1930s, was 'an awful snob .... in that .... he refused to 'know' (recognise socially) anyone but members of the Rifle Brigade and Guardsmen.'[69]

A popular stereotype is that of 'Eton and the Guards' as typified in a later article in a British newspaper discussing the decline of a high street retailer:

68 J. D. Frost, *A Drop Too Many* (London: Cassell, 1980), p.15. Frost, famous for the defence of the road bridge at Arnhem in 1944, would retire as Major General John Frost, CB DSO MC.

69 B. Bond, British Military Policy Between the Two World Wars (Oxford: Clarendon, 1980), p.70.

> [WH] Smith's, they thought, was a law unto itself, an impregnable fortress that could withstand the worst its piffling competitors could throw at it. Management was schooled in the Smith's tradition. That usually meant a stint at Eton and the Guards before going into what was still a family business.[70]

And in a discussion of education in North London:

> Michael Palin, another local resident and parent, apparently used to joke that Gospel Oak and William Ellis school, where my sons later went and where I now also chair the governing body, were the 'Eton and the Guards' of North London.[71]

In fact, this popular stereotype – at least from the perspective of the illustrative example of the brigadiers in 1940, appears to have some slight basis in truth. Examining the group of schools which provided two or more officers to this primary group of brigadiers, the figures are as follows: (regiments listed reflecting the alphabetical order of pupils, not the Army Order of Precedence)

**Table 2.2A Schools Producing More Than One Brigadier**

| | | |
|---|---|---|
| Bradfield (2) | Indian Army (1) | |
| | Royal Engineers (1) | |
| Charterhouse (6) | Infantry (5) | Duke of Cornwall's Light Infantry, Gordon Highlanders, Somerset Light Infantry, Seaforth Highlanders, Cheshire Regiment |
| | Royal Artillery (1) | |
| Cheltenham (9) | Infantry (3) | Bedfordshire Regiment, Cameron Highlanders, Queen's Regiment |
| | Royal Artillery (4) | |
| | Royal Engineers (2) | |
| Clifton (4) | Infantry (2) | South Staffordshire Regiment, Royal West Kent Regiment |
| | Royal Artillery (2) | |
| Dover College (3) | Infantry (2) | Manchester Regiment, Royal Irish Regiment |
| | Army Service Corps (1) | |
| Edinburgh Academy (3) | Infantry (1) | Royal Scots |
| | Royal Artillery (2) | |
| Elizabeth College (2) | Infantry (1) | Essex Regiment |
| | Army Service Corps (1) | |

70 *The Independent*, 12 June 1996.

71 http://www.gospeloak.camden.sch.uk/Fiona%20Millar%20steps%20down.html 'Fiona Millar steps down as chair of governors', Gospel Oak School website, 13 September 2013 accessed 25 September 2016.

| | | |
|---|---|---|
| Eton (12) | Guards (5) | Grenadier Guards (1), Coldstream Guards (3), Irish Guards (1) |
| | Infantry (3) | Argyll & Sutherland Highlanders, Seaforth Highlanders, Durham Light Infantry |
| | Royal Artillery (2) | |
| | Cavalry (2) | 9th Lancers, 12th Lancers |
| Fettes (2) | Infantry (2) | Royal Scots Fusiliers, Seaforth Highlanders |
| George Watson's (2) | Infantry (1) | King's Own Yorkshire Light Infantry |
| | Royal Artillery (1) | |
| Haileybury (2) | Infantry (2) | Lincolnshire Regiment, Royal Scots Fusiliers |
| Harrow (5) | Infantry (4) | Sherwood Foresters, Royal Fusiliers, King's Own Scottish Borderers, the Buffs |
| | Royal Artillery (1) | |
| Lancing (2) | Infantry (2) | North Staffordshire Regiment, The Black Watch |
| Malvern (2) | Cavalry (1) | 7th Dragoon Guards |
| | Army Ordnance Corps | |
| Marlborough (6) | Infantry (3) | Royal Warwickshire Regiment, Essex Regiment, Durham Light Infantry |
| | Royal Artillery (2) | |
| | Royal Engineers | |
| Radley (2) | Guards (1) | Irish Guards |
| | Infantry (1) | West Yorkshire Regiment |
| Repton (4) | Infantry (2) | West Yorkshire Regiment, Oxford & Buckinghamshire Light Infantry |
| | Royal Artillery (1) | |
| | Indian Army (1) | |
| Rugby (8) | Cavalry (1) | 6th Dragoons |
| | Infantry (3) | Bedfordshire Regiment, Norfolk Regiment, Sherwood Foresters |
| | Royal Artillery (2) | |
| | Royal Engineers (2) | |
| Sherborne (2) | Infantry (2) | Lincolnshire Regiment, Sherwood Foresters |
| St Paul's (2) | Infantry (1) | Royal Berkshire Regiment |
| | Royal Engineers (1) | |
| Tonbridge (2) | Infantry (1) | York & Lancaster Regiment |
| | Royal Artillery (1) | |
| Uppingham (3) | Infantry (1) | Middlesex Regiment |
| | Royal Artillery (2) | |
| Wellington (10) | Infantry (2) | King's Royal Rifle Corps, Rifle Brigade |
| | Royal Artillery (4) | |
| | Royal Engineers (4) | |

| | | |
|---|---|---|
| Wimbledon (2) | Infantry (1) | Gloucestershire Regiment |
| | Royal Artillery (1) | |
| Winchester (9) | Cavalry (2) | 16th Lancers (2) |
| | Infantry (6) | Cameron Highlanders, Gordon Highlanders (2), Royal Sussex Regiment, Cameronians, King's Royal Rifle Corps |
| | Royal Artillery (1) | |

The immediate conclusion from this listing, aside from supporting the assertion that 'Eton and the Guards' may have a factual basis with 5 out of 12 Old Etonians joining Guards Regiments, and the Coldstream Guards in particular, no line infantry regiment particularly predominates. There is also little correlation between the geographical location of the school and the county or area infantry regiments joined by those from particular schools. This in itself is not particularly significant because of the influence of factors such as family ties, history and traditions; the fashionability or smartness of certain regiments and the varying levels of supplementary income required to be able to bear the expenses of being part of them. Seeing that four of the six Wykehamist infantry officers would join Scottish regiments, nearly as far as it is possible to go away from Scotland within the British Isles, the tenuousness of a connection between the location of the school and joining regiments associated with the area is clear. The inverse is true; apart from 'Eton and the Guards' only one officer from the 78 infantry officers within the larger group of 156 joined a regiment local to the school he attended.

The regiment or corps most represented among the group outside the infantry is the Royal Artillery, with 24 individuals. Between 1899 and 1924, the Royal Regiment of Artillery was divided into two branches and one sub-branch, the Royal Field Artillery and its sub-branch the Royal Horse Artillery, and the Royal Garrison Artillery.[72] Although this distinction prevailed during the initial period of service of several officers in the group, particularly during the First World War, the amalgamation of the Royal Artillery into a single body in 1924 is deemed more significant going into the interwar period for comparative purposes. The 24 officers are therefore counted as Royal Artillery, regardless of original, pre-1924 commissioning branch, throughout. The Royal Engineers, also trained at RMA Woolwich, received 11 officers from this group of schools at varying points.

Of the six cavalry officers, Eton and Winchester produced two officers apiece, the other two being from Rugby and Malvern. The one common regiment was the 16th Lancers, where Claude Nicholson and John Clark, both Wykehamists, would later both serve together despite the six years' difference in age (Clark the elder of the two).

Almost all of the public school entrants to the Brigade of Guards, five of six in the group, were Old Etonians. The Coldstream Guards predominates with three. There is a

72 Although technically correct in strict terms, in day to day operations there was little practical distinction between the RFA and the RHA

seven-year spread of dates of birth (1890–1897) among the three Coldstreamers; given that the eldest (Merton Beckwith-Smith) spent three years after Eton at Oxford, they will have overlapped in the regiment, albeit in different battalions. Similarly, the two Irish Guards officers, John Fitzgerald and Frank Witts, have a four-year difference in age, Fitzgerald being the elder but as Beckwith-Smith, his three years at Oxford makes them contemporaries in terms of first service in the regiment.

With regard to county infantry regiments, there is no single dominant regiment in terms of original commissioning. Scottish regiments, however, stand out as a regiment of first choice. The single most numerous is the Gordon Highlanders, with three officers born in a narrow window (1889–1892). These three contemporaries came from Charterhouse, Winchester, and Glenalmond; none of them was a graduate. The two officers of the Seaforth Highlanders were directly contemporary, being born in 1891 and 1892; they attended Charterhouse and Eton respectively.

The seven-year age difference between the two officers of the Royal Scots Fusiliers (born 1886 and 1893 respectively) reduces the possibility of them being direct regimental contemporaries; one was educated at Fettes, the other at Haileybury. The two officers of the Argyll and Sutherland Highlanders are highly unlikely to have been regimentally contemporary, as they are separated by 19 years of age (1877 and 1896). The elder was an Old Etonian, and in 1940 was one of the officers 'dug out' of retirement for their skills and who served in the rear areas of the BEF. The other Scottish regiments, with a single officer apiece, were the Highland Light Infantry and the King's Own Scottish Borderers, the subjects being educated at Mercer's, and Harrow.

It is noteworthy that none of the officers in the group began their careers in any of the Welsh country regiments, the Royal Welsh Fusiliers,[73] The Welsh Regiment or the South Wales Borderers. Irish regiments are not highly represented either, with only three – two of whom were commissioned into the Royal Irish Rifles and one the Royal Irish Regiment. The latter was educated at Dover College; the two Rifles officers at Downside and the Royal Belfast School. The five-year age difference between these two Rifles officers (born 1889 and 1894) makes it less likely that they were directly contemporary within the regiment.

There is a wide spread of English county regiments among the brigadiers. Starting first with the nationally based smart regiments, the four officers were divided equally between the King's Royal Rifle Corps and the Rifle Brigade. The King's Royal Rifle Corps officers, born in 1894 and 1896 and educated at Wellington and Winchester respectively, were regimental contemporaries. The Rifle Brigade officers were two years apart (born 1890 and 1892); although the younger of the pair came from Wellington, the elder was one of the officers whose initial schooling remains unlocated; neither attended university. The two officers of the Bedfordshire Regiment, both among the eldest officers in the sample being 53 and 54 years of age in 1940, were also regimental

73 Although the archaic nomenclature 'Welch' had been used informally by the regiment, the official change from 'Welsh' did not occur until *Army Order 56* of 1920.

contemporaries on first commissioning in 1904 and 1905. They were schooled at Rugby and Cheltenham. The two officers from the Durham Light Infantry, which was held in particular esteem in the English North-East, had too much of an age difference (six years, being born in 1887 and 1893) to be direct contemporaries; they too were products of Eton and Marlborough respectively. The West Yorkshire Regiment's two officers were closer in age and therefore contemporaneous (born 1889 and 1891 respectively); the latter, John Gawthorpe, is also a singular exception to the assertion that schoolboys did not join regiments associated with the areas in which they were schooled; he attended Wakefield from 1905–1909.

In their early careers, the two officers commissioned into the Essex Regiment were contemporaries as they were born in 1891 and 1892; the first was educated in the Channel Islands and the latter at Marlborough, so while not connected by a school they joined their regiment close together. The Lincolnshire Regiment's three officers were widely spread in schools and age: the eldest born in 1882, the youngest in 1891 with the man in the middle born in 1889. Their education came from Glenalmond, Haileybury and Sherborne respectively. There was also an eleven-year spread in age between the officers first commissioned into the Royal Berkshire Regiment in this group; the eldest born in 1886, was educated at Weymouth College. The younger officers, born in 1896 and 1897, the first of whom went to Shrewsbury (the second is in the group of those undetermined for education) were regimentally contemporary.

With respect to officers commissioned into what were then termed 'services', e.g. logistics and ordnance, the difficulty in determining contemporary early service is compounded by the wide area in which their formations served. Also, few of the officers in this group who served in the Army Ordnance Corps (as it then was) and the Army Service Corps (ditto) received a public school education and none went to university – indicating that university graduates were furthermore a social elite on three levels, possessing a public school and university education within an elite – army officers – and an elite within that group, as they rose to senior rank. The eight officers who originally joined the Army Service Corps were born between 1882 and 1891; only four are known to have been educated at public school but none was common to any single school; only two (born in 1882 and 1883) will have been commissioned closely together. For the Army Ordnance Corps, both were born in 1884, but only one received a public school education, at Malvern, and neither attended university – one was commissioned into the Regular Army in 1903; the other was mobilised as a Territorial in 1914, further reducing the potential for their having been connected as junior officers.

For comparison, looking one or two echelons upwards – to divisional and corps command (in the BEF) or to force level (in Norway) – it is immediately apparent that among the brigadiers' senior commanders in 1940, public schools again predominate. Of the three corps commanders in France,[74] Michael Barker, Alan Brooke and Ronald

74 Major L. F. Ellis, *The Campaign in France & Flanders – Official History of the Second World War* (London: HMSO, 1953), *Appendix A: British Forces Engaged*, pp.375–99.

Adam, Barker and Adam were educated at Malvern and Eton respectively. Brooke was privately educated in France. Of the 13 divisional commanders deployed to France in 1939–1940, 11 were public school educated, with one privately tutored (Major General E. A. Osborne, 44th Division) and one whose education is unrecorded (Major General W. N. Herbert, 23rd Division). In the BEF, no schools predominate among the group, although the commanders of 2nd, 46th and 48th Divisions (Major Generals H. C. Loyd, H. O. Curtis and A. F. A. N. Thorne, respectively) were all Old Etonians, but none of their subordinate brigadiers were.[75]

There is little commonality of school, either, between the other divisional commanders and their subordinate brigadiers, except when Brigadier F. H. N. Davidson took over temporary command of 2nd Division between 16 and 20 May as this meant that the divisional commander and the officer commanding the division's junior brigade, Noel Irwin, were both Marlburians. (Irwin would be promoted major general and took over command of the division from Davidson on 20 May).[76] One conjunction of the school of the divisional commander and his subordinates comes in the 51st (Highland) Division, where its commander, Major General V. M. Fortune and two of his three brigade commanders were Wykehamists. (Fortune attended from 1897–1901; George Burney of 153 Brigade, 1905–1908 and Arthur Stanley-Clarke of 154 Brigade 1901–1905). There is no firm evidence to suggest that Fortune had any influence over their appointment based purely on their place of education. The chances of their overlapping are slight, being only in the year of departure and arrival, and all three served in different regiments; the Black Watch, the Gordon Highlanders and the Cameronians respectively.

With regard to the NWEF in Norway, all senior field commanders (at brigade, ad hoc 'Force' and NWEF HQ)[77] were public school alumni, but with a wide variety of schools represented. The sole school with two representatives in Norway was Repton, Charles Phillips (146 Brigade, Repton 1903–1908) and Herbert Smyth (15 Brigade, Repton 1910–1914).

The number of direct personal linkages between officers via school, university and first commissioned service is not widespread among the group as a whole. It is not possible to measure all of the indirect linkages, for example through siblings being contemporaries with other men among the group overall. The influence of such combinations would be more significant in later service when specifics such as time at school, in the public schools which house one resided, time and place as an undergraduate would 'level' into a general connectivity through mutual awareness and loyalties based on the school and university overall and also that concept of being a gentleman.

Moving into wider society – both civil and military – connections of school and regiment, regardless of the precise period spent within them act as a common point of

75 Ellis, *The Campaigns….*, pp.375–80.
76 Ellis, *The Campaigns…*, p.375.
77 T. K. Derry, *The Campaign in Norway*, History of the Second World War: United Kingdom Military Series (London: Her Majesty's Stationery Office, 1952), Appendix B: List of Forces Engaged, pp.263–267.

reference. The strength of such ties varied, depending on interpersonal relationships, but as the example of Frost shows, a sense of connection to more senior officers of the same regiment could raise expectations of support for the advancement of careers among juniors, exploiting paternalistic expectations. The pattern of advancement had a common template and seniors maintained or resurrected the notion that an officer should be a gentleman. The importance of school connections was along the broader principle of having attended the right kind of school rather than from being a direct contemporary.

Overall, the patterns of groups of old boys from the various schools attended by the brigadiers show that there is no clear indication of school groups, or factions developing among the officers in the 1940 group, as times of attendance were spread out or overlapping across extended periods, even with those schools, such as Eton, Wellington and Winchester which provided multiple candidates for commissions. There is no evidence of a clear-cut, significant self-helping clique emerging based purely on the basis of school attended. Equally, there is no direct grouping of specific schools to regiments, removing this as a source of self-supporting groups. It can therefore be stated that with regard to this specific group of officers no individual school is particularly dominant over any other in the supply of officers, nor is there any direct linkage between particular schools and particular regiments. Even the connection of Eton to the supply of officers to the Guards Regiments is dissipated by the lack of a dominant single regiment within this group. While the 'old school tie' connection cannot be entirely dismissed due to the commonality of experience even if separated by gaps in time, in respect of this specific group its influence is of lesser impact.

## Family Connections

The social and educational origins of British Army officers from 1800–1970 were examined in a series of articles in the 1970s by the sociologist C. B. Otley.[78] Otley argued that the link between the provision of officers from the nobility and landed gentry was at first eroded by the abolition of purchase, but had 'nothing to fear' as the public schools continued to supply a constant stream of 'suitably processed' young men.[79] The First World War had permitted access to the officer class to a wider range of society if only out of necessity.[80] However, a rapid reapplication of pre-war social norms combined with the very expense of living as an officer – which varied between distinct regiments and

78 C. B. Otley, 'The Social Origins of British Army Officers' in *The Sociological Review* Vol. 18 (2), July 1970, pp.213–239; C. B. Otley, 'The Educational Background of British Army Officers' in *Sociology*, Vol. 7 (2) May 1973, pp.191–209; C. B. Otley, 'Militarism and Militarization in the Public Schools, 1900–1972' *The British Journal of Sociology*, Vol. 29 (3) September 1978, pp.321–339.

79 Otley, The Social Origins…', p..216.

80 G. Sheffield, *Leadership in the Trenches: Officer-Man Relations on the Western Front* (London, Macmillan, 2000), p.100.

corps, based on expectations of the level of uniforms, supply of horses (for example, with cavalry officers being required to supply and maintain ponies for polo and hunting) reduced the impact of this process. Fashionable regiments of higher social standing, such as the Guards, Rifles and cavalry were more expensive to bear the cost of living in by comparison with county regiments, services and the Royal Artillery and Royal Engineers. Stephen Badsey further suggests that even in regiments not deemed smart, where an officer's pay might have sufficed to cover routine living, a supplementary income was needed to sustain an image of 'conspicuous display and consumption' beyond the actual costs of soldiering.[81]

Otley, combining earlier work by Razzell and Janowitz, proved that the percentage of scions of the 'upper class' continued to decline as a proportion of all British Army officers up through the 1920s and 1930s. Their influence remained, however, as the senior (or General) officers of the time, the 'rarified' levels, as Otley describes them, reflected the social make up of their group a generation or two before, when they joined the army. Consolidating the findings of Janowitz, Razzell and his own investigations, Otley found that the sons of the upper classes had declined, by 1939, to 22 percent of the army's elite, with 78 percent from the middle classes, whereas on the verge of the First World War this was a 35/65 split.[82]

In terms of educational background, Otley describes the period 1870–1939 as the 'institution of examination-dominated selection' producing a 'two-tier' system with school education to 18 as the bottom tier, competitive selection intervening and a college training – at the RMC or RMA – as the top tier. This entry system endured, substantially unchanged, until the Second World War.[83]

Otley's findings were that in 1910, from 347 entrants to Sandhurst, 68.6 percent came from the 'major' public schools, 23.3 percent from other public schools (91.9 percent of the total) with the remainder from private education. (There were no products of grammar schools). By 1917, with 1,087 entrants to the shortened war course, 79.7 percent came from the public schools, 7 percent from private education and 4.8 percent from grammar schools. (The balance came from other/unknown educational origins). By 1920, public schoolboys had gone back up to 83 percent of the intake, which remained constant give or take a few tenths of a percentage point, until 1939; the percentage of grammar schoolboys rose from 4.2 percent in 1917 to 5.1 percent in 1939.[84] In contradiction to Otley, however, the growth in the number of officers from grammar schools is not borne out among the 1940 group (and as will be shown later nor is it with officers serving in Normandy in 1944). This indicates that while the social basis of officer candidates was changing, it would not be reflected at the brigadier level for the majority of the Second World War.

81 S. Badsey, *Doctrine and Reform in the British Cavalry 1880–1918* (Aldershot: Ashgate, 2008) p.67.
82 C. B. Otley, 'The Social Origins of British Army Officers' in *The Sociological Review* Vol. 18 (2), July 1970, p.218.
83 C. B. Otley, 'The Educational Background of British Army Officers' in *Sociology*, Vol. 7 (2) May 1973, p.193.
84 C. B. Otley, 'The Educational Background…' p.197.

Frost's examination of the family and educational backgrounds of the senior commanders (divisional and above) in British Second and Eighth Armies in 1944–45 agrees with Otley's findings that officers with aristocratic or landed backgrounds declined markedly in comparison with the rise of those from middle class backgrounds, which, he states, mirrors the post-war decline in the economic fortunes of the landed (or as Otley also labels them, 'monied') classes.[85] He notes that only two officers in Second Army and one in Eighth Army were from aristocratic backgrounds.[86] While Otley observes a decline in the number of officers who were the sons of officers themselves from the First World War until the 1950s (when it began to reverse), 10 of 26 in Second Army and 5 of 25 in Eighth Army in 1944–45 were the sons of army officers.

With regard to 1940, allowing for 14 officers from the whole group of 156 whose initial education was untraced, and 5 more who were public school educated but from schools that were neither CG nor HMC, 84 percent of the whole group were products of the public school system. With the officers who progressed, only one had an untraced early education and only two attended non-CG/HMC schools, meaning that 95 percent were public schoolboys. As to their family backgrounds, 31 of the overall group in 1940 were the sons of military officers ranging in rank from major[87] to lieutenant general,[88] 20.1 percent of the whole group. 13 of these 31 progressed beyond brigadier, 22 percent of the group of officers advancing, or 8 percent of the whole group. If this group is extended to grandfathers, 9 of the group had grandfathers (paternal or maternal) who had served in the Army or Royal Navy; 7 of these had both a father and a grandfather who had served.

**Table 2.3 1940 Brigadiers with Officer Father or Grandfather**

**(Names in Bold Are Officers Progressing After 1940)**

| | 1940 | FATHER | GRANDFATHER (IF OFFICER) |
|---|---|---|---|
| **BARKER** | **10 BDE** | **MAJ GEN SIR GEORGE BARKER** | |
| **BECKETT** | **CRA 15 DIV** | **BRIG-GEN WTC BECKETT** | **MAJ GEN CS THOMASON IA** |
| **BOND** | **CRE I CORPS** | **MAJ GEN SIR FG BOND** | |

85 M. R. Frost, 'Preparation is Key: The effect of the pre-war years on Senior Command in the British Army, 1944–45' (Unpublished PhD thesis, King's College London 2017).

86 M. R. Frost, 'Preparation is…' p.57.

87 Charles Phillips' father, Major G. E. Phillips DSO RE, was killed in action in Somaliland in 1902 when his son was 13. Phillips senior had been a pioneer in British Army aviation, having commanded Balloon Sections, RE in Africa and during the 2nd Boer War. H. Driver, *The Birth of British Military Aviation* (London, Royal Historical Society, Studies in History Series, 1997), p.311.

88 Geoffrey Franklin, whose father was Lieutenant General Sir William Franklyn KCB, latterly Military Secretary. He was also the brother of Lieutenant General Sir Harold Franklyn, GOC 5th Division and 'Frankforce' in the BEF of 1940.

| | 1940 | FATHER | GRANDFATHER (IF OFFICER) |
|---|---|---|---|
| BURNEY | 153 BDE | BRIG-GEN HH BURNEY | MAJ GEN JT COKE |
| CHEVENIX-TRENCH | SIG OFF IN CHF | COL C CHEVENIX-TRENCH | |
| CHICHESTER-CONSTABLE | 139 BDE | LT COL WGR CHICHESTER-CONSTABLE | |
| CHIPPINDALL | CRE III CORPS | COL WH CHIPPINDALL | |
| CHURCHILL | 151 BDE | COL AG CHURCHILL | LT GEN SIR WILLIAM PAYN |
| CURREY | HQ NWEF | LT COL HC CURREY | |
| DUNCAN | CRA III CORPS | | ADM SIR WILLIAM EDMONSTONE |
| FOX-PITT | 20 GDS BDE | LT COL WA FOX-PITT | |
| FRANKLYN | CRA 4 DIV | LT GEN SIR WILLIAM FRANKLYN | |
| **GOLDNEY** | **DRASC III CORPS** | **COL WH GOLDNEY** | |
| HAMILTON, H | AAQMG II CORPS | BRIG GEN WG HAMILTON | GEN SIR HUGH GOUGH |
| **HOGG** | **BASE AREA NWEF** | **MAJ GEN GC HOGG** | |
| **HORROCKS** | **11 BDE** | **COL WH HORROCKS** | |
| **HUDSON** | **2 BDE** | **LT COL HE HUDSON** | |
| KENT-LEMON | HQ NWEF | LT COL W KENT-LEMON | |
| **LAWSON** | **CRA 48 DIV** | **LT COL WA LEVY-LAWSON (Yeo.)** | **LT GEN SIR FREDERICK MARSHALL** |
| **PHILLIPS** | **146 BDE** | **MAJ GE PHILLIPS** | |
| PHIPPS | CRE II CORPS | LT COL EVA PHIPPS | |
| ROUPELL | 36 BDE | LT COL FF ROUPELL | |
| **SCHREIBER** | **CCRA II CORPS** | **BRIG GEN AL SCHREIBER** | |
| **STOPFORD** | **17 BDE** | **COL SIR LIONEL STOPFORD** | **V/ADM SIR MONTAGU STOPFORD** |
| THORPE | BASE CMDT CHERBOURG | COL J THORPE | |
| TILLY | 1 TK BDE | LT COL JC TILLY | |
| TOMES | OC 2ND ECHELON | LT COL A TOMES | |
| **UTTERSON-KELSO** | **131 BDE** | **CAPT WE UTTERSON-KELSO** | |
| **WHITAKER** | **7 GDS BDE** | **COL SIR ALBERT WHITAKER Bt** | **COL J CROKER** |
| WHITEHEAD | AAG BEF | LT COL E WHITEHEAD | |
| WILLIAMSON | CRA MED ARTY III CORPS | CAPT CH WILLIAMSON | |

**Table 2.4 Officers from Aristocratic and Titled Families**

| OFFICER | FATHER | MOTHER | GRANDFATHER | GRANDMOTHER |
|---|---|---|---|---|
| BARKER, E | MAJ GEN SIR EVELYN BARKER | HON LADY CLEMENCY BARKER | JOHN HUBBARD, 1ST BARON ADDINGTON | HON MARIA NAPIER, dtr OF 9TH LORD NAPIER |
| BARRETT | SIR HUGH SCOTT-BARRETT | | | |
| BLUNT | | | SIR HENRY GORDON KCB | |
| DAVIDSON | SIR LEYBOURN DAVIDSON | | | |
| DOWNE | JOHN DAWNAY, 9TH VISCOUNT DOWNE | | 8TH VISCOUNT DOWNE (P). SIR WILLIAM FFOLKES, 3RD BARONET (M) | LADY HENRIETTA FFOLKES dtr, of GEN SIR CHARLES WALE |
| FRASER | 19TH LORD SALTOUN | | | |
| GAMMELL | SIR SYDNEY GAMMELL | | | |
| JARDINE | SIR JOHN JARDINE, 1ST BARONET | | | |
| LAURIE | SIR WILFRED LAURIE, 5TH BARONET | | SIR EMILIUS LAURIE, 4TH BARONET | |
| LAWSON | WILLIAM LEVY-LAWSON, 4TH BARON BURNHAM | | 1ST BARON BURNHAM (P). LT GEN SIR FREDERICK MARSHALL (M) | |
| LEESE | SIR WILLIAM LEESE 2ND BARONET | | SIR JOSEPH LEESE, 1ST BARONET | |
| PERCEVAL | SIR WESTBY PERCEVAL | | | |
| SMITH | RT HON SIR HUBERT CLEMENTI-SMITH | | | |
| SOMERSET | GEORGE SOMERSET, 3RD LORD RAGLAN | LADY ETHEL PONSONBY | 2ND LORD RAGLAN (P); 7TH EARL OF BESSBOROUGH (M) | |
| WHITAKER | COL SIR ALBERT WHITAKER, 1ST BARONET | | | |

The number of officers who came from the aristocracy[89] (Table 2.4) were similarly in a minority; only 15 of the whole group, 9.7 percent, came from such backgrounds (of whom four were Baronets), with only 8 of those 15 progressing. All four Baronets were promoted after 1940. Even fewer officers were sons of clergymen, (Table 2.5) with only seven (4.5 percent), having family connections who were so employed, including Brian Horrocks whose grandfather-in-law was the Reverend J. C. Moore. Four of these seven officers (2.5 percent of the whole group, 6.7 percent of the officers advancing) advanced in rank during the war.

**Table 2.5 Officers with Relatives who were Clergy**

| | FATHER | GRANDFATHER | FATHER IN-LAW |
|---|---|---|---|
| HAWKESWORTH | REV. JOHN HAWKESWORTH | | |
| HOPWOOD | REV CANON HOPWOOD | | |
| HORROCKS | | | REV JC MOORE |
| SCHREIBER | | REV JOHN SCHREIBER | |
| SMITH | | REV JOHN SMITH | |
| SWAYNE | RT REV BISHOP WS SWAYNE | | |
| WITTS | REV CANON FRANCIS WITTS | REV EDWARD WITTS<br>REV CANON GD BOURNE | |

Although most of the remainder whose fathers' profession can be traced were the sons of professional men or gentlemen of independent wealth or private means, no specific professions predominate. The use of the UK National Census to identify many of these officers' fathers' occupation is often inconclusive, as in many cases these officers were at school in 1901, or under training or serving in 1911, especially among those officers who were past their mid-forties when in France or Norway. Furthermore, some officers could not be positively identified in the 1891 Census due to multiple instances of names, which were not further qualified or expanded to include further Christian names. Equally, not all officers who had entries in *Who's Who* listed their fathers' professions.

Away from the sons or grandsons of officers of either the Army or the Royal Navy, a wide range of professions were represented among other officers' fathers, with no particular professional group dominant. By means of example, Kenneth Anderson and Clifford Beckett were sons of railway engineers, both of whom worked in India; Donald

89 In this case 'aristocracy' is extended to cover those who were sons of Baronets and those who were the sons of men who received knighthoods in the course of their professions, not just those of the Peerage.

Banks' father had a stationery business, but his great-grandfather had founded Banks' Brewery in Wolverhampton. Arthur Archdale's father was also a brewer – in Baldock, Hertfordshire but he did not own the business. Claude Gill's father was a shipbuilder at Rochester in Kent.[90] Archibald Beauman's father had been a stockbroker and Percy Clark's an Associate of the Royal College of Art and external examiner for the University of Cambridge.

John Crocker's father had been the company secretary of a gold mining firm; Francis Davidson's father had been a plantation owner in Ceylon. Lawyers were not especially represented, with only Oliver Leese's father, a barrister, William Duncan's father, a Scottish advocate and Geoffrey Franklyn's father in law, a barrister and a Fellow of the Royal Statistical Society. Four fathers had been diplomats or colonial officials. Colin Gubbins' father, John, was a specialist in Anglo-Japanese affairs at the Foreign Office, having been appointed Companion of the Order of St Michael and St George (CMG) for his part in negotiating the Anglo-Japanese Treaty of Commerce and Navigation in 1894.[91] Sir John Jardine KCIE, 1st Baronet, father of Brigadier Colin Jardine, 2nd Baronet, had been a senior official in the Bombay Civil Service;[92] Christopher Perceval's father, Sir Westby Perceval KCMG, as well as serving as an MP in New Zealand, became the Agent-General (now High Commissioner) to the United Kingdom, for which he was knighted. Hubert Clementi-Smith's father, Sir Cecil, was a Privy Counsellor and former Treasurer of Hong Kong; his career culminated as Governor of the Straits Settlements, for which he was advanced to GCMG in 1892 (having been knighted, KCMG in 1886).[93] William Cave-Browne's father, Edward, had ended his career as the Accountant-General of the India Office and appointed Commander of the Order of the Star of India.[94]

Although very few of the officers could be described as having emerged from working, or lower class, backgrounds,[95] neither do they fit a social stereotype of the officer corps as being dominated by the aristocratic or land-owning classes. In this sense, they defy the archetype claimed by Barnett and Williamson,[96] that the aristocratic and upper classes

90 The Cambridge Alumni Database, University of Cambridge http://venn.lib.cam.ac.uk/ accessed 1 May 2019.
91 I. Nish, 'John Harrington Gubbins, 1852–1929' in *Britain and Japan: Biographical Portraits* (London, Japan Library, 1997).
92 *India Office List 1891*, (London, HMSO, 1891).
93 The Cambridge Alumni Database, University of Cambridge http://venn.lib.cam.ac.uk/ accessed 1 May 2019.
94 Details of other fathers' professions from Who Was Who online; https://www.ukwhoswho.com/ Accessed 2 May 2019.
95 One exception is Brigadier A. J. 'Tommy' Clifton, who spent 7 years, 224 days in the Royal Field Artillery, rising to the rank of sergeant. Born in 1887, he was commissioned in 1909 which means he must have joined the Army as a Boy Soldier aged 14. *HYAL* January 1942, p.125
96 C. Barnett, *The Desert Generals* (London, William Kimber, 1960) p.130 and W. Murray, 'British Military Effectiveness 1919–1939' in W. Murray, W. and R. Millett (eds), *Military Effectiveness*, volume 2: The Interwar Period (Cambridge, CUP, 1988), p.105.

still dominated, and were still the main source of supply to the British officer cadre up to, into and beyond the First World War. Otley's assertion that this dominance had weakened, with Frost's analysis of certain senior commanders in 1944 being in harmony with the former's findings is also borne out by examination of the 1940 brigadiers in this study. This shows that the trend was maintained into the Second World War, although as will be discussed in a later chapter, at least with D-Day brigadiers there was some reassertion of the social background of the 'officer type'.

Barnett also asserts that the abolition of purchase in 1870 theoretically opened up the officer ranks to a wider section of society and not just those with the means to buy their way in. In reality the very cost of living as an army officer – which could be, depending on the social fashionability of the regiment, beyond an officer's pay and in some cases far beyond – could act as a disincentive to join for those without some form of private income. Therefore, in the judgement of the Akers-Douglas Committee of 1902 which sought to examine how to attract a wider social band of officer candidates to serving in the army 'many suitable candidates are precluded from entering the Service for no other consideration than the insufficiency of their private income.'[97] Although this was mitigated by the need for more, and experienced officers during the First World War broadening the social base, the return to peacetime soldiering reasserted pre-war patterns and the re-emergence of a more socially typical candidate for advancement.[98]

## Conclusions

By far the majority of the 1940 group were taught at British public schools. An officer would typically be public school educated and from the upper tiers of society. Officers from well-established families who could afford to provide a private income to their sons to supplement their army salary possessed an advantage, unsurprisingly, over those who needed to live on their pay. Anecdotally, Brigadier Shelford Bidwell, a junior officer in the 1930s, said that his father gave him £50 per year to supplement his pay in the Royal

97 C. Barnett, *Britain and Her Army 1509–1970: A Military, Political and Social Survey* (London, Allen Lane, 1970), p.346.

98 An indirect relative of the author was Captain B. F. Whiteley DCM of the King's Royal Rifle Corps. He joined the Army as a rifleman in 1899, fought in the Boer War and remained in the Army after 1902. On the outbreak of war in 1914 he was a sergeant and was rapidly advanced first to colour sergeant and then to company sergeant major. He received a Distinguished Conduct Medal at the First Battle of Ypres in October 1914 and was commissioned in the field in December 1914. Severely wounded in January 1915, he would not return to the Western Front until August 1918. Promoted captain, he served in North Russia in 1919. Married with two children, he resigned his commission in early 1920. Family lore suggested that his resignation was precipitated by his wife's refusal to uproot the family to go to India, but in his private memoir he also mentioned concern at being unable to live as expected by the regiment solely on his captain's salary. (Captain B. F. Whiteley DCM 'My War, 1914–1918'; unpublished typescript ms. 1951).

Artillery. Neil Ritchie's family had accrued a fortune in business in Canada, leaving him well established; he returned to these interests after retirement from the army.

Only 39 officers in the group of 156 gained their commissions after 1913, with two brigadiers, exceptionally young in 1940 terms, being commissioned in the 1920s. The majority, therefore, were products of the Victorian/Edwardian officer selection and training process – and the social norms which applied to it. As the First World War progressed, the demand for officers would outstrip the ability of the traditional routes of supply such as the public schools, the scions of the gentry, the clergy and the land-owning classes, both as casualty rates increased and as the army expanded in size. The class-based bar would lower as more officers were promoted from the ranks on the basis of practical and battle experience. However, this bar would rise again from the 1920s.

Post-war, the old preferences would begin to reassert themselves, where officers who did not 'fit in' would face varying degrees of ostracism and even pressure to leave the army. However, the future brigadiers considered here had already proved themselves 'suitable' on active service, the majority, 121 of the 156, having one or more decorations for gallantry and distinguished service during the past war or between the wars, which would lend them an advantage in resisting and overcoming such pressures in comparison to contemporaries without them. (The issue of possession of decorations is discussed in more detail in the next chapter).

Although a public school education is sufficiently prominent among the officers to lead one to conclude that it was a prerequisite (albeit an implied rather than a mandated one) to remain in the army and build a career after the First World War, the group is not dominated by the seven 'great' public schools and two day-schools of the Clarendon Group. No single school absolutely dominates the group, and although Eton, Cheltenham, Wellington and Winchester figure prominently, Bowman and Connelly's assertion that the Edwardian officer corps was dominated by a small group of six schools is not completely reflected in this group, as only one-third of it came from these schools, even though the CG and HC produced the majority of over half of them.

A university education was much less common, as it was a minority experience across the country overall. The officers in the group who were graduates remained a minority group within a minority of the population, although being a graduate was of itself no impediment to progression to high rank.

Officers who continued as professional soldiers after the First World War, regardless of their means of initial entry to the profession of army officer, were still products of the public school system. Public school alumni reasserted their dominance of the profession in the interwar period.

130 officers of the group of 156 who served in, and survived through to the end of, the First World War were ahead, if only through good fortune, of the statistical trend. Whether they had enhanced networks between them is difficult to prove with certainty, but subsequent commemoration of the dead within schools, universities and regiments acted as a unifying force between those with common experience, or communal connection.

Although the popular assertion linking 'Eton and the Guards' may have a loose factual basis from the number of Old Etonian officers within this group – five, three of whom served with the Coldstream Guards – no other line or county infantry regiment or regiments particularly predominates among them. There is also little correlation between the geographical location of the school and the county or area infantry regiments joined by those from particular schools. This in itself is not particularly significant due to the influence of factors such as family ties, history and traditions; the 'fashionability' of certain regiments and the varying levels of supplementary income required to be able to bear the expenses of being part of them.

The number of immediate and direct personal linkages between officers via school, university and first commissioned service is not widespread among the group as a whole. The influence of such conjunctions would be more significant in later service when specifics such as time at school, in the public schools which house one resided, time and place as an undergraduate would 'level' into a general connectivity through mutual awareness and loyalties based on the school and university overall and also that concept of being a gentleman.

Otley's assertion that the percentage of scions of the 'upper class' continued to decline as a proportion of all British Army officers up through the 1920s and 1930s has some applicability to this group, but its influence remained, however, as the senior officers of the time reflected the social make up of their group a generation or two before, when they actually joined the army.

As to family backgrounds, although the largest minority of the whole group of 1940 brigadiers, a fifth, were the sons of military officers ranging in rank from major to major general, 20.1 percent of the whole group, they were still a minority. This statistic remains largely constant among the officers who advanced in rank after 1940, with 22 percent of the group of officers advancing having fathers who had served previously.

No specific professions are predominant among the relatives of other officers in the group, either among those who advanced or among those who did not. Although very few of the officers could be described as having emerged from working, or lower class, backgrounds, neither do they fit a social stereotype of the officer corps as being dominated by the aristocratic or land-owning classes. In this sense, they defy the stereotype claimed by Barnett and Williamson,100 that the aristocratic and upper classes still dominated, and were still the main source of supply to, the British officer cadre up to, into and beyond the First World War.

With schools and regiments of initial commissioning proving inconclusive as definitive providers of advantage to higher rank promotion, factors such as professional education are now examined to identify whether, and to what extent, it favourably influenced an officer's suitability for higher promotion.

# 3

# The Interwar Period, 1919–1939: Education, Training and Postings

> I am glad Sir, that you have no Staff College officers on your staff, I do not like Staff College officers. My experience of Staff College officers is that they are conceited, and they are dirty! Brains? I do not believe in brains …. my Military Secretary, and a damned good one he is too, is the stupidest man I ever came across.
>
> Attributed to Prince George, Duke of Cambridge,
> Commander-in-Chief of the Forces (1856–1895)[1]

> The Staff College has been devised to restrain and curb officers who are unable to remain at the official level of proficiency.
>
> *The Young Officer's Guide to Knowledge*
> The Senior Major (1915)[2]

This chapter examines two issues which could influence the potential for advancement of the officers in the group who remained in the army during the interwar years, from 1919 to 1939. Although the return to peacetime soldiering meant large-scale reductions in manpower, at the same time promotion structures based on seniority and a lack of incentives for older officers with little prospect of advancement to retire, meant that a younger officer would need to show that he was distinct from his peers to gain advancement.

The first issue considered is those avenues open to junior officers for professional education in the period between the First World War and the mid-1930s, including the successful completion of courses such as the Army Staff College and whether successful admission to, and completion of, such education was influential in post-1940 advancement. It will also explore whether shared experience of such courses created enduring

1 http://regimentalrogue.com/quotes/quotes_officers1.htm accessed 1 July 2019. The quotation has proven impossible to attribute definitively to the speaker.
2 Attributed to Captain C. G. Massie Blomfield (Aldershot: Bourne Press, 2nd Edition 1915).

networks between students which may have been influential later in their careers. This will be followed by an examination of whether service overseas, be it in staff postings or attached service in armies of the empire and so on had any influence over advancement, or generated subgroups and networks within the main grouping.

It should be noted that it is not intended to examine the precise nature of the education, such as the syllabus, provided on such courses as this is discussed elsewhere.[3] The primary aim is to view whether the time spent in such establishments was a potential generator of networks. Consideration will also be given as to whether such networks were immediate (for example, through being direct contemporaries) or indirect, through being connected as graduates of such courses.

Despite having recently engaged successfully in the largest scale war the British Army had ever experienced, with the return of peace and demobilisation attitudes towards the profession of soldiering quickly reverted to pre-war norms. It was as if the war just won was an aberration, and the changes the army had gone through were not to be replicated or extended. Education of officers was one area where this attitude was particularly visible, where prejudices and custom would reassert themselves as the army returned to 'normal'. Even after the Second World War, Montgomery noted that '…we did not properly check up on the lessons of the [First World] war,'[4] notwithstanding his own role in redrafting the second post-war edition of the official manual *Infantry Training* in 1931.[5]

In the interwar period, there were three formal avenues for the continued professional education and training of army officers: the Senior Officers' School with branches at Sheerness in the UK and at Belgaum in India, the Staff Colleges at Camberley in the UK and Quetta in India, and from 1927 the Imperial Defence College in London. The first was an innovation from the First World War, established in 1916 by Brigadier General R. J. Kentish. It was originally intended for officers of the British Army who aspired to battalion command and to ensure that all such candidates received suitable training. This was a role which had traditionally rested with battalion commanders. At the time and increasingly after the cessation of hostilities some took its very existence to imply that they were incapable of preparing their officers adequately. The School attempted to widen officers' outlook by including in its syllabus subjects that were not immediately military but led to an appreciation of the wider political, geographical and technological environment in which the British Army would operate.[6]

3 For example, in works such as B. Bond, *The Victorian Army and the Staff College* (London, Methuen, 1972); A. G. Duncan, 'The Military Education of Junior Officers in the Edwardian Army' (unpublished PhD thesis, University of Birmingham, 2016)

4 'Opening address delivered by Field Marshal the Rt. Hon. Viscount Montgomery, CIGS, on the occasion of Exercise Evolution, Staff College, Camberley, 14 August, 1946' London, Imperial War Museum, Major General R. Briggs Papers, MSS 66/76/1.

5 D. French, 'Doctrine and Organisation in the British Army, 1919–1932' in *The Historical Journal,* 44 (2) (2001), pp.497–515.

6 See G. Kennedy and K. Neilson, in *Military Education, Past Present and Future* (Connecticut: Praeger, 2002), p.111.

With the massive expansion of the British Army in the First World War, the demand for qualified staff officers at all levels of command outstripped the ability of pre-war structures to produce them. The closure of the Staff College on the outbreak of war in August 1914 – as the pupils and the directing staff were needed immediately for front line service – did not help the situation. When Hooge Chateau was shelled by the Germans at 13.25 on 31 October 1914, among the extensive casualties were the staffs of Major General Monro (commanding 2nd Division) and Major General Lomax (commanding 1st Division) which had co-located there to plan the defence of Ypres. Seven staff officers were killed[7] and a further four were wounded, one mortally, removing them from duty at a critical point. (Lomax was so badly hurt he had to be evacuated home and subsequently died of his wounds; Monro, though injured, continued in command).[8]

Apart from the obvious tactical error of combining such essential personnel in one location, it underlined the shortage of supply of such specialists. Additional demand would stem from the need to place qualified Regular Army staff officers with the newly forming and expanding Territorial and New Army divisions at home and latterly in France, which had not generated their own staffs organically. From 40 qualified staff officers serving with the BEF on its initial deployment to France, by the spring of 1915 the total number of staff officers at army, corps and divisional level had risen to 300.[9] Out of necessity, at junior levels, front line officers with some experience would be invited, first, to become what were titled 'Staff Learners' to determine whether they had the ability to fill staff posts and, indeed, whether they wished to do so.

Staff schools were initially established in France in early 1916, but after the experience of the Battle of the Somme, both a senior and junior staff school were established at Hesdin. The courses lasted six weeks and took 20 students at a time, each. The former prepared officers for postings as GSO1s and Assistant Adjutant and Quartermaster General; the latter prepared GSO2s. A comparable school to Hesdin was formed in Cambridge in 1917, and the Staff College at Camberley restarted short staff courses later that year, but this did not endure long as it became a tactical school for senior officers in 1918.[10] GSO1s and 2s were appointed by GHQ, GSO3s and Brigade Majors were appointed at Army level.

Qualifications for staff postings also relaxed as the war went on; until the summer of 1916, potential staff officers either had to be a p.s.c., to have held a staff position, or to have successfully completed a staff course (including a month's service as a Staff Learner). The rules were further relaxed in 1917, with candidates for staff postings in the UK no longer being required to have passed a staff course, but they had to have been

7 S. Robbins, *British Generalship during the Great War: The Military Career of Sir Henry Horne* (London: Rutledge, 2016), p.73.
8 B. Brice, *The Battle Book of Ypres* (2014 reprint of 1927 original), p.141.
9 P. Harris, *The Men Who Planned the War: A Study of the Staff of the British Army on the Western Front 1914–1918* (London: Routledge, 2017), p.50.
10 TNA WO 256/15, 'Summary of Schools for Training in the British Expeditionary Force, Winter 1916–Spring 1917'.

a Staff Learner for a month. In September 1917, this relaxation was also applied to the most junior GSOs, GSO3s, in operational theatres overseas.[11]

From the whole 1940 group of 156, 55 of them served as GSOs on active service (for the purposes of this analysis, officers serving in the UK, such as on the staff of home commands, schools and the War Office are included). This represents 35.7 percent of the whole. Of these 55, 42, or 76 percent of the sub-group were either already, or would become, Staff College graduates between the world wars, 27.7 percent of the whole 1940 group. The combination of staff service and subsequent attainment of a Staff College qualification were therefore a significant minority within the group.

Of the 55 serving as GSOs, 22 officers were promoted beyond brigadier during the course of the Second World War (40 percent of the sub-group). Of these 22, only three did not attend Staff College. This suggests that the combination of front line service as a GSO and a p.s.c. – with 19 out of 55 officers being so qualified, (35.4 percent of the sub-group and 12.3 percent of the whole) while far from decisive, was a positive influence towards selection for further promotion. By comparison, among the remaining 99 officers who did not serve as GSOs during the First World War (even though several did between the wars after attending Staff College) the proportion of Staff College graduates is slightly lower, with 37 out of the 99, or 37.3 percent. Of the 99. the number of officers advancing beyond brigadier is the same – 37, and the same percentage.

Army promotion prospects stagnated in the 1920s and 1930s due to blockages caused by a lack of funding to allow career progression or to encourage ageing officers with little prospect of further promotion to retire. The system of promotion for officers up to major was still based on the concept of regimental seniority, whereby an officer could only be promoted when a vacancy emerged in the higher rank within his regiment, usually through retirement. This could result in long waits for advancement. The latter was exacerbated by the historic system of half pay. As described above, the concept of half pay allowed officers of the British Army (and Royal Navy) to be put into semi-retirement during periods of peace, when fewer command positions were available. While his services were not immediately needed, the officer would receive half of his original pay. This ensured that officers would be financially supported to some extent while they waited to be recalled to active duty.[12] However, as mentioned previously if an officer chose to retire or resign while on the half pay list, his pension would also be reduced by half.[13]

11 Details on staff qualifications from C. Messenger, *Call to Arms: The British Army 1914–1918* (London, Cassell, 2005), pp.361–365.

12 Alphabetical Register of Army Officers on Half Pay, 1737–1921, TNA PMG 4; General office files of the Paymaster General in relation to military pensions, 1730–1969, TNA PMG 74. Public Records Office Records Information Leaflet No.123 *British Army Pensions* (1997).

13 The half pay system was a legacy of the system of purchase of commissions, although purchase was abolished in 1871. Army officers did not receive a formal pension until 1921 and the system of half pay endured into the 1930s. A. P. C. Bruce (1980) *The Purchase System in The British Army 1660–1871*, Royal Historical Society Studies in History Series

Any officer with ambition would have to find avenues to render him distinctive amongst his contemporaries to impress selection boards for further promotion. Attached service overseas was one option, either in staff posts or with Imperial or Colonial units, such as Kenneth Anderson serving as the GSO1 at Deccan Command in India from March 1936 to December 1937[14] or Wilson Crewdson, Staff Colonel at HQ Hong Kong in 1938,[15] and George Martin, who after serving as a GSO2 at the Royal Military College in Canada from 1931–33 and a year at the War Office, again went abroad in 1935 as a GSO2 at HQ Gibraltar.

For many others, this would be an application to the Staff College, either for a competitive place by examination or through the much scarcer route of nomination by the candidate's commanding officer. For example, in 1926, in response to a Parliamentary Question from the Member of Parliament for Barnstable, Sir Basil Peto, the Secretary of State for War, Sir Lamington Worthington-Evans[16] responded that there were 440 entrants for the entrance examination for admission to Camberley. There were 34 vacancies open for competition, of which 22 were for British Army officers, and about 16 vacancies to be filled by nomination, of which 10 were for British Army officers.[17] These figures were generally typical in the 1920s, but by the end of the decade, the pressure on places was increasing.

In 1926 Worthington-Evans had added that the limitations of accommodation at Camberley was 'a very difficult matter' preventing expansion of the course. On average, the annual intake at both Camberley and Quetta was just over 50 for each, making just over 100 places for each year across the two colleges. (In 1925, the prevailing number for each intake was officially declared to be 57 at Camberley and 53 at Quetta).[18] Despite the apparent pressure for places via either route, there was also what has been described as a 'suspicion' of the Staff College among regimental commanders and some senior officers.[19]

Competition for places at Camberley grew as the 1920s progressed, notwithstanding the rigorous process required even to get to sit the competitive examination. The number of candidates applying for the College doubled in under four years – from 193 in 1923

(London: RHIstS, 1980) and D. W. Allen, 'Compatible Incentives and the Purchase of Military Commissions' in *The Journal of Legal Studies*, vol. 27, no.1 (January 1998), pp.45–66 (University of Chicago Law School).

14 *HYAL* January 1938.

15 *HYAL* January 1940.

16 Secretary of State for War, 1924–1929.

17 STAFF COLLEGE, CAMBERLEY (ADMISSION). *Hansard*, House of Commons Deb 16 February 1926 vol. 191 c1697 (House of Commons Library) the size of the course was a particular issue for Peto, who had pressed the War Office on the same issue in 1925 and would again in 1927.

18 STAFF COLLEGES (CAMBERLEY AND QUETTA). House of Commons Deb 10 March 1925 vol. 181 cc1104-05 (House of Commons Library)

19 D. French, *Military Identities: The Regimental System, the British Army, and the British People c. 1870–2000* (Oxford: Oxford University Press, 2005), p.153.

to 400 in 1926. By 1927, the ratio of applicants to places was running at 9:1. In 1929, there were 409 applicants for 56 places.[20] To get to this stage, an officer had to have been deemed suitable, and of a sufficient standard, just to be considered. An officer's commanding officer had to declare the candidate 'suitable' to apply, and he had to sustain this for two years on what was called the 'Selected List' before being allowed to sit the examination.[21] Furthermore, if an officer were successful in passing the test but did not achieve a place on the next course, he would be required to sit the examination again on re-applying.

Success on the course was no guarantee of advancement to the upper ranks of the army. However, exposure to some of the directing staff, either the College's commandants or instructors, could mark promising officers for later advancement through passive talent spotting as the former advanced to higher ranks. This was particularly marked in the mid-1920s when Brooke and Montgomery were serving there as instructors. Brooke was a General Staff Officer Grade 1 (GSO 1), or Senior Instructor, as a lieutenant colonel from 1923–1926. Montgomery taught there as a major (GSO 2, staff instructor) from 1926–1929; and would also serve as the Chief Instructor at Quetta from 1934–1937.[22] Both would later promote to senior positions in the army during the Second World War, and advance the careers, of officers that they had taught at Camberley (see below).

Such patronage was not solely restricted to Montgomery and Brooke. Arthur Percival gained a place on the 1923 course via the nomination of his commanding officer, as was permitted at the time. It was said in the army that although Percival was technically too old (at 36) for Staff College, Winston Churchill had exerted pressure for him to be accepted as he had been impressed with his conduct both in North Russia in 1919–1920 and against the Irish Republican Army during the Irish Civil War.[23] Having gained entry to Camberley, Percival first came to the attention of John Dill, who was instructing. The link would be renewed when Percival was himself posted to Camberley as an instructor and Dill was Commandant. Dill would describe Percival as 'the best officer I have seen in a long time' to the Director of Army Staff Duties and Dill would seek to appoint him to posts in his subsequent commands, the link only being broken when Percival was posted away from France in early 1940 upon promotion to major general to command 43rd (Wessex) Division. This was a post he held for only three months before returning to London in June to become Assistant CIGS, under Dill.

Dill had recommended Percival for appointment to a post as major general (General Staff) at Army level, but another candidate was selected without Dill's knowledge. Both

20 TNA WO 279/57 'Report from a Conference Held at the Staff College' 1927; TNA WO 279/70 'Report from a Conference Held at The Staff College', 1930.

21 Staff College (Camberley) Regulations War Office (London: HMSO, 1930).

22 M. Frost, 'The British and Indian Army Staff Colleges in the Interwar Years' in D. Delaney, R. Engen, and M. Fitzpatrick, *Military Education in the British Empire, 1815–1949* (Vancouver, University of British Columbia Press, 2018), pp.156–157.

23 C. Kinvig, *Percival of Singapore* (London: Brassey's, 1996), p.89.

men were said to hold the other 'in high mutual regard'.[24] Dill had also been the BGS at Camberley from 1919–1922 when the cadres admitted on wartime merit, rather than competition or nomination, attended; he taught Alan Brooke when the latter attended the first course at the newly opened Imperial Defence College in 1927.[25] Although by the time of Dill's return to Camberley in 1931 as Commandant, and where he remained until 1934, most of the 1940 brigadiers, both progressing and not, had already passed through. From the 1940 group, Miles Dempsey, James Steel and Brian Horrocks were pupils under Dill, and all three progressed to General's rank in the course of the war.

Recent scholarship has argued that the training provided at Camberley and Quetta in the first half of the twentieth century was inadequate and left graduates unprepared for the roles and challenges these officers would face during war.[26] However, the notion that the Staff College was the gold standard of officer training in the British Army was persistent and enduring to the extent that whatever the practical reality, the perception of it being so was unshakeable.

The 1924 intake at Camberley, which graduated at the end of 1925,[27] was notable in producing 33 officers who advanced to general officer rank during the Second World War. The 1925 Camberley class also produced the most 1940 brigadiers who progressed in rank, with seven, Richard Bond, Gerald Gartlan, Noel Irwin, William Morgan, Vyvyan Pope, John Swayne and Daryl Watson therefore directly contemporary with those officers above. Of the 32 1940 brigadiers who did not progress to major general, but were Staff College graduates, all came from the 1925 class.

**Table 3.1 Staff College, Camberley: 1925 Graduates Advancing to General Rank**

| NAME | REGIMENT | WW2 HIGHEST RANK | WW2 COMMAND |
|---|---|---|---|
| IVO THOMAS | RA | LT GEN | GOC 43 DIV |
| DOUGLAS GRAHAM | CAMERONIANS | MAJ GEN | GOC 50 DIV |
| MICHAEL CREAGH | 7H | MAJ GEN | GOC 7 ARMD DIV |
| READE GODWIN-AUSTIN | SWB | LT GEN | QMG INDIA |
| GUY ROBINSON | NORTHAMPTON | MAJ GEN | GOC NORTHERN DIST |
| ARCHIBALD NYE | LEINSTER | LT GEN | VCIGS |

24 Kinvig, *Percival…*, pp.95, 110, 112.
25 A. Danchev, *Very Special Relationship: Field Marshal Sir John Dill and the Anglo-American Alliance, 1941–44* (London, Brassey's, 1986), p.47.
26 For example, A. G. Duncan, 'The Military Education of Junior Officers in the Edwardian Army' (unpublished PhD thesis, University of Birmingham 2016) and E. Smalley, *The British Expeditionary Force 1939–40* (London, Palgrave Macmillan, 2013) and D. French, 'Colonel Blimp and the British Army: British Divisional Commanders in the War against Germany, 1939–1945' in *The English Historical Review*, Vol. 111 (444) (1996), p.1200.
27 'Staff College: List of Graduates' *The Times*, London, issue 44198, 17 February, 1926, p.11.

| NAME | REGIMENT | WW2 HIGHEST RANK | WW2 COMMAND |
|---|---|---|---|
| NOEL BERESFORD-PIERCE | RA | LT GEN | GOC S CMD (INDIA) |
| RUFUS LAURIE | SEAFORTH | MAJ GEN | GOC 52 DIV |
| JOHN REEVE | RB | MAJ GEN | DEP ADJ GEN ME |
| NOEL NAPIER-CLAVERING | RE | MAJ GEN | DEP ADJ GEN EGYPT |
| HUMFREY GALE | ASC | LT GEN | DEP CHF STAFF SHAEF |
| CLIFFORD MALDEN | R SUSSEX | MAJ GEN | GOC 2 DIV (DIED 1941) |
| WILLOUGHBY NORRIE | 11H | LT GEN | GOC XXX CORPS |
| GEOFFREY RAIKES | SWB | MAJ GEN | GOC SUDAN |
| FREDERICK HYLAND | RE | MAJ GEN | DEP CDR GIBRALTAR |
| THOMAS RIDDELL-WEBSTER | CAMERONIANS | LT GEN | QMG TO THE FORCES |
| SYDNEY WASON | RA | LT GEN | GOC 1 AA CORPS (RTD 1942) |
| JAMES HARTER | RF | MAJ GEN | GOC N MIDS DIST |
| GERALD BRUNSKILL | R SUSSEX | MAJ GEN | DIR SPECIAL WPNS |
| OTTO LUND | RA | MAJ GEN | DIRECTOR RA |
| GERALD FITZGERALD | INDIAN ARMY | MAJ GEN | GOC LUCKNOW DIST |
| GEORGE LAMMIE | R SCOTS | MAJ GEN | DIR QUARTERING, WO |
| LANGLEY BROWNING | RA | MAJ GEN | GOC RA TRG |
| ROBERT STUDDERT | RA | MAJ GEN | D/MGO (INDIA) |
| LIONEL FINCH | LANCS FUS | MAJ GEN | DIST CDR HOME |
| BEF/NWEF BRIGADIERS | | | |
| RICHARD BOND | RE | MAJ GEN | CDR, RE |
| GERALD GARTLAN | R IR RIF | MAJ GEN | MGGS N CMD |
| NOEL IRWIN | ESSEX | LT GEN | E ARMY, BURMA |
| WILLIAM MORGAN | RA | LT GEN | CGS, MED |
| VYVYAN POPE | N STAFFS | MAJ GEN | GOC XIII CORPS (KIA 1941) |
| JOHN SWAYNE | SOM LI | LT GEN | CGS, INDIA |
| DARYL WATSON | RF | LT GEN | GOC W CMD |

The extended, progressing group was typical in one aspect; with the exception of one grammar school pupil and one who appears to have gone no further than prep school, public schools were again the predominant source of education. Wellington and Cheltenham were dominant, with four old boys each, followed by Eton with three and Clifton, George Watson's and Marlborough with two each.

Among those officers who served both as GSOs on active service during the First World War and also graduated later from Staff College there were a number of groups of contemporaries. Arthur Archdale, Archibald Beauman and Frederick Bissett were at Camberley in 1920 (none of whom progressed after 1940). Merton Beckwith-Smith, Raleigh Chichester-Constable, Henry Currey, James Gammell, Graham Leventhorpe, Eric Miles and Richard Wooten were GSOs who graduated from Camberley in 1922 (of whom four of these seven, Beckwith-Smith, Gammell, Miles and Wooten, advanced). In 1923, Geoffrey Franklyn, Gerald Gartlan, John Halstead, Douglas Pratt, George Roupell, 'Jacky' Smyth and 'Monty' Stopford (again seven, of whom five were promoted – Gartlan, Halstead, Pratt, Smyth and Stopford) were contemporaries. In 1926, John Clark, William Duncan, Humfrey Gale, Cyrus Greenslade and Geoffrey Mansergh (five, of whom only Clark and Gale progressed) were students together. The only other sub-group among these doubly qualified officers was the 1927 set, comprised of Evelyn Barker, John Hawkesworth and 'Kit' Woolner, all of whom progressed. Therefore, of five groups of officers totalling 22, 14 were promoted after 1940.

## The Senior Officers' School

The Senior Officers' School opened at Aldershot in 1915 and endured until its closure in 1961. Originally conceived as a wartime expedient, in 1920, it was put on the permanent peacetime establishment. In 1925 it was 'temporarily' transferred to Sheerness, into barracks vacated by the Royal Garrison Artillery the year before.[28] Its final location, from 1939, was Erlestoke Park in Wiltshire. The parallel establishment at Belgaum in India closed in 1939. The continued existence of the Senior Officers' School after the end of the First World War was questioned in some quarters, not least on grounds of cost. In 1920, Sir Archibald Williamson MP, the Financial Secretary to the War Office, declared in Parliament that:

> It is necessary for all officers of the Regular Army, with the exception of the Royal Army Medical Corps and the Royal Army Veterinary Corps, to undergo a course at this school before they can be considered fit for promotion to the rank of substantive Lieut.-Colonel. This procedure is required in the interests of the higher tactical training of officers and of the training and administration of units, and to ascertain the fitness of officers to command troops.[29]

These remarks underline the perception that the aim of the Staff Colleges both at Camberley and Quetta was to prepare their candidates for 'higher', e.g., general officers' commands, even if when attending they were several steps in rank, and/or years from any such appointment, if at all.

28 'Army Senior Officers School' in *The Scotsman*, 11 January 1924, p.11; Hansard, House of Commons Deb 26 February 1924, vol. 170 cc231-32. (House of Commons Library)
29 *Hansard*, HC Deb 30 March 1920 vol. 127 cc1057-58. (House of Commons Library)

In the interwar period, the Senior Officers' School had a high throughput, with three courses of three months' duration each year with a total of up to 126 students[30] (i.e. 42 per course) from all three services. Priority was given to those serving in Home Forces, with places equalling a third of the total open to officers serving in the Rhine Army and the Middle East.[31] Its very existence was frequently debated in the 1920s as battalion commanders felt it their place to train and prepare their junior officers for later command of battalions. When CIGS, Sir George Milne[32] expressed understanding for this view, but in turn believed that a lack of common doctrinal teaching at this devolved level could be overcome by retaining the school. He also resisted a proposal from Sir Edmond Ironside, when the latter was Commandant at Camberley,[33] that the School be disbanded in favour of forming a War College, where a select few graduates of the Staff Colleges would spend a year later in their careers learning the requirements of higher level command. Milne rejected this suggestion on two practical grounds; first, the continuing lack of consistent standards in training, and second, a fear that the spilt would produce antagonistic groups of officers prepared to be staff officers but not commanders, and commanders not necessarily proficient in staff work.[34] (Personal antagonism between Ironside and Milne, exacerbated by the former's desire to accelerate army reform along the lines proposed by J. F. C. Fuller and Basil Liddell Hart, also cannot be ruled out as a factor.)[35]

The School's courses were reformed in 1932, reducing the number to two per year and replacing the third three-month course with four courses of two weeks' duration intended specifically for lieutenant colonels of the Territorial Army, 'for higher tactical training and actual command of troops, so that a higher number of TA commanders may receive this instruction to assist in the training of their troops.'[36] The number of vacancies on the two remaining courses for regular officers was not increased to compensate for the loss of capacity.[37] Although there had been places at the School for a 'select number'

30 For example, the 36th Course, which completed in September 1931, had 41 students, including a rear admiral, rather more senior than the typical intake and senior in rank to the school's commandant, who was an army brigadier. *Hampshire Telegraph*, 18 September 1931, p.20.
31 *The Times*. London, issue number 42671, 17 March 1921, p.21.
32 Field Marshal Sir George Milne was CIGS from February 1926 until his retirement from the Army in January 1933.
33 Ironside was Commandant of the Staff College from 1922 to 1926.
34 D. French, 'Officer Education and Training in the British Regular Army 1919–1939' in G. Kennedy & K. Neilson (eds), *Military Education, Past, Present & Future* (New Haven, Praeger, 2002), p.118.
35 John C. Cairns, 'Ironside, (William) Edmund, first Baron Ironside (1880–1959)' in *Oxford Dictionary of National Biography*, online ed. accessed 13 Apr 2018.
36 *The Times*, London, issue 46076, 8 March 1932), p.20.
37 For example, the 39th Course at the Senior Officers' School, the Second Course of 1932, comprised 35 Army officers of the rank of major or lieutenant colonel (including one major from the Indian Army); 2 captains, RN; 2 lieutenant colonels Royal Marines and 2 Squadron leaders RAF – a total of 41 candidates. *The Times*, London, issue 46115, 23 April 1932, p.8.

(unspecified) of TA lieutenant colonels in the 1920s and 1930s, this was the first time that a specific course tailored to the TA had been provided.[38] In this regard, the School was more advanced than the Staff College, which did not admit Territorials until 1938.

Defining a set of possible connections between the School's students is complicated as a complete list of course attendees does not exist. Although the directing staff are listed in the *HYAL* as part of the list of Educational Establishments, no comprehensive lists of its graduates survive. Lists of those graduating appear intermittently but erratically in newspapers in the interwar period, but their usefulness is reduced by several being only partial, being captioned 'among those to pass through .... were...'[39]

A posting as an instructor to the school could be variable in duration, from as long as three years in some cases (e.g. Henry Currey) to a few months, or, in the extreme case of Edmond Schreiber, 18 days. (Schreiber was posted away almost before taking up post in order to become the BRA in Southern Command to fill an urgent vacancy).[40] Some of the other 1940 brigadiers did serve as instructors at the School, including Alfred Hopwood, Henry Currey, Jack Churchill, John Crocker and Edmond Schreiber.

**Table 3.2 1940 Brigadiers: Instructors at The Senior Officers' School**

| NAME | 1940 | SCHOOL | REGT | STAFF COLLEGE | SEN O OFFS SCH |
|---|---|---|---|---|---|
| CHURCHILL | 151 BDE | ETON | DURHAM LI | 1919 | OCT 35-OCT 37 |
| CROCKER | 3 ARMD BDE | AT HOME | TANK CORPS | 1929 QUETTA | APR 37-FEB 38 |
| CURREY | HQ NWEF | BRADFIELD | R IR RIF | 1922 | NOV 33-OCT 36 |
| HOPWOOD | NWEF BASE | GLENALMOND | LINCOLN R | 1919 | SEP 33-SEP 35 |
| SCHREIBER | CCRA II CORPS | WELLINGTON | RA | 1925 | 8-26 SEP 1938 |

Churchill and Hopwood, while Staff College graduates together, just missed serving simultaneously at Sheerness, but Churchill and Crocker were contemporaries between April and October 1937. Hopwood and Currey served there together for nearly two years, from November 1933 to September 1935. However, another 1940 connection was that the then Brigadier Wilfrid 'Tommy' Lindsell served as Commandant of the school from September 1933 to May 1935, making him a contemporary of Hopwood and Currey. Lindsell served as the BEF's Quartermaster General in France. (Gort had

38 *The Times*, London, 8 March 1932. p.6
39 *Hampshire Telegraph*, 18 September 1931, p.20.
40 N. Smart, Biographical Dictionary of British Generals of the Second World War (Barnsley: Pen & Sword Military, 2005), p.281.

served as the Chief Instructor at Sheerness for 11 months in 1926–1927, too early to have encountered any of the brigadiers serving under him in France in 1940).[41]

Having graduated from the school, or having been directing staff thereof, did not proffer any particular advantage to officers in terms of advancement or the generation of networks. Its commandants up to the mid-1930s were, in the main, officers late in their careers for whom command of the school represented their professional swansong and were limited in their ability to influence the careers of former subordinates. Of the five, only Crocker and Schreiber advanced to major general or above during the course of the war. No officers from the Indian Senior Officers' School in Belgaum served in France or Norway.

## The Imperial Defence College

The Imperial Defence College was established at 9 Buckingham Gate in London in 1927 to instruct senior officers in the defence of the British Empire and as such was designed for officers destined for the highest ranks of the army. However, as established it differed from Ironside's rejected proposal in that it was tri-service and senior civilians were admitted. Students were of the rank of lieutenant colonel or equivalent and above (on its early courses, some substantive majors with a brevet of lieutenant colonel were admitted). Of all the officers who served as brigadiers in France and Norway, only nine were graduates of the College:

**Table 3.3 Imperial Defence College Graduates**

| NAME | 1940 | INITIAL ED | REGT | STAFF COLLEGE | IDC CLASS |
|---|---|---|---|---|---|
| BOND | CRE I CORPS | WELLINGTON | RE | 1926-27 | 1933 |
| DAVIDSON | CRA I CORPS | MARLBOROUGH | RA | 1923-24 QUETTA | 1935 |
| GARTLAN | 5 BDE | DOWNSIDE | R IRISH; RUR | 1923-24 | 1937 |
| IRWIN | 6 BDE | MARLBOROUGH | ESSEX | 1924-25 | 1936 |
| MILES | 126 BDE | HARROW | KOSB | 1922-23 | 1934 |
| PERCIVAL | BGS I CORPS | RUGBY | BEDFORDS | 1923-24 | 1937 |
| POPE | BGS II CORPS | LANCING | N STAFFS; RTR | 1924-25 | 1934 |
| SWAYNE | BGS BEF | CHARTERHOUSE OXFORD (TRINITY) | SOMERSET LI | 1925-26 | 1933 |
| WEST | ASST MIL SEC | KING'S CANTERBURY | RE | 1927-28 | 1938 |

41 *HYAL* December 1938, pp.13–20.

The eight IDC contemporaries were therefore Bond and Swayne in 1933; Miles and Pope in 1934 with Gartlan and Percival following in 1937, leaving Davidson in 1935, Irwin in 1936, and West in 1938, as the officers who did not graduate together from Buckingham Gate. However, if the conjunction between time at Staff College and the IDC is considered, Gartlan and Percival are doubly connected by being direct contemporaries at both, in 1923–1924 and 1937 respectively. All the nine IDC graduates fulfilled the intent of the course at least in part; six progressed to major general[42] and three to lieutenant general,[43] Alan Brooke, having been a student at the IDC in 1927 returned to the College as an instructor in 1932, remaining until 1934 – and would therefore have taught Bond, Swayne, Miles and Pope.

In terms of 'talent spotting' by the Commandant of the College itself, the sole Commandant of the IDC from the army in the period was the then Major General Robert Haining in 1935–1936, when Davidson and Irwin were students. Haining went on to significant postings thereafter, including the Director of Military Operations and Intelligence in 1936, GOC British Forces in Palestine and Transjordan in 1938, GOC Western Command in 1939 and Vice Chief of the Imperial General Staff in 1940.[44] After a period in the Middle East in the summer of 1941 in a post, Intendant General, specially and specifically created by Churchill[45] to ensure continuity of supplies to theatre, and especially those coming from the United States, Haining retired in 1942. In an immediate sense, therefore, his influence over the careers of his students would only have been indirect, as their postings (save for Davidson's subsequently following him as Director of Military Operations and Intelligence) did not directly coincide; neither served under him in Palestine nor in the War Office or subsequently. Although attendance on the IDC course was a factor in the advancement of the 1940 brigadiers to higher rank, the direct influence of the army commandants on their students' careers is not an influential factor.

## Attached Service Overseas

A second route for an officer seeking to make himself appear distinctive among his peers was to apply for attached service overseas, in command or staff postings in the armies of the British Empire and Commonwealth. Service overseas in the interwar period, attached, on loan or in staff postings was a common occurrence among the 1940 group, with 86 of them (including some officers who served more than once, in different parts of the world), having done so. By far the most common region was India, with 33 officers

42 Bond, Davidson, Gartlan, Miles, Pope and West. As Pope was killed in action in 1942, whether he may have progressed further is a matter of conjecture.
43 Irwin, Percival, and Swayne.
44 Liddle Hart Centre for Military Archives, King's College, London: Sir John Dill Papers DILL 3/1/14 1940 15 April 1941 – 5 November: Correspondence while CIGS; letters from Haining.
45 Hansard HC Deb 09 July 1941, vol. 373 cc165–167.

serving there between 1919 and 1938. Nine served in East, West or South Africa, seven in Palestine, six apiece in Egypt and Gibraltar, five in China, four in Malaya, three apiece in Iraq and Turkey and two in the British Military Mission to Finland. Among the single instances were an observer at the Schleswig Plebiscite in 1920, and Instructors at the Royal Military Colleges of Canada and Australia.

The 'Overseas Service Reconciliation' table below indicates the number of officers from the overall group who served in overseas postings from 1918–1939 and the areas in which they served, along with the percentage of the sub-group who advanced in rank. (These figures include officers who served in more than one overseas theatre, as will be shown later).

**Table 3.4 Overseas Service Reconciliation**

| OVERSEAS THEATRE | NUMBER OF OFFICERS | OFFICERS ADVANCING | PERCENTAGE |
|---|---|---|---|
| INDIA | 33 | 17 | 45.5 |
| AFRICA | 9 | 6 | 66.6 |
| PALESTINE | 7 | 5 | 71.4 |
| EGYPT | 6 | 1 | 16.6 |
| GIBRALTAR | 6 | 1 | 16.6 |
| CHINA | 5 | 1 | 20.0 |
| MALAYA | 4 | 3 | 75.0 |
| IRAQ | 3 | 0 | 0.0 |
| TURKEY | 3 | 1 | 33.3 |
| FINLAND | 2 | 0 | 0.0 |
| SINGLE POSTING | 8 | 3 | 37.5 |
| TOTALS | 86 | 38 | 44.1 |

Therefore, over half of the whole group, 54 percent, served overseas on varying forms of attached duty in the interwar period, making it a sufficiently influential factor in the careers of those who reached brigadier by 1940. However, with less than half of this total figure, 44 percent, advancing beyond that rank, having served overseas in the interwar period is not decisively influential as a factor in advancement of itself.

## Postings to India

Although the largest single area of operational service between the two world wars, comparison of contemporary service among the officers in India is of reduced immediate usefulness due to the wide geographical area covered and a lack of precise location detail in the records. It is worthy of mention here in a similar manner to that of having attended the same schools, as a certain commonality of experience would apply in later years, however tangential. Table 3.4A arranges the officers serving in India alphabetically; Table 3.4B arranges them into groups by period served. Table 3.4C lists them as groups of contemporaries, arranged by two-year time frames as this was the predominant posting duration among the group, although officers could, and did, serve for both longer and shorter tours of duty, or served in overlapping postings within the same period of service. For example, Arthur Clifton spent seven years in India in three separate specialist postings connected to armoured cars and armour. 'Jackie' Smyth, unsurprisingly for an officer commissioned into the Indian Army and who was awarded a Victoria Cross with the Indian contingent on the Western Front in 1915, spent most of the period 1919–1939 in staff posts in India, save for a period in the mid-1920s at the Staff College, Camberley. At the other extreme, Frederick Roupell spent only three months in India, in two postings, in 1920. (Names in bold in all following tables listed indicate officers progressing beyond brigadier after 1940).

**Table 3.4A Overseas Postings 1919–1939: India**

| NAME | 1940 | 1940 POSTING | POST INDIA | DATES |
|---|---|---|---|---|
| **ANDERSON** | **BEF** | **11 BDE** | **GSO 1 DECCAN DIST** | **MAR 36-DEC 37** |
| ARCHDALE | BEF | CRA 42 DIV | BDE MAJ | MAY 23-JUL 24 |
| BLAKE | NWEF | CHF MED OFF (RUPERTFORCE) | OC HOSPITALS | 1933-38 |
| CHENEVIX-TRENCH | BEF | SIG OFF IN CHF BEF | CHF SIG OFF INDIA | MAR 27-FEB 31 |
| CHURCHILL | BEF | 151 BDE | GSO 2 | JAN 29-DEC 32 |
| CLIFTON | BEF | 2 LT ARMD RECCE BDE | ADVISER ARM CARS<br>CMDT ARM CARS (I)<br>CHF INST RTC SCH (I) | MAR 18-OCT 20<br>DEC 21-JUL 23<br>JUL 23-MAR 25 |
| **DAVIDSON** | **BEF** | **CRA I CORPS** | **GSO 2**<br>**BDE MAJ** | **NOV 25-MAY 27**<br>**MAY 27-NOV 29** |
| DAWES | BEF | DA/QMG II CORPS | DA&QMG | MAR 21-SEP 23 |
| DE CORDOVA | BEF | 35 BDE | STAFF CAPT | SEP 24-NOV 28 |
| EDEN | BEF | CRA 51 DIV | DAAG | MAY 26-OCT 28 |
| FRANKLYN | BEF | CRA 4 DIV | STAFF GHQ (I) | APR 32-APR 36 |
| GREENSLADE | BEF | DQMG DIR QTRG BEF | GSO 2 | NOV 35-OCT 36 |
| GRIFFIN | BEF | BASE CMDT | INST, SMALL ARMS SCH (I) | MAR 21-MAR 23 |
| **GUBBINS** | **NWEF** | **SCISSORFORCE** | **GSO 3** | **APR 26-FEB 28** |
| **HOGG** | **NWEF** | **BASE AREA ANDALSNES** | **DAAG**<br>**BDE MAJ** | **MAR 24-JUL 26**<br>**JUL 26-MAR 28** |
| **JARDINE** | **BEF** | **MIL SEC BEF** | **DAAG**<br>**BDE MAJ** | **MAR 24-DEC 25**<br>**DEC 25- FEB 27** |
| **KING** | **BEF** | **D/ENG IN C BEF** | **GSO 1 (RE)**<br>**CRE (DIV)**<br>**DEP CHF ENG (I)** | **FEB 33-OCT 35**<br>**OCT 35-JAN 37**<br>**JAN 37-SEP 39** |
| **LEESE** | **BEF** | **DCGS HQ BEF** | **INST SC QUETTA** | **SEP 38-SEP 39** |
| LEVENTHORPE | BEF | CRA 1 DIV | DAAG | OCT 28-OCT 32 |
| **MORGAN** | **BEF** | **CDR SPT GP 51 HD** | **GSO 2** | **JAN 32-JAN 35** |
| PHIPPS | BEF | CRE II CORPS | SO, TO CHF ENG | OCT 18-NOV 20 |

| NAME | 1940 | 1940 POSTING | POST INDIA | DATES |
|---|---|---|---|---|
| **PRATT, F** | **BEF** | **CC MED ARTY I CORPS** | **INST, SCH OF ARTY** | **DEC 29-DEC 33** |
| PYNE | NWEF | CRE IV CORPS | CHF RE CL 2 | SEP 26-MAR 30 |
| **ROBB** | **BEF** | **9 BDE** | **GSO 3** | **AUG 26-AUG 30** |
| ROSSITER | BEF | 6 AA BDE | DAAG<br>DA&QMG | FEB-MAR 20<br>APR-MAY 20 |
| **SMYTH** | **BEF** | **127 BDE** | **BDE MAJ<br>GSO 3<br>GSO 2** | **OCT 19-JUN 20<br>JAN-NOV 22<br>NOV 25-NOV 29** |
| STAVELEY | BEF | CCMA II CORPS | DA&QMG<br>DAAG | DEC 28-MAR 31<br>MAR 31-DEC 32 |
| **STEELE** | **BEF** | **132 BDE** | **STAFF CAPT** | **NOV 19-JUL 20** |
| **SWAYNE** | **BEF** | **BGS BEF** | **ADC TO GOC W CMD** | **FEB 21-APR 23** |
| SWINTON | BEF | CRA MED ARTY | INST, SCH OF ARTY | DEC 31-DEC 35 |
| THORPE | BEF | BASE CMDT CHERBOURG | DAG | DEC 31-APR 35 |
| **WATSON** | **BEF** | **BGS III CORPS** | **SPEC. EMPD.<br>CMDT SEN OFFS SCH** | **MAY 36-JAN 37<br>JAN 37-DEC 38** |
| **WOOLNER** | **BEF** | **8 BDE** | **GSO 2<br>BDE MAJ** | **MAY 30-MAR 32<br>APR 32-MAY 34** |

**Table 3.4B Degrees of Contemporaneousness by Date: India**

| NAME | 1940 | 1940 POSTING | POST INDIA | DATES |
|---|---|---|---|---|
| PHIPPS | BEF | CRE II CORPS | SO TO CHF ENG | OCT 18-NOV 20 |
| CLIFTON | BEF | 2 LT ARMD RECCE BDE | ADVISER ARM CARS | MAR 18-OCT 20 |
| **SMYTH** | **BEF** | **127 BDE** | **BDE MAJ** | **OCT 19-JUN 20** |
| **STEELE** | **BEF** | **132 BDE** | **STAFF CAPT** | **NOV 19-JUL 20** |
| ROSSITER | BEF | 6 AA BDE | DAAG | FEB-MAR 20 |
| ROSSITER | BEF | 6 AA BDE | DA&QMG | APR-MAY 20 |
| **SWAYNE** | **BEF** | **BGS BEF** | **ADC TO GOC W CMD** | **FEB 21-APR 23** |
| **GRIFFIN** | **BEF** | **BASE CMDT** | **INST, SMALL ARMS** | **MAR 21-MAR 23** |
| DAWES | BEF | DA/QMG II CORPS | DA&QMG | MAR 21-SEP 23 |
| CLIFTON | BEF | 2 LT ARMD RECCE BDE | CMDT ARM CARS (I) | DEC 21-JUL 23 |
| **SMYTH** | **BEF** | **127 BDE** | **GSO 3** | **JAN-NOV 22** |
| ARCHDALE | BEF | CRA 42 DIV | BDE MAJ | MAY 23-JUL 24 |
| CLIFTON | BEF | 2 LT ARMD RECCE BDE | CHF INST RTC SCH (I) | JUL 23-MAR 25 |
| **JARDINE** | **BEF** | **MIL SEC BEF** | **DAAG** | **MAR 24-DEC 25** |
| **HOGG** | **NWEF** | **BASE AREA ANDALSNES** | **DAAG** | **MAR 24-JUL 26** |
| DE CORDOVA | BEF | 35 BDE | STAFF CAPT | SEP 24-NOV 28 |
| **DAVIDSON** | **BEF** | **CRA I CORPS** | **GSO 2** | **NOV 25-MAY 27** |

| NAME | 1940 | 1940 POSTING | POST INDIA | DATES |
|---|---|---|---|---|
| **SMYTH** | **BEF** | **127 BDE** | **GSO 2** | **NOV 25-NOV 29** |
| **JARDINE** | **BEF** | **MIL SEC BEF** | **BDE MAJ** | **DEC 25- FEB 27** |
| **GUBBINS** | **NWEF** | **SCISSORFORCE** | **GSO 3** | **APR 26-FEB 28** |
| EDEN | BEF | CRA 51 DIV | DAAG | MAY 26-OCT 28 |
| **HOGG** | **NWEF** | **BASE AREA ANDALSNES** | **BDE MAJ** | **JUL 26-MAR 28** |
| **ROBB** | **BEF** | **9 BDE** | **GSO 3** | **AUG 26-AUG 30** |
| PYNE | NWEF | CRE IV CORPS | CHF RE CL 2 | SEP 26-MAR 30 |
| **CHENEVIX-TRENCH** | **BEF** | **SIG OFF IN CHF BEF** | **CHF SIG OFF INDIA** | **MAR 27-FEB 31** |
| **DAVIDSON** | **BEF** | **CRA I CORPS** | **BDE MAJ** | **MAY 27-NOV 29** |
| LEVENTHORPE | BEF | CRA 1 DIV | DAAG | OCT 28-OCT 32 |
| STAVELEY | BEF | CCMA II CORPS | DA&QMG | DEC 28-MAR 31 |
| CHURCHILL | BEF | 151 BDE | GSO 2 | JAN 29-DEC 32 |
| **PRATT, F** | **BEF** | **CC MED ARTY I CORPS** | **INST, SCH OF ARTY** | **DEC 29-DEC 33** |
| **WOOLNER** | **BEF** | **8 BDE** | **GSO 2** | **MAY 30-MAR 32** |
| STAVELEY | BEF | CCMA II CORPS | DAAG | MAR 31-DEC 32 |
| THORPE | BEF | BASE CMDT CHERBOURG | DAG | DEC 31-APR 35 |
| SWINTON | BEF | CRA MED ARTY | INST, SCH OF ARTY | DEC 31-DEC 35 |
| **MORGAN** | **BEF** | **CDR SPT GP 51 HD** | **GSO 2** | **JAN 32-JAN 35** |
| FRANKLYN | BEF | CRA 4 DIV | STAFF GHQ (I) | APR 32-APR 36 |
| **WOOLNER** | **BEF** | **8 BDE** | **BDE MAJ** | **APR 32-MAY 34** |
| **KING** | **BEF** | **D/ENG IN C BEF** | **GSO 1 (RE)** | **FEB 33-OCT 35** |
| BLAKE | NWEF | CHF MED OFF (RUPERTFORCE) | OC HOSPITALS | 1933-38 |
| **KING** | **BEF** | **D/ENG IN C BEF** | **CRE (DIV)** | **OCT 35-JAN 37** |
| GREENSLADE | BEF | DQMG DIR QTRG BEF | GSO 2 | NOV 35-OCT 36 |
| **ANDERSON** | **BEF** | **11 BDE** | **GSO 1 DECCAN DIST** | **MAR 36-DEC 37** |
| **WATSON** | **BEF** | **BGS III CORPS** | **SPEC. EMPD.** | **MAY 36-DEC 38** |
| **KING** | **BEF** | **D/ENG IN C BEF** | **DEP CHF ENG (I)** | **JAN 37-SEP 39** |
| **LEESE** | **BEF** | **DCGS HQ BEF** | **INST SC QUETTA** | **SEP 38-SEP 39** |

Table 3.4C indicates groupings of overlap between officers; as noted above, the size of India and the lack of exact data as to officers' precise postings means that although they were not necessarily serving in the same space (for example, in GHQ India) they were contemporaries in-theatre. Thus, Archdale, Clifton and De Cordova were in India together in the 1920s, and Churchill, Staveley, Thorpe and Woolner in the late 1920s and early 1930s. Blake's service from 1933–1938 in command of a number of medical units, including two British Military Hospitals, placed him in India in common with King, Thorpe, Swinton and Woolner at various points, but their paths did not cross in 1940, as

Blake served in Norway when the others were in France. (Although Davidson served in two posts in India, they were continuous and are therefore considered as a single posting).

**Table 3.4C Groups of Contemporaries, India 1919–38**
**Postings to Africa (Including South Africa)**

| 1919-1920 | 1920-1922 | 1922-1924 | 1924-1926 | 1926-1928 | 1928-1930 | 1930-1932 | 1932-1934 | 1934-1936 | 1936-1938 |
|---|---|---|---|---|---|---|---|---|---|
| Clifton | Clifton | Archdale | Archdale | Davidson | Chenevix-Trench | Churchill | Blake | Blake | Anderson |
| Phipps | Dawes | Clifton | Clifton | De Cordova | Churchill | Pratt, F. | King | Franklyn | Blake |
| Rossiter | Griffin | De Cordova | Davidson | Eden | Davidson | Staveley | Morgan | King | King |
| Smyth | Smyth | Hogg | De Cordova | Hogg | Leventhorpe | Swinton | Swinton | Morgan | Leese |
| Steele | Swayne | Jardine | Hogg | Robb | Pyne | Thorpe | Thorpe | Swinton | Watson |
| | | Smyth | Jardine | Smyth | Robb | Woolner | Woolner | Thorpe | |
| | | | Smyth | Pyne | Staveley | | | | |

**Table 3.4D Overseas Postings 1919–1939: Africa**

| NAME | 1940 | 1940 POSTING | POSTING AFRICA | DATES |
|---|---|---|---|---|
| BURNEY | BEF | 153 BDE | ATT. RWAFF LT COL | JUN 24-JUN 30 |
| **DEMPSEY** | **BEF** | **13 BDE** | **GSO 2 SA DEF FORCE** | **MAY 37-JAN 38** |
| **GRANT** | **BEF** | **154 BDE** | **ATT. RWAFF LT COL** | **OCT 24-OCT 30** |
| GREEN | BEF | "A" BDE 51 HD | ATT. RWAFF LT COL | AUG 30-JUL 34 |
| KENT-LEMON | NWEF/ BEF | 15 BDE "B" BDE BEAUMAN FORCE | MAJ. ATT KAR LT COL CO 3/KAR | MAR 23-DEC 26 JAN 27-DEC 29 |
| **PERCIVAL** | **BEF** | **BGS I CORPS** | **ATT. RWAFF GSO 2** | **APR 25-JAN 29** |
| **PRATT, F** | **BEF** | **C MED ARTY I CORPS** | **EMPLD SA DEF FORCE** | **OCT 35-OCT 36** |
| **STOPFORD** | **BEF** | **17 BDE** | **GSO 2 TO INSP GEN RWAFF & KAR** | **MAY 32-JUN 36** |
| **WOOLNER** | **BEF** | **8 BDE** | **SURVEY DUTY GOLD COAST** | **MAY 20-SEP 23** |

The next group is of those officers who served in Africa (including South Africa). Nine officers served there between 1919 and 1939; postings tended to be of longer duration, two to three years or more, save for Frederick Pratt, who served in South Africa for one year only in 1935–1936. Two 1940 officers in this group served simultaneously in Africa first, between 1920 and 1923 but were unlikely to have served directly together, as 'Kitt' Woolner was engaged in mapping and survey duty in the Gold Coast whereas Arthur Kent-Lemon arrived in Africa in 1923 to serve with a battalion of the King's African Rifles. They overlapped between March and September 1923, when Woolner departed.

Four officers subsequently coincided with Kent-Lemon; Woolner again, for six months in 1923; George Burney,[46] from 1924 and across Kent-Lemon's two postings from 1923 to 1929; Donald Grant, who arrived in Africa 18 months after Kent-Lemon, in November 1924 and Arthur Percival, between April 1925 and January 1929. However, Kent-Lemon was the only officer who served with the King's African Rifles, ultimately commanding its 3rd Battalion.[47] Grant, Burney and Percival served with the Royal West African Frontier Force; the latter gained experience in bush fighting which he wrote up in 1927 for publication.[48] (Burney and Grant would go on to serve together in 51st (Highland) Division in France in 1940). The next small group was that of Michael Green and 'Monty' Stopford, serving in Africa simultaneously between May 1932 (when Stopford arrived) and July 1934, when Green departed, after four years' service in Africa.[49] Frederick Pratt was also on the Continent when Stopford was serving, but was in South Africa on attachment. Although Miles Dempsey would also serve with the South African Defence Force in a staff posting in 1937–1938, he did not coincide there with any other officers. Therefore, while service in Africa offered, proportionately, a good chance of later advancement (with six of nine officers who served there doing so) the disparity and spread of their service mitigates against a specific bloc of officers.

## Postings to Palestine

**Table 3.4E Overseas Postings 1919–39: Palestine**

| NAME | 1940 | 1940 POSTING | POSTING PALESTINE | DATES |
|---|---|---|---|---|
| BARRETT | BEF | D/JAG | EMPD. | SEP-DEC 36 |
| **BERNEY-FICKLIN** | **BEF** | **15 BDE** | **T/BDE CDR** | **OCT 38-JUL 39** |
| **MC MULLEN** | **BEF** | **DG TRANSPORT** | **ASST DIR TPT** | **JAN 36-JAN 37** |
| **RAMSDEN** | **BEF** | **25 BDE** | **GSO 1** | **JAN SEP 39** |
| **RITCHIE** | **BEF** | **BGS II CORPS** | **GSO 2/GSO 1** | **JAN 38-AUG 39** |
| SMYTH, H | NWEF | 15 BDE | BDE MAJ/GSO 2 | JAN 35-MAR 37 |
| **UTTERSON-KELSO** | **BEF** | **131 BDE** | **CDR LofC TPS** | **JUN-NOV 36** |

46 Burney had served with the Nigeria Regiment (West African Frontier Force) in 1917. *HYAL* December 1938 p.227.

47 Lieutenant Colonel J. Moyse-Bartlett, *The King's African Rifles* (Aldershot: Gale & Polden, 1956), p.438.

48 Major A. E. Percival, 'The West African Frontier Force' in *The Army Quarterly*, XV, 1927, pp.91–99. The WAFF was granted a Royal Charter in 1928.

49 Green returned to Africa after Dunkirk to command a Brigade Group in Sierra Leone, and as 'Commander, Sierra Leone'. A. Stewart, 'The Quiet Colony of Sierra Leone' in A. Jackson, Y. Khan, and G. Singh (eds), *An Imperial World At War*' (Abingdon: Routledge, 2017), p.15; Joslen, *Orders of Battle*, vol. 2 p.440.

With the exceptions of Herbert Smyth and Donald McMullen, who were already serving there, the remaining five officers who served in Palestine in the interwar period did so during the time of the Arab Revolt against the British Mandate from April 1936 to August 1939. (McMullen was 'double-hatted' in that he was Assistant Director, Transport Egypt, Palestine and Transjordan).[50] Except for Neil Ritchie, who arrived in Palestine initially as the commanding officer of 1st Battalion, the King's Own Regiment but remained first as a GSO2 and then a GSO1, all served in staff postings. With the establishment of a GOC's command in Palestine in September 1936, all holders of the post until the end of the revolt in August 1939 were officers of considerable repute who would advance to higher command in 1939–1945. Lieutenant General Sir John Dill, later CIGS, was first, from September 1936-October 1937; he was succeeded by the then Lieutenant General Sir Archibald Wavell, later Commander-in-Chief Middle East and Viceroy of India (August 1937-April 1938), Lieutenant General Sir Robert Haining, later Vice Chief of the Imperial General Staff (April 1938-July 1939) and Lieutenant General Michael Barker (July 1939-February 1940).[51] From 1932–1938, all served under the High Commissioner, General (Retd) Sir Arthur Wauchope, who was initially admired by both sides, but after 1936 came to be seen as too favourable towards Jewish immigration while not strict enough on Arab rebels in return to stem the revolt. Due to his advanced age and declining health, he resigned in February 1938.[52]

Wauchope's patronage of these officers is likely to have been at best indirect, although he and Herbert Smyth were products of Repton, albeit over 20 years apart; Wauchope in the late 1880s and Smyth not until 1910. Wauchope served initially in the Argyll & Sutherland Highlanders; none of the others did, even though Ritchie and Utterson-Kelso served in Scottish regiments, the Black Watch and the Royal Scots Fusiliers respectively.

While John Dill served as Commandant of the Staff College from 1931–1934, the only p.s.c.'s in this group were Ritchie and Smyth, both of whom preceded Dill's tenure there, nor were they taught by him when he was an instructor at Camberley.

## Postings to Egypt

The next largest group was of those officers serving in Egypt. There is little overlap in the early period, save between James Hamilton and Arthur Kent-Lemon between February 1920 and April 1921. Whether they interacted directly is unlikely as Hamilton was serving with British forces and Kent-Lemon with the Egyptian Army. Donald

50 *HYAL* December 1938, p.233.

51 Barker commanded I Corps in France in 1939–1940 but suffered a complete nervous breakdown, requiring his replacement by Harold Alexander. Alan Brooke described him as, 'overwrought and impossible to deal with.' A. Danchev and D. Todman (eds), *War Diaries 1939–1945: Field Marshal Lord Alanbrooke* (London: Weidenfeld and Nicholson, 2001), pp.64–65.

52 M. Bunton, 'Wauchope, Sir Arthur Grenfell' in *DNB* (Oxford: OUP, 2008) *https://www.oxforddnb.com* accessed 6 March 2020.

McMullen (serving simultaneously as Assistant Director, Transport for Egypt, Palestine and Transjordan) and Clement Tomes are more likely to have crossed paths as they were serving in senior staff postings at GHQ and with the Egyptian Army when they coincided in 1936. Tomes actually returned to the UK in March 1939 and retired from the army but was recalled on the outbreak of war.

**Table 3.4F Overseas Postings 1919–39: Egypt**

| NAME | 1940 | 1940 POSTING | POSTING EGYPT | DATES |
|---|---|---|---|---|
| BLAKE | NWEF | CHF MED OFF (RUPERTFORCE) | CO FD AMB | 1926-31 |
| HAMILTON | BEF | 144 BDE | BDE MAJ<br>GSO 3 | FEB-DEC 20<br>APR 21- OCT 23 |
| KENT-LEMON | NWEF/<br>BEF | 15 BDE<br>"B" BDE BEAUMAN FORCE | EMPLD. W. EGYPTIAN ARMY | JAN 17-APR 21 |
| **MC MULLEN** | **BEF** | **DG TRANSPORT** | **ASST DIR TPT** | **JAN 36-JAN 37** |
| SHILSTONE | BEF | 3 AA BDE | CHF INST, MIL MISS. TO EGYPTIAN ARMY | JUN 37-DEC 38 |
| TOMES | BEF | OC 2ND ECHELON | BRIG I/C ADMIN | MAR 35-DEC 38 |

## Postings to Gibraltar

**Table 3.4G Overseas Postings 1919–1939: Gibraltar**

| NAME | 1940 | 1940 POSTING | POSTING GIBRALTAR | DATES |
|---|---|---|---|---|
| ARCHDALE | BEF | CRA 42 DIV | GSO 2 | AUG 24-MAY 27 |
| BARRY, J | BEF | CRA 5 DIV | GSO 2 | NOV 32-JAN 36 |
| CURREY | NWEF/<br>BEF | GHQ NWEF<br>GHQ BEF | BRIG. DA&QMG | OCT 36-DEC 39 |
| HAMILTON, H | BEF | AAQMG 2 DIV | GSO 2 | MAR 31-JAN 33 |
| LAURIE | BEF | 157 BDE | ASST MIL SEC | NOV 24-FEB 27 |
| VALLENTIN | BEF | CRA 1 DIV | GSO 2 | MAR-DEC 38 |

Arthur Archdale and Sir John Laurie overlapped during the latter's service in Gibraltar from 1924–1927 and served in the same headquarters when General Sir Charles Monro was Governor and commander there. While Monro was held in high esteem during his tenure, due to the exertions of his service in the First World War he would die of cancer in 1929 soon after returning, term expired, in 1928.[53] His opportunity to influence the careers of two still relatively junior officers was limited. Hugh Hamilton arrived

53 D. Cassar, 'Monro, Sir Charles Carmichael, Baronet' in *DNB* (Oxford, Oxford University Press, 2008) *https://www.oxforddnb.com* accessed 6 March 2020.

in Gibraltar in March 1931; his period of service alongside John Barrie was rather brief, the latter arriving in November 1932 and the former departing in January 1933. Both served there under General Sir Alexander Godley (Governor, August 1928-October 1933) during the latter's last tour of duty before retirement from the army.

As Godley was an infantryman, with Hamilton a sapper and Barrie a gunner, there was no regimental connection between them; as he had also left the Staff College prematurely in 1900 to fight in South Africa, the ties between them as graduates were weaker. Godley had commanded New Zealanders on the Western Front during the First World War. Despite a firm reputation as a trainer of raw troops and adept in organisation, he was considered '...a picture of austerity and dedication. Aristocratic in outlook, he remained aloof from all but his intimates...'[54] Again, his influence over the careers of junior subordinates at this late stage was as limited as it was unlikely.

Although Barry left just as the Gibraltar garrison was being reinforced in response to the declining situation in Spain which resulted in the outbreak of the Spanish Civil War 1936–1939, 'Harry' Currey arrived in October 1936 with Claude Vallentin following him in March 1938, having been a student at the Royal Naval Staff College at Greenwich in 1936–1937. Both served latterly and directly under Edmund Ironside when he was Governor in 1938–1939, prior to his appointment as CIGS.

## Postings to China

**Table 3.4H Overseas Postings 1919–39 China**

| NAME | 1940 | 1940 POSTING | POSTING CHINA | DATES |
|---|---|---|---|---|
| BARRETT | BEF | D/JAG | EMPD. W. SHANGHAI DEF FORCE | APR 27-MAY 28 |
| CHURCHILL | BEF | 151 BDE | DAA & QMG SHANGHAI DEF FORCE | JAN 27-NOV 28 |
| HOPWOOD | NWEF | BASE AREA | CDR TIENTSIN AREA | SEP 35-DEC 38 |
| **MILES** | **BEF** | **126 BDE** | **BDE MAJ SHANGHAI DEF FORCE** | **JAN 27-JUN 28** |
| ROUPELL | BEF | 36 BDE | GSO 2 CHINA | OCT 34-NOV 35 |

Of the officers who served in a posting to China, four overlapped with each other, however briefly. (China Command was a pre-war independent command, responsible for the British possessions of Hong Kong and Kowloon, and the British concessions in the Chinese cities of Shanghai and Tientsin.) Command of the British Troops in China was a major general's appointment. Due to the activity of the National Revolutionary

54 'GODLEY, General Sir Alexander John' from A. H. McLintock (ed.), *An Encyclopaedia of New Zealand* (Auckland: R. E. Owen for the Government of New Zealand, 1966).

Army (led by Chiang Kai Shek) within China from 1925, the international garrisons were reinforced. The British dispatched the Shanghai Defence Force, equivalent to a three-brigade division, under the command of Major General Sir John Duncan (hence it's also being known as Duncan Force). His second in command was the then Colonel The Viscount Gort, later Commander-in-Chief of the BEF.[55] Eric Milligan and Jack Churchill arrived with the first wave of reinforcements, dispatched via Hong Kong, in January 1927.[56] The Honourable Hugh Barrett followed in April, overlapping with Milligan until his departure in May 1928.

The Tientsin Area was responsible for the British concession in the Chinese city of Tientsin (now called Tianjin). The city of Tientsin was captured by Japanese troops on 30 July 1937. Japan, however, respected the international concessions in the city and the British troops remained in situ. Alfred Hopwood remained in command of the area, as a local brigadier from 27 September 1935 until he was relieved at the end of 1938. Although George Roupell coincided in China with Hopwood, he was based on the staff of the GOC British Troops in China, Major General Arthur Bartholomew, who had assumed command in 1935, having served very briefly under Bartholomew's predecessor, Lieutenant General Oswald Borrett.[57] Either General's influence on their former subordinates would again have been limited.

## Postings to Malaya

**Table 3.4I Overseas Postings 1919–1939: Malaya**

| NAME | 1940 | 1940 POSTING | POSTING MALAYA | DATES |
|---|---|---|---|---|
| CAVE-BROWN | BEF | DIR OF WORKS | CHF ENG MALAY STATES | MAY 35-FEB 38 |
| HUDSON | BEF | 2 BDE | GSO 2 STRAITS SETTLEMENTS | NOV 28-MAR 32 |
| **MILES** | **BEF** | **126 BDE** | **GSO 1 MALAYA** | **FEB-DEC 38** |
| **PERCIVAL** | **BEF** | **BGS I CORPS** | **GSO 1 MALAYA** | **MAR 36-MAR 38** |

Again, all the officers who served in Malaya and the Straits Settlements were in staff postings at headquarters level, but across the times spent would have served under several different GOCs; Major General Sir Casimir Van Straubenzee (1927–1929), Major

55 K. Stevens, 'Duncan Force' – the Shanghai Defence Force in 1927 & the Career of Captain Ronald Spear' in *Journal of the Royal Asiatic Society Hong Kong Branch*, vol. 48 (2008), pp.151–174.

56 TNA FO 371/63436 'The Dispatch of Shanghai Defence Force to Shanghai in 1927' (March 1928).

57 Bartholomew returned from China in 1938 and immediately retired from active service on grounds of age. Borrett left China a matter of six weeks after Roupell's arrival in the autumn of 1935.

General Harry Pritchard (1929–31), Major General Ernest Lewin (1934–1935), and Major General William Dobbie (1935–1938). Van Straubenzee was already well past retirement age when appointed (being 61) and retired from the army when Pritchard – himself being an advanced 58 years old on appointment – relieved him. However, Pritchard's final job before retirement in 1933 was as the Commandant of the Royal School of Military Engineering at Chatham and would therefore have been familiar with and aware of the careers of those sapper officers passing up their career chain. William Cave-Brown and Arthur Percival would have crossed paths due to coinciding; both would also have served under William Dobbie, who had been Pritchard's predecessor at the Royal School of Military Engineering and therefore also have been familiar with those sappers progressing.

Although Dobbie himself was retired on grounds of age in 1939, a chance encounter with Edmund Ironside, when the latter was CIGS, led to Dobbie being offered command on Malta, which he took up on promotion to lieutenant general. However, the strain of command under siege broke his health and he retired again – being temporarily replaced by his CRA, Clifford Beckett, who had served in France in 1940 as the CRA of 15th Division. (Beckett, in turn, was replaced by William Robb, who had commanded 9 Brigade in France in 1940).

## Postings to Iraq

**Table 3.4J Overseas Postings 1919–39: Iraq**

| NAME | 1940 | 1940 POSTING | POSTING IRAQ | DATES |
|---|---|---|---|---|
| CHIPPINDALL | BEF | CRE III CORPS | CHF ENG IRAQ | FEB 33-SEP 37 |
| **CLARK** | **BEF** | **CHF ENG, ADV AIR STR FORCE** | **ATT IRAQI ARMY<br>CHF ENG (AIR)** | **MAR 28-AUG 32<br>MAR 37-DEC 38** |
| WARREN | BEF | 4 BDE | ATT IRAQI ARMY | SEP 28-SEP 32 |

British involvement in Iraq was confirmed after the Iraqi Revolt of 1920 against the proposed British Mandate of Mesopotamia,[58] thereafter Kingdom of Iraq under British Administration, or Mandatory Iraq. Atypically, in 1922, command of all British forces in the area was passed to the Royal Air Force, while the High Commissioner of the territory until Iraqi independence was agreed in 1932 was a serving or former army officer, except for the period from 1923–1928 when it was Sir Henry Dobbs, an experienced colonial administrator. Both Edward Warren and Percy Clark served there pre-independence as advisers to the Iraq Army; Warren training infantry and Clark training engineers. Clark returned as the Chief Engineer to the Iraqi Air Force in 1937. John

58 Quincy Wright, 'The Government of Iraq' in *The American Political Science Review*, vol. 20, no.4 (1926), pp.743–769. JSTOR, *www.jstor.org/stable/1945423* accessed 21 April 2020.

Chippindall, as an engineer by background and training, was responsible for several key infrastructure projects including the construction of the military airfield and airport at Habbaniya, for which he received a CBE in 1937.[59] Although these officers performed with some distinction, the opportunities for patronage based purely on these postings were slight.

## Postings to Turkey and Constantinople

**Table 3.4K Overseas Postings 1919–1939: Turkey/Constantinople**

| NAME | 1940 | 1940 POSTING | POSTINGS | DATES |
|---|---|---|---|---|
| FOX-PITT | BEF | 20 GDS BDE | STAFF CAPT TURKEY | MAR-OCT 23 |
| GREENSLADE | BEF | D QUARTERING | STAFF CAPT TURKEY | JUL 21-OCT 23 |
| **PRATT, F** | **BEF** | **C MED ARTY I CORPS** | **STAFF CAPT CONSTANTINOPLE** | **AUG 20-JAN 21** |

Frederick Pratt was attached to the staff of the British Mission to Constantinople for four months in 1920–1921. Cyrus Greenslade, who arrived in Turkey some six months after Pratt's departure, served in two postings in Turkey from 1921–1923, firstly on special deployment to the Turkish Gendarmerie in 1921–1922 and from 1922–1923 on the staff of the British Mission to Constantinople. This was during the second stage of British occupation from 1918–1923, which followed the Treaty of Sevres in 1920. William Fox-Pitt was also present in this final phase, which ended in 1923 following the conclusion of the Turkish Civil War of 1919–1922. The end of the war led to the establishment of a Turkish Republic and the revision of the earlier peace treaty with the Allied powers.

## Postings to Finland

John Fitzgerald and Cyrus Greenslade both served on the headquarters staff of the first British Military Mission to Finland and the Baltic States in 1920, established under General Sir Hubert Gough in 1919, to observe and report on the general military situation, and to assist those states in preparing for defence against any Bolshevik action against them resulting from the civil war under way in Russia.[60]

59 Obituary in *Journal of the Royal Engineers*. Vol. LXXXVIII; 3 (September 1974), (Chatham: Royal Engineers, 1974), p.190.

60 Copy of Orders from General Sir Henry Wilson, CIGS, to General Sir Hubert Gough, dated 4 June 1919; United States Congressional Serial Set, Senate Documents, vol.7610 May-November 1919, pp.37–40.

**Table 3.4L Overseas Postings 1919–1939: Finland**

| NAME | 1940 | 1940 POSTING | POSTINGS | DATES |
|---|---|---|---|---|
| FITZGERALD | BEF | 156 BDE | GSO 3 BRIT MIL MISS FINLAND | MAY 19-JUN 20 |
| GREENSLADE | BEF | D QUARTERING | BRIT MIL MISS FINLAND | JUN 19-JAN 20 |

## Single Postings

**Table 3.4M Overseas Posting 1919–1939: Single Postings**

| NAME | 1940 | 1940 POSTING | POSTINGS | DATES |
|---|---|---|---|---|
| MILLIGAN | BEF | 1 AA BDE | INST IN GUNNERY, MALTA | JAN 32-FEB 35 |
| CLOUGH | BEF | DIR SURVEY | ALBANIAN FRONTIER COMMN.<br>N. RHODESIA BORDER COMMN. | JUL-AUG 25<br>APR 28-JUL 30 |
| **MILES** | **BEF** | **126 BDE** | **GSO 3 SCHLESWIG PLEBISCITE** | **1920** |
| **MORGAN, W** | **BEF** | **BGS I CORPS** | **MIL ATTACHE BUDAPEST** | **JAN 29-MAY 31** |
| **PRATT, D** | **BEF** | **1 ARMY TK BDE** | **INST, MILITARY ART R MIL COL AUSTRALIA** | **DEC 29-JAN 33** |
| ROUPELL | BEF | 36 BDE | INST, R MIL COL CANADA | MAR 29-APR 31 |
| STAFFORD | BEF | CHF ENG | E. SOMALILAND SVY | JUN 29-JUL 31 |
| TOMES | BEF | OC 2ND ECHELON | BDE MAJ BRIT TPS SUDAN | NOV 24-MAY 25 |

By its nature, a single posting is unlikely to generate networks unless the officers concerned served alongside others who rose to prominence. On Malta, Eric Milligan was serving as a Gunnery instructor while 'Ivo' Thomas, later to command 43rd (Wessex) Division in North-West Europe, was serving as a GSO2 on the island from 1932–1936.[61] However, Milligan's career stalled after Dunkirk, with his reverting to lieutenant colonel and being placed on retired pay in 1941. (His involvement in a well-publicised divorce in 1941 which led to the setting of a legal precedent would not have stood in his favour socially). Pratt, a lieutenant colonel on his arrival in Australia, served briefly and atypically (as historically the post was intended for a brigadier or major general) as the Commandant of the Royal Military College when it was relocated in a reduced form from Duntroon to Sydney in 1931. The move was politically contentious in a period of drastic defence cuts. He was quickly replaced by Brigadier F. B. Heritage, an Australian officer who had been the College's commandant in the 1920s.[62] Roupell's posting to the Royal Military College of Canada in 1929 was to act as an assistant to its deputy commandant, the then Lieutenant Colonel George Pearkes VC with the specific aim of preparing Canadian

61 *HYAL* January 1942, p.1400.
62 C. Coulthard-Clark, Duntroon: The Royal Military College of Australia, 1911–1986 (Sydney: Allen & Unwin, 1986), p.82.

candidates for entry to the Staff College at Camberley.[63] Both had been awarded the Victoria Cross on the Western Front, Roupell in 1915 at the Second Battle of Ypres[64] and Pearkes in 1917 at the Third Battle of Ypres.[65]

## Multiple Overseas Service

Those officers who undertook multiple overseas tours in the interwar period were as follows:

**Table 3.4N Officers with Multiple Overseas Tours**

| ARCHDALE | BEF | CRA 42 DIV | BDE MAJ INDIA | MAY 23-JUL 24 |
|---|---|---|---|---|
| | | | GSO 2 GIBRALTAR | AUG 24-MAY 27 |
| BARRETT | BEF | D/JAG | EMPD. W. SHANGHAI DF | APR 27-MAY 28 |
| | | | EMPD. PALESTINE | SEP-DEC 36 |
| BLAKE | NWEF | CHF MED OFF (RUPERTFORCE) | CO FD AMB EGYPT | 1926-31 |
| | | | OC HOSPITALS INDIA | 1933-38 |
| CHURCHILL | BEF | 151 BDE | DAA/QMG SHANGHAI DF | JAN 27-NOV 28 |
| | | | GSO 2 INDIA | JAN 29-DEC 32 |
| KENT-LEMON | NWEF/ BEF | 15 BDE/ B BDE BEAUMAN | EMPLD. W. EGYPT | JAN 17-APR 21 |
| | | | MAJ. ATT KAR | MAR 23-DEC 26 |
| | | | LT COL CO 3/KAR | JAN 27-DEC 29 |
| **MILES** | **BEF** | **126 BDE** | **GSO3 SCHLESWIG** | **1920** |
| | | | **BDE MAJ SHANGHAI DEF** | **JAN 27-JUN 28** |
| | | | GSO 1 MALAYA | FEB-DEC 38 |
| **PRATT, F** | **BEF** | **CC MED ARTY I CORPS** | **INST, SCH OF ARTY I** | **DEC 29-DEC 33** |
| | | | **EMPLD SA DEF FORCE** | **OCT 35-OCT 36** |
| **PERCIVAL** | **BEF** | **BGS I CORPS** | **ATT. RWAFF GSO 2** | **APR 25-JAN 29** |
| | | | GSO 1 MALAYA | MAR 36-MAR 38 |
| **WOOLNER** | **BEF** | **8 BDE** | **SURVEY GOLD COAST** | **MAY 20-SEP 23** |
| | | | **GSO2 INDIA** | **MAY 30-MAR 32** |
| | | | **BDE MAJ INDIA** | **APR 32-MAY 34** |

63 P. Oldfield, Victoria Crosses on the Western Front: Third Battle of Ypres, 1917 (Bradford, Pen & Sword, 2017), p.293; R. Roy, For Most Conspicuous Bravery: A Biography of Major-General George R. Pearkes, VC (Vancouver: University of British Columbia Press, 2011), p.107.

64 K. Brazier, *The Complete Victoria Cross* (Barnsley: Casemate, 2017), p.7.

65 R. Roy, For Most Conspicuous Bravery…, p.110.

## Officers Progressing with Overseas Postings

Breaking out those officers with overseas postings in the interwar period who progressed, in order to examine possible linkages of school, regiment or attendance at Staff College presents the following results:

**Table 3.40 Officers with Overseas Service 1919–1939 Progressing: School, Regiment & Staff College**

| INDIA[66] | | SCHOOL | REGT | STAFF COLLEGE |
|---|---|---|---|---|
| SMYTH | BEF | REPTON | INDIAN ARMY | 1924 |
| STEELE | BEF | ROYAL BELFAST | R IRISH | 1931 |
| SWAYNE | BEF | CHARTERHOUSE | SOM LI | 1925 IDC 1935 |
| DAVIDSON | BEF | MARLBOROUGH | RA | 1924 QUETTA IDC 1935 |
| JARDINE | BEF | CHARTERHOUSE | RA | 1922 |
| GUBBINS | NWEF | CHELTENHAM | RA | 1928 QUETTA |
| HOGG | NWEF | CHELTENHAM | RE | 1922 QUETTA |
| ROBB | BEF | GEORGE WATSON'S | KOYLI | NO |
| MORGAN | BEF | CLIFTON | RA | 1928 QUETTA |
| KING | BEF | FELSTEAD | RE | NO |
| ANDERSON | BEF | CHARTERHOUSE | SEAFORTH | 1927 |
| WATSON | BEF | MERCER'S | HLI | 1924 |
| LEESE | BEF | ETON | C GDS | 1927 |
| AFRICA | | | | |
| DEMPSEY | BEF | SHREWSBURY | R BERKS | 1930 |
| GRANT | BEF | ? | A&SH | NO |
| STOPFORD | BEF | WELLINGTON | R BDE | 1923 |
| PALESTINE | | | | |
| BERNEY-FICKLIN | BEF | RUGBY | NORFOLK | NO |
| RAMSDEN | BEF | BATH COLLEGE | WI REGT | NO |
| RITCHIE | BEF | LANCING | BW | 1929 |
| UTTERSON-KELSO | BEF | HAILEYBURY | RSF | NO |
| GIBRALTAR | | | | |
| LAURIE | BEF | ETON | SEAFORTH | NO |
| MALAYA | | | | |
| HUDSON | BEF | SHERBORNE | N&D | 1926 |
| SINGLE POSTINGS | | | | |

66 Excluding Pratt, F and Woolner, included in the "Multiple Postings" table below

| MORGAN, W | BEF | GEORGE WATSON'S | RA | 1925 |
|---|---|---|---|---|
| PRATT, D | BEF | DOVER COLLEGE | R IRISH | 1923 |
| MULTIPLE POSTINGS | | | | |
| MC MULLEN | BEF | BRADFIELD | RE | NO |
| MILES | BEF | HARROW | KOSB | 1922 & IDC 1934 |
| PERCIVAL | BEF | RUGBY | BEDFORDS | 1923 & IDC 1935 |
| PRATT, F | BEF | CHELTENHAM | RA | NO |
| WOOLNER | BEF | MARLBOROUGH | RE | 1927 |

Firstly, with one exception, Donald Grant, whose educational background could not be traced, all the advancing officers were educated at public schools. Of these, nearly a third (nine officers) attended Clarendon Group schools. Among those who served in India, Cheltenham (Gubbins, Hogg, Pratt) and Charterhouse (Anderson, Jardine and Swayne) predominate. In India, it was not an absolute that an officer be a graduate of Staff College to take up a posting in a junior position, in Robb's case as a GSO3, or even as a senior post, such as King, who served as a GSO1 but did so by virtue of serving in specialist engineer postings where professional technical knowledge outweighed formal staff qualifications. The officers serving in India included four graduates of the Staff College at Quetta (Davidson, Gubbins, Hogg and Morgan) – unique among the group of officers who progressed and had overseas service, as no other Quetta graduates served overseas. However, none of them were contemporaries at Quetta. No single regiment predominates in the India group as a whole. Gunners and sappers represent a significant minority, being nearly a quarter – three of 13 – of those who served and advanced in rank. Furthermore, with one exception all of these officers served in general staff posts, not specialist engineer or artillery jobs; with the exception of Arthur King, who was not a Staff College graduate.

There are few overall conjunctions or patterns among the remaining officers who had interwar overseas service and advanced after 1940. It is significant that of the four officers who served in Palestine, three of them were not Staff College graduates. Since all four served there just before or during the Arab Revolt, this most likely reflects urgent need following an upsurge in operations, requiring the filling of vacancies outstripping the available supply of Staff College trained candidates. This would also be the situation in France in 1939–1940, where retired officers were 'dug out' for rear area and some supporting arms posts in order to place suitably qualified officers in staff postings.

## Conclusions

With the return of peace and demobilisation, attitudes towards the profession of soldiering quickly reverted to pre-war norms. It was as if the recently won war was an aberration, and the changes the army had gone through were not to be replicated or extended. Education of officers was one area where this attitude was particularly visible, where prejudices and custom would reassert themselves as the army returned to 'normal'. This chapter has shown that officers who wished not only to sustain a career in the interwar army but wished to progress would find it necessary to make themselves distinctive with respect to other officers and potential rivals. The two paths were to seek overseas postings either in staff positions or on attached service, or to acquire higher professional educational qualifications, such as graduation from Staff College or the Imperial Defence College. However, neither path was any guarantee of progression to the higher ranks of the army, and service in some areas overseas, such as Egypt, Iraq and Gibraltar, offered little or no advantage at all. Overseas service, therefore, did not generate any particular blocs of officers favoured for advancement.

Some pre-war attitudes towards professional education of officers did reassert themselves, notwithstanding the increased interest in and demand for its limited places as a means of professional distinctiveness. One manifestation of this was the deep-seated suspicion among some senior officers of the continued existence of the Senior Officers' School, latterly at Sheerness. This school was intended to prepare officers for battalion command (a role traditionally, and inconsistently resting in commanding officers) and inculcate a wider world view in its students. Graduating, or having been directing staff thereof did not proffer any particular advantage to officers in terms of advancement or the generation of networks. As most of its commandants were late in their careers and retired thereafter, their ability to act as patrons or to influence the careers of former subordinates was therefore limited.

Officers who served as GSOs during the First World War, and especially those who subsequently graduated from Staff College had an edge over those who had not. This was significant, but not singularly decisive as several officers who had not served in staff posts during the First World War but did graduate from Camberley and Quetta did progress after 1940. While the value and applicability of the type of training offered at Staff College has been debated in recent literature, perception of its status endured and enhanced an officer's prospects. Attendance at the Imperial Defence College after 1927 when it was founded, was an influential factor in advancement. All the officers who attended it from the group were promoted to higher command during the war, and it also generated small, but close groupings of officers as minor networks, in one case reinforced by the officers being contemporaries both at Camberley and Buckingham Gate.

The single most influential path for advancement, whatever the actual value of the education offered, remained the successful completion of Staff College at Camberley or Quetta. The assessment by French that Brooke and Montgomery used their times there as directing staff in later years to 'talent spot' is well-founded, but other officers such as John Dill also identified pupils they would later act as patrons for. Camberley also produced clusters of officers who would reach general's rank during the war. The supply of qualified staff officers remained inadequate to meet the demand of the BEF in 1940, as indicated by the number of officers recalled from retirement to fill gaps in certain administrative and support posts, whether or not such officers were p.s.c. An officer who was public school educated, had served in junior staff officer's post during the First World War, was a Staff College graduate and who had served overseas between 1919–1939, was therefore possessed of advantages ahead of his contemporaries.

Commanders of the 21st Army Group, May 1945. (Sergeant Malin, AFPU)

Evelyn Hugh Barker.

Horatio Pettus Mackintosh (known as Horatio).

Alan Francis Brooke.

Colin McVean Gubbins, 1944.

John Tredennick Crocker.

Richard Dawnay (10th Viscount Downe), 1940.

Francis Henry Norman Davidson, 1943.

Ian Cameron Grant.

James Melvill Hamilton, 1950.

James Stewart Steele, 1949.

John George 'Jacky' Smyth VC, 1947.

Neil Methuen Ritchie, 1946.

Vyvyan Vavasour Pope (KIA October 1941).

The Hon. Nigel Fitzroy Somerset.

Noel Irvine Whitty.

Christopher Geoffrey Woolner.

Hugh Kenyon Molesworth Kindersley.

Colin Muir Barber (Nickname "Tiny").

William Robert Norris Hinde ("Looney").

Bernard Law Montgomery.

Headstone of Gordon King Archibald.
Nottingham Road Cemetery, Mansfield.

4

# Officers Progressing Beyond Brigadier, 1940–1945

> On the morning of 1 June [1940] the situation around Dunkirk was this: 195,000 troops had been embarked, of which about 160,000 were British. This left around 40,000 British and an unknown number of French.... In addition, most of the senior commanders were now also in Britain: Brooke, Adam, Montgomery, Franklyn. Petre, Osborne, Thorne, Martel *and many of the Brigadiers*. Here was the nucleus around which a future British Army might be built.[1]
>
> *When Britain Saved The West*, Robin Prior (Author's emphasis)

The aim of this chapter is to examine the officers from the 1940 group more closely and to determine the linkages between them to identify connections and groupings. The intention is to establish whether these were sufficiently distinctive to explain, in part, their professional survival and advancement after 1940. This research reveals that the general contention which initiated this research, that merely serving in France or Norway was the career graveyard of officers at the level of brigadier, is open to challenge.

Of the 156 officers who served in those operational theatres during the spring of 1940, 58 of them, 37.9 percent of the total, advanced to the rank of major general or above during the course of the war. While still a minority, being more than one-third of the group is a considerable proportion when not all officers could expect to advance to such a rank. The January 1940 *HYAL* contains 503 major generals.[2] When officers such as those on the Retired List, major generals holding honorary rank such as Royal Colonels of regiments, and retired officers granted the rank on their retirement, are excluded, the total falls to just under 200 serving officers, including officers holding temporary rank.

1 Robin Prior, *When Britain Saved The West: The Story of 1940* (London: Yale University Press, 2015), p.131.

2 This figure does not include colonels on the retired list granted honorary rank on retirement.

This chapter will examine questions including, which elements in their professional and personal backgrounds were influential in their advancement beyond brigadier. For those who rose higher than major general, consideration will be given to whether there were any further distinctions, or evidence of groupings, such as their schools, regiments, attendance at Staff College, war service and possession of decorations. While these methods have already been employed in previous chapters, it is intended to show that as the cohorts reduced in number, which factors predominated among the smaller groups. For example, as will be shown in Chapter 6, the proportion of public school educated officers serving as brigadiers in Normandy in 1944 actually increased in comparison with 1940, when it might have been expected that a larger army would be recruiting from a wider pool of potential officers from more diverse social and educational backgrounds.

The army had not been static in attempting to reform the officer corps after Dunkirk. In 1941, the Army Council reduced the maximum ages for the appointment to command positions in the field army, with a further reduction expected to have been implemented by 1943. The maximum age for field force command, unless the officer possessed unspecified 'special qualifications' was to be 50 years old.[3] Had this later rule been applied strictly to the complete 1940 group, 15 officers, 9.6 percent of the total, would have reached this limit by or in 1943. A further 13 officers, 8.4 percent of the group, would reach that age before the end of the war in August 1945, suggesting that 18 percent of the 1940 group, some 28 officers, would have been notionally ineligible for advancement on grounds of age. Twenty-two would not have reached the age of 50 and faced possible compulsory retirement under the 1941 rules before the cessation of hostilities. These figures include officers who retired or were subsequently killed in action after 1940.

On 10 May 1940, 64 of the whole group, 41.3 percent, were aged 50 or above. In the advancing group, 9 officers (5.2 percent) would not have reached 50 by the end of the war; 3 would have by 1945; 3 by 1944; 10 by 1943; 5 by 1942 and 15 by 1941. The remainder were aged 50 or above, the eldest being 53. Therefore, only 12 of the 58, or 20.8 percent of the group, would have survived to command in the field by the end of the war, at least in Europe in May 1945, had this criterion been strictly applied. Among the officers who advanced to high command or eminence who would have been affected by this were 'Monty' Stopford (47 in 1940), Kenneth Anderson (48 in 1940), Frederick Morgan (46 in 1940) and John Hawkesworth (47 in 1940).

From the group of 58 officers who progressed, 21 reached the rank of lieutenant general by the end of the war, representing 36.2 percent of the group of officers advancing in rank and 13.7 percent of the overall group of 1940 officers, fewer than one in seven. The 58 are examined in more detail below.

3 D. French, 'Doctrine and Organization in the British Army, 1919–1932' in *The Historical Journal*, vol. 44 no.2 (2001), p.79.

## Age Profile

As noted earlier, the average age of the officers in the overall group is 49.23 years, the youngest being 36[4] and the eldest 63.[5] 67 were below 49 years old in 1940, 69 were older. Both the youngest and eldest from the group were serving in France, including several older officers recalled from retirement to fill administrative posts. Some of the latter were in their late fifties and even sixties. For the group only serving in France, 140 of the group, the average was only slightly lower, at 49.22. The smaller group which served in Norway also had an average age equalling the overall group, 49.23, but the spread among ages was closer; the youngest 43[6] and the eldest 54.[7] However, when the officers who did not progress beyond brigadier after 1940 are filtered out, the average age in the overall group drops to 47.76, with the age range being comparable to the Norway group – 42[8] to 53.[9] Of the six officers in Norway who progressed,[10] the average age climbs back to 48.83 as four of them were aged 50 and above. The average age of officers who did not progress was higher than the overall average, at 50.16.

## Education

The educational background for two of the officers in the whole advancing group was untraced;[11] of the remaining 56, one was home schooled[12] and all the others were products of the public school system. Table 5.1 indicates the schools these officers attended and demonstrates the percentage of attendees from those schools who rose to General officer rank after 1940. Eliminating those schools with a sole attendee – whose success rate in producing a general officer from within the main 1940 group would of course be 100 percent – and schools from which no-one progressed, whose success rate would be zero, leaves a spread from 100 percent to 30 percent – the latter figure influenced by those who attended Wellington.

4 Acting Brigadier, the Viscount Downe, commanding 69 Infantry Brigade.
5 Brigadier Gervase Thorpe, commanding Base Depot, Cherbourg.
6 There were two 43-year olds; Acting Brigadier Colin Gubbins, commanding Scissorforce and Brigadier Herbert Smyth commanding. 15 Brigade.
7 Brigadier Henry Currey, BGS HQ NWEF.
8 Acting Brigadier Richard McCreery, commanding 2 Armoured Brigade and Acting Brigadier Neil Ritchie, BGS II Corps.
9 Brigadier Arthur Percival, BGS I Corps and Brigadier Herbert Stewart, commanding 152 Brigade.
10 Gubbins of Scissor Force; Gammell, BGS HQ NWEF; Phillips, 146 Brigade; Wootten, Chief Admin Off; Hogg, Base Area Commander Andalsnes and Morgan, 148 Brigade.
11 Halstead, Robb and Slater; Halstead was born and initially educated in Australia.
12 John Crocker.

**Table 4.1 Officers Progressing to Major General or Above: Schools Attended**

| SCHOOL | 1940 GROUP ATTENDEES | MAJ GEN OR HIGHER | INDIVIDUALS PROGRESSING |
|---|---|---|---|
| BATH COLLEGE | 1 | 1 | RAMSDEN |
| BRADFIELD | 2 | 1 | MCMULLEN |
| CHARTERHOUSE | 6 | 3 | ANDERSON, JARDINE, SWAYNE |
| CHELTENHAM | 9 | 4 | GRANT, GUBBINS, HOGG, PRATT, F |
| CLIFTON | 4 | 2 | LEE, MORGAN F |
| DOVER COLLEGE | 3 | 2 | GOLDNEY, PRATT, D |
| DOWNSIDE | 1 | 1 | GARTLAN |
| ETON | 12 | 7 | BECKWITH-SMITH, LAURIE, LAWSON, LEESE, MC CREERY, NORMAN, WHITAKER |
| FELSTED | 1 | 1 | KING |
| FETTES | 1 | 1 | STEWART |
| GEORGE WATSON | 1 | 1 | MORGAN, W |
| HAILEYBURY | 1 | 1 | UTTERSON-KELSO |
| HARROW | 5 | 2 | MILES, MORGAN H |
| KING'S CANTERBURY | 1 | 1 | WEST |
| LANCING | 2 | 2 | POPE, RITCHIE |
| MARLBOROUGH | 6 | 3 | DAVIDSON, IRWIN, WOOLNER |
| MERCER'S | 1 | 1 | WATSON |
| RADLEY | 2 | 1 | TILLY |
| REPTON | 4 | 2 | PHILLIPS, SMYTH |
| ROYAL BELFAST | 1 | 1 | STEELE |
| RUGBY | 8 | 3 | BERNEY-FICKLIN, PERCIVAL, WOOTTEN |
| SHERBORNE | 2 | 2 | GRIFFIN, HUDSON |
| SHREWSBURY | 1 | 1 | DEMPSEY |
| ST BEES | 1 | 1 | HAWKESWORTH |
| ST PAUL'S | 2 | 1 | GALE |
| TONBRIDGE | 2 | 1 | BECKETT |
| UPPINGHAM | 3 | 1 | HORROCKS |
| WELLINGTON | 10 | 3 | BOND, SCHREIBER, STOPFORD |
| WINCHESTER | 9 | 3 | CLARK, GAMMELL, WILSON |
|  | 102 | 54 |  |

**Table 4.2 Schools Producing More Than One Brigadier in 1940: Progression 'Success Rate'**

| SCHOOL | IN 1940 GROUP OVERALL | SUCCESS | SUCCESS % | |
|---|---|---|---|---|
| BRADFIELD | 2 | 1 | 50.0 | MCMULLEN |
| CHARTERHOUSE | 6 | 3 | 50.0 | ANDERSON, JARDINE, SWAYNE |
| CHELTENHAM | 9 | 4 | 44.4 | GRANT, GUBBINS, HOGG, PRATT F |
| CLIFTON | 4 | 2 | 50.0 | LEE, MORGAN F |
| DOVER COLLEGE | 3 | 2 | 66.6 | GOLDNEY, PRATT D |
| ETON | 12 | 7 | 58.3 | BECKWITH-SMITH, LAURIE, LAWSON, LEESE, MC CREERY, NORMAN, WHITAKER |
| HARROW | 5 | 2 | 40.0 | MILES, MORGAN H |
| LANCING | 2 | 2 | 100.0 | POPE, RITCHIE |
| MARLBOROUGH | 6 | 3 | 50.0 | DAVIDSON, IRWIN, WOOLNER |
| RADLEY | 2 | 1 | 50.0 | TILLY |
| REPTON | 4 | 2 | 50.0 | PHILLIPS, SMYTH |
| RUGBY | 8 | 3 | 37.5 | BERNEY-FICKLIN, PERCIVAL, WOOTTEN |
| SHERBORNE | 2 | 2 | 100.0 | GRIFFIN, HUDSON |
| ST PAUL'S | 2 | 1 | 50.0 | GALE |
| TONBRIDGE | 2 | 1 | 50.0 | BECKETT |
| UPPINGHAM | 3 | 1 | 33.3 | HORROCKS |
| WELLINGTON - | 10 | 3 | 30.0 | BOND, SCHREIBER, STOPFORD |
| WINCHESTER | 9 | 3 | 33.3 | CLARK, GAMMELL, WILSON |
| | 89 | 42 | 47.1 | |

Table 4.2 indicates that a small group of the public schools therefore retained its dominant position not only in the production of officers overall but was an influencing factor among those successful in advancing beyond brigadier. Eighteen schools with more than one successful officer produced 47 percent of the overall total. If the schools which produced only one or two successful candidates are omitted the remainder highlights that traditional, core sources of army officers predominate. The group comprises Cheltenham, Clifton, Eton, Harrow, Marlborough, Rugby, Wellington and Winchester; Dover College is the exception. Members of the seven 'great' schools of the Clarendon Group[13] are still prominent; Eton with seven officers, Charterhouse, Rugby

13 Eton, Charterhouse, Harrow, Rugby, Shrewsbury, Westminster and Winchester; see Chapter 2.

and Winchester with three apiece and Harrow with two – 18 of the 42 successful, 42.8 percent of the total.

**Table 4.3 Degrees of Contemporaneousness, Schools Producing More Than One Progressing Officer**

| SCHOOL | NAME | YEARS |
|---|---|---|
| CHARTERHOUSE | SWAYNE | 1904-08 |
| | ANDERSON | 1905-09 |
| | JARDINE | 1907-10 |
| CHELTENHAM | HOGG | 1901-06 |
| | GRANT | 1904-09 |
| | PRATT, F. | 1906-10 |
| | GUBBINS | 1909-14 |
| CLIFTON | MORGAN F. | 1908-12 |
| | LEE | 1910-14 |
| DOVER COLLEGE | GOLDNEY | 1901-05 |
| | PRATT D. | 1906-10 |
| ETON | BECKWITH-SMITH | 1903-07 |
| | LAWSON | 1904-08 |
| | NORMAN | 1904-08 |
| | LAURIE | 1906-10 |
| | LEESE | 1907-11 |
| | WHITAKER | 1909-14 |
| | MCCREERY | 1910-15 |
| HARROW | MORGAN | 1901-06 |
| | MILES | 1906-09 |
| LANCING | POPE | 1905-11 |
| | RITCHIE | 1911-15 |
| MARLBOROUGH | DAVIDSON | 1906-10 |
| | IRWIN | 1906-10 |
| | WOOLNER | 1907-11 |
| REPTON | PHILLIP | 1903-08 |
| | SMYTH | 1908-12 |
| RUGBY | PERCIVAL | 1901-06 |
| | WOOTTEN | 1903-08 |
| | BERNEY-FICKLIN | 1906-10 |
| SHERBORNE | GRIFFIN | 1905-09 |
| | HUDSON | 1906-10 |
| WELLINGTON | SCHREIBER | 1903-07 |
| | BOND | 1904-08 |
| | STOPFORD | 1906-10 |
| WINCHESTER | CLARK | 1906-10 |
| | GAMMELL | 1906-10 |
| | WILSON | 1910-15 |

As can be seen from the table, relatively few of the officers in the group progressing were exact school contemporaries (as in they attended together during exactly the same years). However, as described in Chapter 2, the impact of this would mitigate over time as the very fact of having attended the school would become more significant as individuals moved on in life and encountered other alumni from eras different to their own – the 'old school tie'. The effect of having attended together (however loosely) should not, however, be completely discounted as in many cases they would have been aware of their fellow pupils and the same masters. This degree of overlapping attendance is examined below.

## Degrees of Contemporaneousness

***Exact Contemporaries***

The number of exact contemporaries – individuals whose period of attendance directly overlapped – is small; 6 of the 58, or 10.3 percent. These six came from three of the 18 schools producing major generals from the 1940 group. At Eton, it was Lawson and Norman (1904–1908), with Davidson and Irwin (1906–1910) at Marlborough and at Winchester, Clark and Gammell (1906–1910). However, by extending this definition to close contemporaries – individuals attending the school plus or minus one year around each other, the alumni networks broaden significantly.

***Close Contemporaries***

At Charterhouse, Swayne and Anderson were close contemporaries, having entered in 1904 and 1905 respectively. At Eton, Beckwith-Smith (entered 1903) was a near contemporary of Lawson and Norman (entered 1904), extending the network to three. Under these terms, Laurie and Leese (arriving 1906 and 1907 respectively) are also close contemporaries. At Marlborough, Woolner (arrived 1907) counts as a close contemporary of Clark and Gemmell. Griffin (arrived 1905) and Hudson (1906) form a close contemporaries group at Sherborne, the only members of the advancing group there and at Wellington, Schreiber (arrived 1903) and Bond (1904) are close contemporaries. Six of the eighteen schools therefore produce close contemporary groups, with three common to the exact group.

***Near Contemporaries***

Near contemporaries, as defined here, are individuals who attended the same school in an overlapping period but were separated by two or more years. Applying this criterion to the schools list means that the three Old Carthusians, Swayne, Anderson and Jardine, become members of this group with Jardine's arrival in 1907 overlapping both. From Cheltenham, two overlapped groups emerge: Hogg, Grant and Pratt with the second being Grant, Pratt and Gubbins, the group pivoting on Pratt 1906–1910. Morgan and Lee, at Clifton, also qualify. Eton, already the single largest contributing school, is also the only school to have all three types of these networks: exact, close and near. In the latter, Lawson, Norman, Laurie and Leese again pivot on 1907; Leese (1907–1911), and Whitaker (1909–1914) are a second near contemporary group, this time pivoting on 1909. Whitaker and McCreery (1911–1915) provide a third grouping. Rugby has two groups (from three officers); Percival and Wootten; Wootten and Berney-Ficklin (Percival's departure in 1906 omits him from bridging the group when Berney-Ficklin arrived). Equally, Stopford's arrival at Wellington in 1906 was just in time to create a close contemporary group with Schreiber (1903–1907) and Bond (1904–1908).

***No Contemporaries***

Dover College, Harrow, Lancing and Repton, while each producing two officers who proceeded to major general, generated no overlapping groups. Miles at Harrow and Smyth at Repton both arrived in the year when the other progressing officer left the school (1906 and 1908 respectively). Pratt arrived at Dover College a year after Goldney had departed; two years passed between Pope's departure from Lancing and Ritchie's arrival.

## Regiment

Among the group of officers who proceeded to general officer rank, no infantry regiments of first commissioning can be determined to be dominant among the group. However, the Guards officers who advanced were all Coldstreamers.[14] No single county or line infantry regiment predominates as a single bloc or route to general's rank. The one county or line regiment with more representatives than any other was the Royal Irish Rifles[15] (the Royal Ulster Rifles after Irish independence in 1922) with three, although one of them would later transfer to the Royal Tank Corps.[16] Three other officers would leave their original regiments for the Royal Tank Corps (these officers were still serving when the Royal Tank Corps was renamed the Royal Tank Regiment in April 1939). There is therefore arguably a Royal Tank Corps/Royal Tank Regiment bloc of four among the group of general officers.[17] The largest single grouping of officers reaching major general's rank or above remained that of the Royal Artillery with 10;[18] the Royal Engineers produced five.[19] The Army Service Corps (Royal Army Service Corps after 1920) group produced three.[20]

14 Beckwith-Smith, Leese and Whitaker.
15 D. Gartlan and Pratt and Steele; Pratt was the transferee.
16 From 1939 the Royal Tank Regiment.
17 Crocker and Pope and D. Pratt and Tilly.
18 Beckett, Davidson, Jardine, Lawson, F. Morgan, W. Morgan, Pratt, Schreiber, Slater and Gubbins.
19 Bond, Hogg, King, West and Woolner.
20 Gale, Goldney and McMullen.

**Table 4.4 General Officers by Original Commissioning**

| BRANCH | BRIGADIERS 1940 | GENERAL OFFICERS POST 1940 | PERCENTAGE PROCEEDING |
|---|---|---|---|
| CAVALRY[21] | 7 | 3 | 42.8 |
| GUARDS | 7 | 3 | 42.8 |
| INFANTRY | 76 | 31 | 40.7 |
| RA | 32 | 10 | 31.2 |
| RE[22] | 16 | 5 | 31.2 |
| ASC | 6 | 3 | 50.0 |
| OTHER/SUPPORT ARMS[23] | 12 | 3 | 25.0 |
| | 156 | 58 | 41.4 |

## War Service Before WW2

'War service' among the progressing officers falls into the following groups:

- Service on the frontline during the First World War, on several fronts
- Service in Russia in 1918–1919 during the Intervention against the Bolsheviks
- Service in India in confrontations on the North-West Frontier and elsewhere in tribal wars in South Asia from 1919–1939
- Service in the Middle East in Iraq and Persia
- Service in Egypt and Palestine, especially during the Arab Revolt of 1936–1939

All the officers progressing beyond brigadier had seen active service in the First World War, eliminating its effect as a distinction between officers who did advance and those who did not. Only 4 of the group of 58 did not serve on the Western Front, indicating the influence of service there on advancement, and its primacy as an operational front. Hogg,[24] who served in Mesopotamia and Egypt and King,[25] who spent the First World War in India on operations against the Mohmands and Swatis[26] countering raids and enforcing a blockade of the Swat Valley, were two of them. The third was Lawson, a pre-war

21 Includes the Tank Corps/Royal Tank Corps.
22 Includes officers who transferred to the Royal Corps of Signals on its formation in 1921.
23 Includes one officer originally commissioned into the Indian Army (Smyth), one into the Yeomanry of the Territorial Force (Gammell), one into the West Indies Regiment (Ramsden).
24 Commanded the Corps Rear Area at Andalsnes in Norway, 1940.
25 Deputy Engineer in Chief, BEF.
26 See, for example *War diary, Army Headquarters India, Frontier Operations*. General Staff India, 1914–1920. 56 vols: vols. 8–10, Aug-Oct 1915 India Office Records and Private Papers Reference: IOR/L/MIL/17/5/4073-5 (British Library).

Territorial, who served at Gallipoli with his Yeomanry regiment, the Buckinghamshire Yeomanry (Royal Bucks Hussars), but did not follow when it moved to France in April 1918. He remained in the Middle East, commanding the Middlesex Yeomanry, until the war's end. The fourth and last was McMullen, who served in Macedonia, Egypt and the Egyptian Expeditionary Force.

Five officers served on Gallipoli for varying periods. Lawson, as noted, with his Yeomanry regiment from August to November, when it moved to Egypt. Beckett landed at Cape Helles on the first day of the landings there on 25 April 1915, leaving for Egypt in mid-June; Davidson also landed at Cape Helles the same day, but remained on the peninsula until evacuated to Egypt in December. Gammell was among the last of those to be evacuated from Gallipoli in January 1916. Although Grant only arrived in August 1915, serving as a staff officer (his original battalion of the Queen's Own Cameron Highlanders did not serve on Gallipoli) he was also one of the last to leave, on 9 January 1916.

Barker, Beckett and McMullen also served, again, for varying durations and at differing times, on the Macedonian front.[27] Barker spent the rest of the war after November 1915 serving there, firstly with his battalion,[28] then in staff postings at divisional headquarters and as a brigade major. McMullen, as a Royal Engineer, was a specialist in railway transportation serving both there and latterly Egypt; he served on the Macedonian front from September 1915 to January 1916.[29] Beckett was present for only just over two months, from April to June 1917.[30] The likelihood of any of these officers' specific paths crossing in this theatre are therefore slim, but as with education the knowledge borne out of shared experience was more significant.

Davidson, Gammell, Grant, McMullen and Smyth all served in Egypt after the Gallipoli campaign and before the formation of the EEF in mid-March 1916, when the latter was established as a regional strategic force. Hogg had missed Gallipoli, remaining in Egypt from December 1914, before transferring to Mesopotamia, where he served until the end of October 1918. Grant, whose First World War active service was predominantly in staff postings, rapidly returned to France but with no active or staff service listed for him in 1917 and a notification of his having been wounded, was most likely in hospital and/or recuperating. Smyth, an Indian Army officer who earned a Victoria Cross in France in 1915, spent four months of 1915 (August to November) in Egypt but the rest of the war in India and on the North-West Frontier.

The officers serving in the EEF after its formation were Beckett (June 1916 to May 1917), Davidson (March to June 1916), Gammell (March to August 1916), Hogg (March to May 1916), McMullen (March 1916 to October 1918), and Ritchie (January

27 Also known as the Salonika Front; in official records it is noted as 'Greek Macedonia, Serbia, Bulgaria, European Turkey and the Islands of the Aegean Sea' e.g., Beckett's entry, *HYAL* January 1940, p.251.

28 4th Battalion, King's Royal Rifle Corps.

29 *HYAL* January 1940, pp.201–202

30 *HYAL* January 1940, p.168

to October 1918). As noted above, Hogg served in Mesopotamia; the only other officer in the group to serve there was Ritchie, who was present at the fall of Baghdad on 11 March 1917 with his battalion, 2/Black Watch. Except for a period absent wounded between June and December 1917, Ritchie spent 23 months in Mesopotamia from January 1916 before returning to Egypt. At some point, therefore, Beckett, Gammell, Hogg and McMullen were all serving in the EEF simultaneously; McMullen and Ritchie would do so in 1918.

Eight officers served in Russia during the British intervention there in 1918–1919. Barker, Berney-Ficklin, Gubbins, Hogg, Horrocks (who was captured in January 1919 and spent 10 months as a Bolshevik prisoner),[31] Hudson, Percival and Pope. There was a direct connection between two of them; Gubbins and Berney-Ficklin (both of whom would serve in Norway in 1940) were both on the headquarters staff of the then Major General Ironside at Archangel in the summer of 1919.[32]

Through the 1920s until the mid-1930s, active service opportunities for officers, especially those of the British Army, were very limited, unless they served in India on the various pacification campaigns against tribal forces from 1919 to 1935, or on the North-West Frontier between 1936 and 1937 and again from 1937 to 1939. Officers desiring advancement, or improvement of their professional prospects, would volunteer for loan service overseas such as training indigenous troops in Africa or India, or in staff postings or attached for active service.[33] The latter, India, is the largest single group of those serving overseas. At various times between the world wars, Anderson, Berney-Ficklin, Bond, Irwin, King, Morgan, Ramsden, Robb, Smyth, Steele, Tilly and West, 12 in total, were on active service in India. Four officers who did not progress, Chichester-Constable, Clifton, Greenwood and Whitehead, served in India at various times in the 1930s. Therefore, service in India was a potential advantage towards later advancement.

King, Slater and Smyth all served during the Third Afghan War between May and August 1919, when the Emir of Afghanistan invaded British India; the short, if intense, campaign ending in an armistice. Anderson, Irwin, Robb, Smyth and West also served during the so-called Redshirt Rebellion on the North-West Frontier between October 1930 and February 1931. In this campaign, Afridi tribesmen rebelled over Imperial encroachment and the loss of grazing land around Peshawar, resulting in the dispatch of a two-brigade strong force to prevent further tribal advances towards Peshawar. West was Mentioned in Dispatches and received a DSO for his part in the campaign, a rare

31 P. Warner, *Horrocks: The General Who Led From The Front* (London: Hamish Hamilton, 1984), p.36.

32 Sir E. Ironside, *Archangel 1919* (London: Constable, 1953) and N. Smart, *Biographical Dictionary of British Generals of the Second World War* (Barnsley: Pen & Sword Military, 2005), p.31.

33 For example, Major General John Frost (of Arnhem renown) volunteered to serve with the Iraq Levies after regimental service in Palestine. 'Obituary: Major-General John Frost' in *The Independent* (London) 24 May 1993. p.27

interwar award of this decoration, which joined the MC he was awarded on the Western Front in 1917.[34]

Two separate campaigns in Waziristan were deemed sufficiently active to attract the award of a clasp to the Indian General Service Medal of 1908 (IGS 08); from 1919–21 and 1921–24.[35] The first was given to those participating in operations in Waziristan on the Bannu Line in October and November 1919, on the Tank Line between October 1919 and December 1921, or occupying posts in the Zhob District between November 1920 and May 1921. Smyth and Steele received the first, William Morgan and Tilly the second. Steele was Mentioned in Dispatches in June 1921[36] for his part in the campaign. Smyth and Steele also served in the same area of operations within Waziristan in 1919–1920, which attracted the award of the clasp 'Mahsud 1919–20', for service on the Taki Zam Line between December 1919 and April 1920. Berney-Ficklin and Smyth were also present during the campaign between February and April 1935 in the Loe Agra area, which was represented by the last clasp to the IGS 08, 'North-West Frontier 1935'.

Smyth, unsurprisingly given his Indian Army background, was the most experienced officer in frontier fighting. By virtue of this he was connected, however indirectly, by operational service in often short duration, if intense, campaigns to Anderson, Berney-Ficklin, Irwin, King, Robb, Slater and West, creating a loose 'India group' within the brigadiers. This was more of a convergence of service than a formal grouping, in comparison with Henry Wilson and Henry Rawlinson serving closely together in Burma in the 1880s.

A new medal was instituted in 1938, to reflect active service on the North-West Frontier from November 1936 to 15 December 1937,[37] and thence from 16 December 1937 to 1 January 1939.[38] For the first, the only officers connected from the group were Bond and Ramsden; both were Mentioned in Dispatches for their service there between November 1936 and January 1937; Bond as the Chief Engineer of the Waziristan Force, Ramsden as the commanding officer of 1st Battalion, the Hampshire Regiment.[39] No officers in either group – advancing or not – qualified for the clasp/medal awarded for service in the 1937–1939 period.[40]

The other campaign medal covering operational service in the interwar period appropriate to the group of officers under discussion was the Army and RAF General Service Medal, instituted in 1918.[41] Prior to the Arab Revolt in Palestine in 1936, the only

34 The *London Gazette*, 6 May 1932, p.2958 'for distinguished services rendered in the field in connection with military operations on the North-West Frontier of India during the period October 1930 to March 1931.'
35 A third clasp 'Waziristan 1925' was awarded, but only to the Royal Air Force.
36 *The London Gazette*, 10 June 1921.
37 Army Order 168, 1938; TNA WO 123/80; the clasp was 'North-West Frontier 1936–37'.
38 Army Order 217, 1940; TNA WO the clasp was 'North-West Frontier 1937–39'.
39 *The London Gazette*, 18 February 1938, p.1073.
40 As checked against the Gradation List for Officers of the Army, *HYAL* January 1940 and *HYAL* January 1942.
41 This medal remained in use until 1962; the clasps awarded and relevant here were 'Iraq' and 'Palestine'.

campaign for which a clasp to this medal was awarded and was common to members of the group was for the Iraqi Revolt of 1920, for those serving between December 1919 and November 1920.[42] Beckett and Smyth both qualified for this medal, although it is unlikely that their paths crossed as Beckett was a captain serving as the adjutant of a unit[43] and Smyth was a brigade major in an Indian Army brigade.[44]

The 1936–1939 Arab Revolt in Palestine[45] generated another group with common experience; five officers from the group served there, Berney-Ficklin, Halstead, Ritchie, Utterson-Kelso and Wootten. This campaign was significant in that several officers who rose to high command during the Second World War served there in senior posts; for example, Richard O'Connor was Military Governor of Jerusalem and GOC 7th Division, where Berney-Ficklin served under him as CO of 2/Highland Light Infantry.[46] Montgomery was GOC 8th Division there and certainly 'talent spotted' junior officers who served under him during the Second World War, such as Ritchie, who had transferred from his 'home' Scottish regiment of the Black Watch to command an English county regiment, 1/King's Own (Royal Lancaster) Regiment in Palestine on promotion to lieutenant colonel in 1938. Another example was Major General Robert 'Bobby' Ross, who commanded the 53rd (Welsh) Division from 1942–1945, particularly in the North-West Europe campaign; although a lieutenant colonel in 1939 and outside the scope of this work, he was known to Montgomery for commanding a battalion in one of the brigades of 8th Division in Palestine, and Monty was a frequent visitor to his headquarters in 1944–1945, which was much remarked upon by Ross' staff.[47]

In summary, several groupings of common interwar operational service emerge from the officers who advanced to major general and beyond.

**Table 4.5 War Service of Officers Progressing**

| THEATRE | NUMBER | NAMES |
|---|---|---|
| **FIRST WORLD WAR: NON-WESTERN FRONT** | | |
| GALLIPOLI | 5 | BECKETT, DAVIDSON, GAMMELL, GRANT, LAWSON |
| EGYPT | 6 | DAVIDSON, GAMMELL, GRANT, **HOGG**, **MC MULLEN**, SMYTH |
| EEF | 6 | BECKETT, DAVIDSON, GAMMELL, **HOGG**, **MC MULLEN**, RITCHIE |
| MESOPOTAMIA | 2 | **HOGG**, RITCHIE |

42 Clasp 'Iraq'.
43 *HYAL* January 1940 p.251.
44 *HYAL* January 1940 pp.191 92.
45 Clasp 'Palestine' to the 1918 General Service Medal.
46 http://regiments.org:80/deploy/uk/reg-inf/074-1.htm (2nd Battalion Highland Light Infantry) accessed 20 January 2016.
47 Patrick Delaforce, *Red Crown and Dragon: 53rd (Welsh) Division 1944–1945* (London: Tom Donovan Publishing,1996) p.37.

| THEATRE | NUMBER | NAMES |
|---|---|---|
| GREEK MACEDONIA | 2 | BARKER, **MC MULLEN** |
| 1919-1939 | | |
| RUSSIA (1918-1919) | 8 | BARKER, BERNEY-FICKLIN, GUBBINS, **HOGG**, HORROCKS, HUDSON, PERCIVAL, POPE |
| INDIA[48] (1919-1939) | 12 | ANDERSON, BERNEY-FICKLIN, BOND, IRWIN, **KING**, MORGAN, RAMSDEN, ROBB, SMYTH, STEELE, TILLY, WEST |
| IRAQ (1920-22) | 2 | BECKETT, SMYTH |
| PALESTINE (1936-39) | 5 | BERNEY-FICKLIN, HALSTEAD, RITCHIE, UTTERSON-KELSO, WOOTTEN |

**Table 4.5A Officers Advancing Who Served in Multiple Theatres, First World War (Excluding Western Front) & 1919–1939**

| | |
|---|---|
| BERNEY-FICKLIN | RUSSIA, INDIA, PALESTINE |
| BECKETT | GALLIPOLI, EGYPT, EEF, IRAQ |
| DAVIDSON | GALLIPOLI, EGYPT, EEF |
| GAMMELL | GALLIPOLI, EGYPT, EEF |
| **HOGG** | **EGYPT, EEF, MESOPOTAMIA, RUSSIA** |
| **MC MULLEN** | **MACEDONIA, PALESTINE** |
| RITCHIE | MESOPOTAMIA, PALESTINE |
| SMYTH | EGYPT, INDIA |

(Officers highlighted in bold did not serve on the Western Front during the First World War)

Aside from the individual campaign groupings, it can be seen that other groups of linked service emerge; Beckett, Davidson and Gammell as a Gallipoli/Egypt/EEF group, expanding to a group of five if Hogg and McMullen's service in Egypt and the EEF is factored in. While a small group set against the overall number of officers, it again shows groupings of shared, varied knowledge and experience. It is significant that other operational fronts from the First World War do not figure in the list of officers advancing after 1940. There are no veterans of the war in East or South-West Africa, or of the Italian campaign of 1917–1918, underlining the perception of these fronts as 'sideshows' to the main effort on the Western Front.

## Staff College

Of the 58 officers promoted to major general or above during the Second World War, 40 of them were Staff College graduates, or 68.9 percent of the total. Thirty-five officers, 22.9 percent of the overall group or 36.7 percent of the non-advancing group, were also

48 Including North West Frontier, Afghanistan and Waziristan.

Staff College graduates. This suggests, due to the similarity of numbers advancing and not advancing, that possessing a p.s.c. in and of itself was not decisive for advancement, even if preferable. 36 of the 40 graduated from Camberley, the remaining 4 from Quetta. These officers are grouped by their year of graduation:

**Table 4.6 Officers Progressing: Staff College Contemporaries**

| GRADUATION YEAR | NUMBER | INDIVIDUALS |
|---|---|---|
| CAMBERLEY | | |
| 1922 | 3 | BECKWITH-SMITH (C GDS); GAMMELL (CAM HDRS); MILES (KOSB) |
| 1923 | 1 | WOOTTEN (BAYS) |
| 1924 | | HALSTEAD (LOYALS); PERCIVAL (BEDFORDS); PRATT (RTR); SCHREIBER (RA); SMYTH (IA); STOPFORD (RB) |
| 1925 | 5 | BOND (RE); GARTLAN (R IRISH); IRWIN (ESSEX); POPE (N STAFFS); WATSON (HLI); |
| 1926 | | CLARK (16L); GALE (ASC); HUDSON (N&D); MORGAN W (RA) NORMAN (9L); SWAYNE (SOM LI) |
| 1927 | | BARKER (KRRC); DAVIDSON (RA); WEST (RE) |
| 1928 | | ANDERSON (SEAFORTH); HAWKESWORTH (E YORKS); JARDINE (RA); LEESE (C GDS); WOOLNER (RE) |
| 1929 | | CROCKER (MIDDX); GUBBINS (RA); MCCREERY (12L); |
| 1930 | | RITCHIE (BW) |
| 1931 | | STEELE (R IRISH); DEMPSEY (R BERKS) |
| 1932 | | HORROCKS (MIDDX) |
| QUETTA | 1 | |
| 1923 | 2 | HOGG (RE) |
| 1927 | 1 | LEE (S STAFFS); DAVIDSON (RA) |
| 1928 | 4 | MORGAN F (RA) |

Only one officer who served as a Brigadier in 1940 graduated from Camberley before 1922[49] and none after 1932. There are several conjunctions and overlaps, where officers beginning the two-year course[50] would have been present as junior students when their senior students were heading towards graduation from the course and would have overlapped in their attendance. They can be classified, therefore, as close contemporaries as with schools above.

49 Archibald Beauman, who graduated from Camberley after the first post-First World War course in December 1919; he was appointed an honorary brigadier on retirement in 1938, but recalled to service from the reserve in 1939, (*HYAL* January 1940 p.1313).

50 The first two Staff College courses post-war, in 1919 and 1920, lasted eight months and a year respectively; the two-year course was reinstituted in 1922, as was entry through competitive examination.

For example, Wootten, who graduated in 1923, would have been present in his first year while Beckwith-Smith, Gammell and Miles were finishing their course in 1922 and been in a similar position to them in 1923, when Halstead, Pratt, Schreiber, Smyth and Stopford were beginning their attendance at Camberley, making Wootten connected to nine other officers by their overlapping attendance. By the same measure, the 1924–1926 'envelope' would be 13 strong in the first period, 1924–25 and 11 in the second, 1925–26 – making this the largest conglomeration of officers under examination. The overlap reduces after 1925 as the number of individuals who were successful in progressing also declines; in 1926–1928 it is seven and eight officers respectively around the 1927 'pivot', and in 1927–1929, both years have an overlap of eight. The highest figure in 1929–1931 is five officers followed by three in 1930–1931. By 1931–1932, it falls to two officers – Horrocks and Dempsey. Despite the direct connection between 1940 brigadiers who advanced to major general and beyond being limited, the 1930–1932 period did still produce many wartime general officers and is a valuable snapshot of officers at a point in their careers for whom the outbreak of war would provide additional impetus to higher rank.

The officers graduating in 1926 could count among their contemporaries several officers who, if not brigadiers in 1940, were destined for high rank later in the war. These included Ronald Scobie,[51] Frank Messervy,[52] Raymond Briggs,[53] Eric 'Dreadnought' Harrison,[54] Henry Willcox,[55] Francis 'Gertie' Tuker,[56] John Swayne,[57] and Ralph Deedes.[58]

Among Dempsey's contemporaries in the Junior Division at Camberley when he arrived there in January 1930[59] were William 'Strafer' Gott,[60] George Hopkinson,[61]

51 Later GOC Tobruk, GOC 70th Division and CGS Middle East. Mead, *The Last Great Cavalryman...*, p.410.

52 Commanded 4th (Indian) Division, 1st Armoured Division, 7th Armoured Division, 7th (Indian) Division and IV Corps during the Second World War.

53 Commanded 2 Armoured Brigade, 1st Armoured Division and was Director, Royal Armoured Corps during the war.

54 A gunner who spent most of the war in Commander or Brigadier, Royal Artillery posts in 12th Division, IX Corps and Northern Ireland: Major General Royal Artillery Allied Forces HQ in North Africa and finally GOC Sussex and Surrey District.

55 Commanded 13 (Infantry) Brigade in France in early 1940; transferred command to Miles Dempsey, who he had taught at Camberley; GOC 42nd (East Lancashire) Division and I Corps from May-October 1941, before being sent to India where he saw out the war.

56 Director of Military Training, India 1940–41; 4th (Indian) Infantry Division 1941–1944 and briefly IV Corps.

57 Head of the British Military Mission to French General Headquarters, 1939–1940; GOC 4th Division 1941; CGS Home Forces 1941; GOC South Eastern Command 1941; CGS (India) 1944–1945.

58 GOC Waziristan District (India) 1941–1943; Military Secretary (India) 1943–1944; Adjutant General (India) 1944–1946.

59 List of contemporaries from N. Smart, *Biographical Dictionary of British Generals of the Second World War* (Barnsley: Pen & Sword Military, 2005), pp.81–82.

60 Later commander, Eighth Army in the Middle East; killed in an air crash 7 August 1942. Smart, *Biographical Dictionary...* p.125.

61 A liaison officer to the Belgians in 1940, later commander of 1 Airlanding Brigade and second commander of 1st Airborne Division, killed in action in Italy on 9 September 1943. Smart, *Biographical Dictionary...* p.158.

James Steele,[62] Maurice Chilton,[63] Arthur Snelling[64] and John 'Crasher' Nichols.[65] In the year above Dempsey, in the senior division (who had arrived in January 1929) were Neil Ritchie,[66] Herbert Lumsden,[67] George Erskine,[68] Ivor Hughes,[69] Harold Redman,[70] and Ian Playfair.[71] The junior division below Dempsey, who started in January 1931, included Brian Horrocks,[72] Sidney Kirkman,[73] Frank Simpson,[74] Joseph Baillon,[75] Arthur Dowler,[76] Thomas 'Pete' Rees,[77] Keith Arbuthnot[78] and Cameron Nicholson.[79]

That the Staff College in the interwar period was a breeding ground for talented officers who would rise to senior command during the Second World War is a difficult claim to dismiss. Although not singularly decisive, it was an advantage. While the value and applicability of the training it provided for those who did reach the higher echelons has been debated,[80] from the perspective of this work, it certainly did generate

62 Latterly GOC 59th Division 1941–1942; II Corps 1942; Director of Staff Duties, War Office 1943. Smart, *Biographical Dictionary*… pp.296–97.
63 Later Dempsey's Chief of Staff at Second Army and Deputy Adjutant General of 21st Army Group.
64 Later Major General in charge of Administration, 14th Army in Burma. Smart, *Biographical Dictionary* …, p.293.
65 GOC 50th (Northumbrian) Division at the Battle of El Alamein in October 1942, but later dismissed by Montgomery and demoted. Smart, *Biographical Dictionary*…, p.233.
66 A Dunkirk contemporary, commander of Eighth Army in 1942 and XII Corps in Normandy in 1944. Smart, *Biographical Dictionary*…, p.272
67 Later commander of 6th Armoured Division, 1st Armoured Division and X Corps in the Middle East; II Corps and VIII Corps before Normandy. Smart, *Biographical Dictionary* …, p.196
68 Commander of 7th Armoured Division in North Africa and Normandy. Smart, *Biographical Dictionary*…, p.96.
69 Commanding 44th Division in North Africa and XXV (Indian) Corps in the Far East. Smart, *Biographical Dictionary*…, p.163.
70 Secretary to the Combined Chiefs of Staff, Washington 1943–1945. Smart, *Biographical Dictionary*…, p.263.
71 Director of Plans, War Office 1940–1942, but better known as the author of the volumes of the *Official History of the Second World War: The Mediterranean and Middle East*, 4 volumes (London: HMSO, 1954–1966).
72 Chief Instructor at Camberley on the outbreak of war. Commanded 11 Brigade in France; XIII Corps in North Africa and XXX Corps in North-West Europe.
73 Commanded 50th Division in the Middle East and XIII Corps in Italy.
74 Deputy Director, and then Director, Military Operations at the War Office, 1942–1945.
75 Chief of Staff, Persia and Iraq Force (Paiforce) and Chief of Staff. Mediterranean Expeditionary Force (MEF).
76 GOC 38th (Welsh) Division; Chief of Administration, Southern Command 1942–1944 and Chief of Administration MEF 1944–1945.
77 Commanded 10th (Indian) Division in the Middle East and 19th (Indian) Division in Burma.
78 Commanded 78th Infantry Division in Italy, 1944–1946.
79 Brigadier General Staff, 1st Army in Tunisia; Commanded 44th (Indian) Division, 21st (Indian) Division and 2nd Division in Burma.
80 For example, in A. G. Duncan, 'The Military Education of Army Officers in the Edwardian Era' (unpublished PhD thesis, University of Birmingham, 2016), pp.187–214 and D. French,

networks of officers known and connected to each other. The key periods for this were from 1922–1926, coinciding with the tenure as Commandant of the then Major General Sir Edmund Ironside and 1924–1928, overlapping between Ironside and Major General Sir Charles Gwynn.

## The Imperial Defence College

All nine officers from the 1940 group who attended the Imperial Defence College before 1939 would progress to major general or above during the Second World War, achieving the College's purpose of preparing officers selected to attend it as preparation for higher command. This should not come as a surprise given the College's reason for existing. (The *HYAL* for January 1940 contains 40 officers still serving who were graduates of the College, including a major general of the Royal Marines and several Indian Army officers). Two were on the 1933 course, Bond[81] and Swayne.[82] In 1934, Miles[83] and Pope[84] and in 1935, Percival[85] and Davidson[86]. Irwin,[87] Gartlan[88] and Gammell[89] followed in 1936, 1937 and 1938 respectively. Furthermore, Bond and Swayne had been direct contemporaries at the Staff College, graduating in 1925.

## Decorated for France 1940

In Chapter 2, it was shown that of the 156 officers making up the 1940 sample, 79.2 percent, or 121, had received at least one decoration for gallantry or distinguished service during the period of the First World War. Of those 121 officers, 54 would advance to major general or beyond after 1940, or 44.6 percent of the whole. However, in order to further examine the case against the assertion which originally triggered this research

'Officer Education and Training in The British Army 1919–1939' in G. Kennedy and K. Neilson, *Military Education and Training: Past, Present and Future*' (Westport: Praeger, 2002), pp.105–128, particularly pp.117–120. Duncan contends that the post-Boer War professionalisation of the Army was enhanced both by the education provided at Staff College and its growing perception as a necessary step for potential advancement to high rank. French states that while a positive experience for most who attended, the training provided was inadequate to meet the demands graduates would face during the Second World War.

81 Chief Engineer, I Corps in France.
82 A BGS and Head of the Liaison Mission to French GHQ.
83 Commanding 126 Brigade of 42nd Division in 1940.
84 BGS II Corps 1940.
85 BGS I Corps 1940.
86 CRA I Corps 1940.
87 Commanding 6 Brigade of 2nd Division to 20 May 1940.
88 Commanding 5 Brigade of 2nd Division.
89 BGS NWEF in Norway.

(that participation in either of 1940's strategic failures was automatically career limiting or terminating) the number of officers who received decorations for gallantry or distinguished service directly as a result of these two campaigns, and who progressed beyond brigadier, will now be examined.

No awards of the Victoria Cross, the highest British award for gallantry, were made to officers at this level in either France or Norway. Three of the 156 were already holders of the VC, all awarded for the First World War: George Roupell, originally from the East Surrey Regiment, who commanded 36 Brigade in France had earned his VC on the Western Front in April 1915 and graduated from the Staff College in 1927; Charles Hudson, originally from the Sherwood Foresters, commanded 2 Brigade in France and had earned his VC in Italy in 1918 and graduated from the Staff College in 1926; John 'Jacky' Smyth commanded 127 Brigade in France, he was originally commissioned into the Indian Army and earned his VC on the Western Front in 1915 while serving with the 15th Ludhiana Sikhs; he graduated from the Staff College at Camberley in 1923, and taught there from 1931–34. All three were from public schools, Roupell from Rossall, Hudson from Sherborne and Smyth from Repton; Roupell and Smyth served as GSOs during the First World War. Of the three, only Hudson was decorated for 1940, appointed Companion of the Order of the Bath.

Smyth and Hudson progressed to major general. Roupell, by virtue of having escaped and evaded capture before being smuggled out of occupied Europe via Spain in 1942, did not. None of the three had much success thereafter. Hudson briefly held a divisional command in the UK, but serious personality clashes with his corps commander led to dismissal and demotion back to colonel, from which he did not recover.[90] Smyth's career was finished after the incident at the Sittang Bridge in February 1942 (see below). Therefore, despite the possession of other apparent advantages for advancement, a Victoria Cross was not a guarantee.

Seventy-three officers received decorations for their services on operations in 1940, ranging from the Mention in Dispatches at the lowest end of the Order of Seniority of British Honours and Awards[91] to a Companion of the Order of Bath (Military Division) at the top. (The number of awards reflects occasional multiple awards to individuals). In between were the Distinguished Service Order and appointment to be a Commander of the Order of the British Empire (Military Division).[92] The breakdown of awards for service in 1940 is shown in the table below:

90 C. Hudson and M. Hudson, *Two Lives 1892–1992. The Memoirs of Charles Edward Hudson, VC, CB, DSO, MC, and Miles Matthew Lee Hudson, also some poems by Charles Edward Hudson* (Privately published by Wilton 65: York, 1992), p.187.

91 *https://www.gov.uk/honours/types-of-honours-and-awards* Official UK Government website, accessed 11 August 2018. This list includes awards instituted since the end of the Second World War.

92 Both the Order of the Bath and the Order of the British Empire were (and still are) divided into Civil and Military divisions, the former distinguished by different forms of insignia, the latter by a slight difference in the ribbon worn, the Military Division having a salmon pink

**Table 4.7 Honours and Awards to The Group for Operations in France or Norway 1940**

| AWARD | NOT PROGRESSING | PROGRESSING | TOTAL[93] |
|---|---|---|---|
| CB (MIL) | 1 | 7 | 8 |
| CBE (MIL) | 17 | 17 | 34 |
| BAR TO THE DSO | 1 | 1 | 2 |
| DSO | 4 | 6 | 10 |
| MID | 21 | 7 | 28 |
| | **44** | **38** | **82** |

Based on pure numbers of awards, it cannot be stated that receipt of a distinction for operations in 1940 was a definitively influencing factor in advancement of itself. Examining the nature of awards granted, however, suggests that the seniority of the award was influential for future advancement. The higher the award, the higher the chance of its contributing to subsequent promotion. Comparing the size of the group of those who progressed with the much larger group of those who did not, indicates a much higher percentage of those in the progression group who held an award. This is even clearer if MiDs are removed.

The Statutes of the Most Honourable Order of the Bath[94] indicate that CBs should be awarded to officers around the rank of rear admiral in the Royal Navy, major general in the army or Royal Marines, or air vice marshal in the Royal Air Force, and in addition must have been Mentioned in Dispatches for distinction in a command position on active service. Officers of supporting arms (e.g. engineers, medical officers, logisticians) may be appointed only for meritorious service in wartime. Numerical limitations on the number of Companions at any one time are suspended at time of war.[95] The Order of the Bath, as the main Order of Chivalry awarded to military officers then and now, is a mark of distinction for outstanding performance on duty or in command. Only one officer who received a CB for France did not advance beyond brigadier;[96] this was Ralph Chenevix-Trench, the Signal Officer in Chief BEF who was 'retired' as the Chief

ribbon with pearl grey edges and a thin pearl grey stripe added to its centre and the Civil Division a salmon pink ribbon with pearl grey edges and no centre stripe. Officers of the rank of lieutenant colonel and above were ineligible for the award of the Military Cross, which was awarded only to officers of the rank of major and below.

93 Total numbers exceed the size of the group as some individuals received more than one award; for example, two officers were Mentioned in Dispatches twice during the period.

94 Anonymous, *The Statutes of the Most Honourable Order of the Bath (Revised 1925)* (London: Harrison and Sons, 1939 published edition), article 17.

95 Anonymous, *The Statutes of the Most Honourable Order of the Bath (Revised 1925)* (London: Harrison and Sons, 1939 published edition), article 25.

96 Chenevix-Trench held the rank of Acting Major General for three weeks while 'specially employed' in May 1940 see Major General R. W. H. Nalder, *The Royal Corps of Signals: a History of its Antecedents and Development (circa 1800–1955)* (London: The Royal Signals Institution, 1958); *The Wire* (The Corps Magazine of the Royal Corps of Signals) vol. XXI

Signals Officer, Home Forces by Montgomery in 1941.[97] His very brief tenure as a major general may explain his appointment as CB in the post-Dunkirk honours list.[98] All the other officers appointed CB for their service in 1940 progressed beyond brigadier.[99]

Award of a Commander of the Most Excellent Order of the British Empire (Military Division) or CBE (Mil) to military officers reflects recognition for work often not in the face of the enemy, such as on headquarters staffs or in command in areas not under fire. That the number of awards was equal between officers advancing and those who did not, aside from coincidence, suggests that the award of a CBE, while a signal recognition of good work, was neither a positive influence over future promotion nor a negative one. Of the 17 recipients who did progress, all but two held posts as senior staff officers in headquarters (such a BGS, for example Ritchie at GHQ BEF and Leese as BGS III Corps) or were the senior officers in charge of support arms at higher formation headquarters, for example Director, Supply or Director, Transport at corps level or above.[100]

The Distinguished Service Order was instituted in 1886 as an award for distinguished or gallant service for officers, at a time when the only other alternatives, apart from meritorious awards of rank, were the Victoria Cross or the Order of the Bath. Despite its status as an award of distinction, it was also known laconically as 'Did Something or Other'. Although its use was expanded during the First World War and it was awarded to junior officers such as subalterns, its primary recipients were intended to be officers of the rank of major and above. (An award to an officer of more junior rank, especially to subalterns or equivalent, was often popularly, if not officially, considered to be a 'near miss' for the award of a Victoria Cross in both world wars). This Order was established to reward officers who exhibited individual instances of meritorious or distinguished service in war. It was usually awarded for service under fire or under conditions equivalent to service in actual combat with the enemy.

Prior to 1943, the DSO could be given only to someone who had already been Mentioned in Dispatches. Ten were awarded to officers of this 1940 group; four to officers who did not progress and six to those who did. There were two bars to the DSO given to two officers who had received their original decoration during the First World War. One progressed beyond brigadier,[101] the other did not.[102] Whether a DSO was

No.245 (July 1940), p.1; B. N. Hall, *Communications and British Operations on the Western Front, 1914–1918* (Cambridge: Cambridge University Press, 2017), p.61,

97 S. Godfrey, *British Army Communications in the Second World War: Lifting the Fog of Battle* (Cambridge: Cambridge University Press, 2013), p.73.

98 The London Gazette, 11 July 1940.

99 Gammell and Wootten, for Norway; Halstead, Hudson, Irwin, Jardine and Lawson for France.

100 The two exceptions, being awarded CBEs in command of fighting formations were: Gartlan (commanding 5 Brigade of 2nd Division) and Ramsden (commanding 25 Brigade of 50th Division).

101 Phillips (commanding 146 Brigade of 49th Division) for Norway; his original DSO had been awarded in 1919 for East Africa.

102 Chichester-Constable (commanding 139 Brigade of 46th Division) for France; his original DSO had been awarded in 1916 for the Western Front.

therefore a contributing element in advancement is not decisively proven but may be considered influential.

The award of 'Mentioned in Dispatches' (or MiD) is one where the name appears in an official report written by a superior officer and sent to high command, in which gallant or meritorious action in the face of the enemy is described. This lowest-level distinction became formalised during the First World War with the issue of certificates and, after 1920, the issue of an oak leaf device worn upon an appropriate campaign medal or ribbon when the latter only are worn. There are no limits to the number of times an individual may be 'mentioned' although in British practice until 2014 only one device is granted regardless of the number of 'mentions' received. Authority to award MiDs is devolved to lower command without the need to refer to higher echelons. As such, it was a ready means to quickly reward service not of a standard for higher recognition. Of the 21 MiDs awarded to officers who did not progress in rank after France and Norway, all but two were to those in staff posts at senior headquarters, including a Deputy Director of Medical Services, a Commander of a Base Area and a Commander of a Rear Echelon base – implying that MiD was used, in this case, to recognise organisational skill rather than leadership in the field.

## 'Patronage' Beyond June 1940

The brigadiers serving in 1940 did not do so in isolation; each was subordinate to a higher commander of one form or another, a major general or higher. This section will examine, firstly, officers in fighting formations to establish if the divisional commander's career post 1940 influenced that of his subordinate. Staff officers at GHQ BEF would be subordinate to the Commander-in-Chief – Gort, the Chief of Staff – Pownall, the Adjutant General – Brownrigg or the Quarter Master General – Lindsell.

Brigadiers in fighting formations in France were subordinate to the divisional commander, some of whom (for example Anderson of 11 Brigade, 4th Division) replaced divisional commanders when they were reassigned or evacuated back to the UK.[103] The smaller force in Norway, based on brigades and ad hoc forces, was more fluid but overall the brigadiers were subordinate to Major General de Wiart (Mauriceforce), Major General Paget, (Sickleforce) and Major General Macksey (Avonforce), with Gubbins, then a brigadier, in command of Scissorforce. After the reorganisation of British forces in Norway on 13 May, Lieutenant General Sir Claude Auchinleck assumed command of the North-West Expeditionary Force.

103 Anderson was reassigned to command 3rd Division when its GOC, Montgomery, replaced Brooke as II Corps' commander on 30 May 1940. Mead, *The Last Great Cavalryman...*, p.48 and Mackie (2018 edition), p.178.

## Careers After 1940

While the charge that the fact of merely serving in France or Norway in 1940 in a brigadier's appointment was career-ending is simple to refute, it cannot be said that it was necessarily a step to success or advancement either. Two elements should be examined more closely. Firstly, whether having been a pupil of Brooke (at the Staff College from 1924–1926 and the Imperial Defence College from 1933–1934) or Montgomery (at Camberley from 1926–1929 and Quetta from 1934–1937) was influential or advantageous, and secondly whether there was a 'coat tails effect' of having served under a divisional commander in 1940. The latter will review whether those commanders took subordinates with them as, when or if they themselves advanced after 1940. The following table outlines the career paths after the summer of 1940 of those officers in the group who progressed to major general or above.

**Table 4.8 Post 1940 Careers of Officers Progressing Beyond Brigadier Taught by Brooke and Montgomery**

| NAME | BEF/ NWEF | COMMAND 1940 | HIGHEST RANK WW2 | POST 1940 SERVICE (THEATRE) |
|---|---|---|---|---|
| ANDERSON | BEF | 11 BDE | LT GEN | GOC 1 DIV 1940 (HOME)<br>GOC VI CORPS 1941 (HOME)<br>GOC II CORPS 1942 (HOME)<br>GOC EASTERN CMD (HOME)<br>GOC 1ST ARMY 1942-43 (NORTH AFRICA)<br>GOC SOUTHERN CMD (HOME) 1944<br>GOC EAST AFRICA 1945 (AFRICA) |
| BARKER, E | BEF | 10 BDE | LT GEN | GOC 54 DIV 1940-42 (HOME)<br>GOC 49 DIV 1944 (NWE)<br>GOC VIII CORPS 1944-45 (NWE) |
| BECKETT | BEF | CRA 15 DIV | MAJ GEN | CRA 15 DIV 1940-41 (HOME)<br>CRA MALTA 1941-42 (MED)<br>A/GOC MALTA 1942 (MED)<br>CDG 4 & 5 AA GPS RA 1943-45 (HOME) |
| BECKWITH-SMITH | BEF | 1 GDS BDE | MAJ GEN | GOC 18 DIV 1941-42 (FE)<br>DIED AS POW 1942 |
| BERNEY-FICKLIN | BEF | 15 BDE | MAJ GEN | GOC 5 DIV 1940-43 (HOME; MED)<br>GOC 48 DIV 1943 (HOME)<br>GOC 54 DIV 1944 (HOME) |

| NAME | BEF/ NWEF | COMMAND 1940 | HIGHEST RANK WW2 | POST 1940 SERVICE (THEATRE) |
|---|---|---|---|---|
| BOND | BEF | C/ENG CRE I CORPS | MAJ GEN | MAJ GEN I/C ADMIN WO 1940-41 (HOME)<br>DEP QMG INDIA 1941-42; (INDIA)<br>ENG IN CHF INDIA 1942-43 (INDIA) |
| CLARK | BEF | 12 BDE | MAJ GEN | GOC 1 CAV DIV 1940 (ME)<br>GOC 10 ARMD DIV 1941 (ME)<br>GOC LofC AFHQ 1942 (MED)<br>DEP MIL GOV SICILY 1943 (MED)<br>CHF ADMIN OFF, AFHQ 1943-45 (MED)<br>HD. SHAEF MISSION NETHERLANDS 1945 (NWE) |
| CROCKER | BEF | 3RD ARMD BDE | LT GEN | GOC 6 ARMD DIV 1940-41 (HOME)<br>GOC 2 ARMD GP 1941 (HOME)<br>GOC IX CORPS 1942-43 (HOME/MED)<br>GOC I CORPS 1943-45 (HOME/NWE) |
| DAVIDSON | BEF | CRA I CORPS | MAJ GEN | DMI, WO 1940-44 (HOME)<br>MAJ GEN BRITISH ARMY STAFF WASHINGTON DC 1944-46 (USA) |
| DEMPSEY | BEF | 13 BDE | LT GEN | BGS 1 CAN DIV 1940-41 (HOME)<br>GOC 46 DIV 1941-42 (HOME)<br>GOC 42 ARMD DIV 1942 (HOME)<br>GOC XIII CORPS 1942-43 (MED)<br>GOC 2 ARMY 1943-45 (HOME/NWE) |
| GALE, H | BEF | DA&QMG III CORPS | LT GEN | MAJ GEN I/C ADMIN S CMD 1941 (HOME)<br>CHF ADMIN OFF HOME FORCES 1942 (HOME)<br>DEP CofS & HD ADMIN SHAEF 1943-45 (HOME/ NWE) |
| GAMMELL | NWEF | BGS NWEF | LT GEN | GOC 3 DIV 1940 (HOME)<br>A/GOC XII CORPS 1941 (HOME)<br>GOC E CMD 1942-44 (HOME)<br>CofS SACMED 1944-45 (MED) |

| NAME | BEF/ NWEF | COMMAND 1940 | HIGHEST RANK WW2 | POST 1940 SERVICE (THEATRE) |
|---|---|---|---|---|
| GARTLAN | BEF | 5 BDE | MAJ GEN | GOC DORSET COUNTRY DIV 1941 (HOME)<br>MAJ GEN STAFF N CMD 1941-44 (HOME)<br>RETD 1944 |
| GOLDNEY | BEF | DRASC III CORPS | MAJ GEN | DIR, S&T GHQ ME 1941-44 (ME)<br>RETD 1944 |
| GRANT | BEF | AQMG BEF | MAJ GEN | ADC TO KING, 1944 RETD 1944 |
| GRIFFIN | BEF | BASE CMDT | MAJ GEN | CDG 11 BDE 1943-44 (MED) |
| GUBBINS | NWEF | SCISSORFORCE | MAJ GEN | CDG AUXILIARY UNITS 1940-41 (HOME)<br>HD, SOE 1941-45 |
| HALSTEAD | BEF | DA&QMG I CORPS | MAJ GEN | MAJ EN I/C ADMIN S CMD 1941 (HOME)<br>VICE QMG 1945 (HOME) |
| HAWKESWORTH | BEF | 12 BDE | LT GEN | DMT, WO 1940-42 (HOME)<br>GOC 4 DIV 1942 (NA)<br>GOC 46 DIV 1943-44 (MED)<br>GOC X CORPS 1944 (MED)<br>GOC BRIT TPS GREECE 1945 (MED)<br>DIED 1945 |
| HOGG | NWEF | BASE AREA ANDALSNES (V CORPS PARTY) | MAJ GEN | MAJ GEN I/C ADMIN N CMD 1940-41 (HOME)<br>RETD 1942 |
| HORROCKS | BEF | 11 BDE (TEMP) | LT GEN | BGS E CMD 1941 (HOME)<br>GOC 44 DIV 1941 (HOME)<br>GOC 9 ARMD DIV 1942 (HOME)<br>GOC XIII CORPS 1942 (ME)<br>GOC X CORPS 1942-43 (ME)<br>GOC IX CORPS 1943 (ME)<br>GOC XXX CORPS 1944-45 (NWE) |
| HUDSON VC | | 2 BDE | MAJ GEN | GOC 46 DIV 1940-41 (HOME)<br>CDG 182 BDE (AS BRIG) 1941-43 (HOME)<br>ADC TO KING 1944-46 |
| IRWIN | BEF | 6 BDE (TO 20 MAY) | LT GEN | GOC 38 DIV 1940-42 (HOME)<br>GOC XI CORPS 1942 (HOME)<br>GOC EASTERN ARMY 1942-43 (INDIA)<br>UNEMPLOYED LIST 1943-44<br>GOC E SCOTLAND (MAJ GEN) 1944-45 |
| JARDINE | BEF | MIL SEC BEF | MAJ GEN | DEP FORTRESS CDR, GIBRALTAR 1942-43<br>DIR, ARMY WELFARE 1943-1945 |

| NAME | BEF/ NWEF | COMMAND 1940 | HIGHEST RANK WW2 | POST 1940 SERVICE (THEATRE) |
|---|---|---|---|---|
| KING | BEF | D/ENG IN C BEF | LT GEN | CHF ENG HOME FORCES 1940-41 (HOME)<br>ENG IN CHF, WO 1941-44 (HOME)<br>SPECIAL ENVOY, WELFARE SEAC 1944-46 |
| LAURIE Bt | BEF | 157 BDE | MAJ GEN | GOC 52 DIV 1940-41 (HOME)<br>DIR, COMB OPS TRG 1942-45 (HOME) |
| LAWSON | BEF | CRA 48 DIV & CDR Y FORCE | MAJ GEN | GOC YORKSHIRE COUNTY DIV. 1941-42 (HOME)<br>DPR (ARMY) 1942-45 (HOME) |
| LEE | BEF | BGS II CORPS | MAJ GEN | GHQ ME 1942-43 (AS BRIG) (ME)<br>DEP CDR BRIT MIL STAFF WASHINGTON 1944-47 (USA) |
| LEESE | BEF | DCGS HQ BEF | LT GEN | CDG 29 BDE 1940-42 (HOME)<br>GOC W SUSSEX COUNTY DIV 1942 (HOME)<br>GOC 15 DIV 1942 (HOME)<br>GOC GDS ARMD DIV 1942 (HOME)<br>GOC XXX CORPS 1943 (MED)<br>GOC LAND FORCES SEAC 1944-45 (FE) |
| MCCREERY | BEF | 2 ARMD BDE | LT GEN | GOC 8 ARMD DIV 1940-41 (HOME)<br>ARMD ADVISER GHQ ME 1941 (ME)<br>CofS TO SACME 1942-43 (ME)<br>GOC X CORPS 1943-44 (MED)<br>GOC 8 ARMY 1944-45 (MED) |
| MCMULLEN | BEF | DG TRANSPORT | MAJ GEN | DIR OF ARMY TRANSPORT, 1940-45 (HOME) |
| MILES | BEF | 126 BDE | MAJ GEN | BGS HOME FORCES 1940-41 (HOME)<br>GOC 42 DIV 1941 (HOME)<br>GOC 56 DIV 1941-43 (HOME/ ME)<br>GOC KENT DISTRICT 1943-44 (HOME)<br>GOC SE CMD 1944-46 (HOME) |
| MORGAN, H | NWEF | 148 BDE | MAJ GEN | GOC 45 DIV 1941-43 (HOME)<br>WO 1943-46 (HOME) |
| MORGAN, W | BEF | CDR SPT GP 51 HD | LT GEN | BGS 1 DIV 1940-41 (HOME)<br>GOC 55 DIV 1941 (HOME)<br>CGS 21 AG 1943 (HOME)<br>GOC S CMD 1944-45 (HOME)<br>CofS SACMED 1945 (MED) |

| NAME | BEF/ NWEF | COMMAND 1940 | HIGHEST RANK WW2 | POST 1940 SERVICE (THEATRE) |
|---|---|---|---|---|
| MORGAN, F | BEF | BGS II CORPS | LT GEN | GOC DEVON & CORNWALL DIV 1941 (HOME)<br>GOC 55 DIV 1941-42 (HOME)<br>GOC I CORPS 1942 (HOME)<br>COSSAC 1943 (HOME)<br>CofS SACEUR 1944-45 (NWE) |
| NORMAN | BEF | 1 LT ARMD RECCE BDE | MAJ GEN | GOC 8 ARMD DIV 1941-42 (HOME/ME)<br>GOC ALDERSHOT DIST 1944-45 (HOME) |
| PERCIVAL | BEF | BGS I CORPS | LT GEN | ASST CIGS 1940 (HOME)<br>GOC 44 DIV 1941 (HOME)<br>GOC MALAYA 1941-42 (FE)<br>POW 1942-45 (FE) |
| PHILLIPS | NWEF | 146 BDE | MAJ GEN | CDG BDE N IRELAND 1940-41 (HOME)<br>GOC GAMBIA & SIERRA LEONE 1942-44 (W AFRICA)<br>RETD 1944 |
| POPE | BEF | BGS II CORPS | MAJ GEN | CDG 3 ARMD BDE 1940 (HOME)<br>DIR, AFVs WO 1941 (HOME)<br>GOC XXX CORPS 1941 (ME)<br>KIA NORTH AFRICA 1941 |
| PRATT, D | BEF | 1 ARMY TK BDE | MAJ GEN | MAJ GEN AFVs BRIT MIL STAFF WASHINGTON 1942-43 (USA)<br>DEP DIR GEN BRIT MIL SUPPLY STAFF WASHINGTON 1943-45 (USA) |
| PRATT, F | BEF | CC MED ARTY I CORPS | MAJ GEN | CCRA, X CORPS 1940-41 (HOME)<br>BRIG, RA SE CMD 1941-42 (HOME)<br>CCRA V CORPS 1942-43 (MED)<br>BRIG RA 15 AG 1943-44 (MED)<br>MAJ GEN I/C TRG, RA 1944-45 (HOME)<br>ADC KING 1944-46 |
| RAMSDEN | BEF | 25 BDE | MAJ GEN | GOC 50 DIV 1940-42 (HOME/ ME)<br>GOC XXX CORPS 1942 (ME)<br>A/GOC 8 ARMY 1942 (ME)<br>GOC 3 DIV 1942-43 (HOME)<br>GOC SUDAN DEF FORCE 1944-45 (E AFRICA) |

| NAME | BEF/ NWEF | COMMAND 1940 | HIGHEST RANK WW2 | POST 1940 SERVICE (THEATRE) |
|---|---|---|---|---|
| RITCHIE | BEF | BGS II CORPS | LT GEN | GOC 51 DIV 1940-41 (HOME)<br>DCGS HQ ME 1941 (ME)<br>GOC 8 ARMY 1941-42 (ME)<br>GOC 52 DIV 1942-43 (HOME)<br>GOC XII CORPS 1943-45 (HOME/NWE) |
| ROBB | BEF | 9 BDE | MAJ GEN | CMDT, SEN OFFS SCH 1940-41<br>CDG 73 BDE 1941-43<br>GOC MALTA 1943-45 |
| SCHREIBER | BEF | CCRA II CORPS | LT GEN | GOC 61 DIV 1940 (HOME)<br>GOC 45 DIV 1940-41 (HOME)<br>GOC W CMD 1941-44 (HOME)<br>GOC SE CMD 1944 (HOME)<br>GOV & CinC MALTA 1944-45 (MED) |
| SLATER | BEF | 4TH AA BDE | MAJ GEN | BRIG RA 9 ARMY 1941-42 (IRAQ)<br>GOC 7 AA DIV 1942 (HOME)<br>GOC 4 AA GP 1942 (HOME) |
| SMYTH VC | BEF | 127 BDE | MAJ GEN | CDG 3 BDE 1940 (HOME)<br>GOC 17 DIV 1941-42 (FE)<br>RETD 1942 |
| STEELE | BEF | 132 BDE | LT GEN | GOC 59 DIV 1942 (HOME)<br>GOC II CORPS 1942 (HOME)<br>DCOS HQ ME 1942-43 (ME)<br>DCOS 18 AG 1943 (ME)<br>DIR, ARMY STAFF DUTIES 1943-45 (HOME) |
| STEWART | BEF | 152 BDE | MAJ GEN | ADC KING 1941-44 (HOME)<br>RETD 1944 |
| STOPFORD | BEF | 17 BDE | LT GEN | GOC 56 DIV 1941 (HOME)<br>CMDT, STAFF COLL 1942 (HOME)<br>GOC XII CORPS 1942-43 (HOME)<br>GOC XXIII CORPS 1943-45 (FE)<br>GOC 12 ARMY 1945 (FE) |
| SWAYNE | BEF | BGS BEF | LT GEN | DCGS HOME FORCES 1940-42 (HOME)<br>GOC 4 DIV 1942 (HOME)<br>CGS HOME FORCES 1942 (HOME)<br>GOC SE CMD 1942 (HOME)<br>CGS, INDIA 1944 (INDIA) |
| TILLY | BEF | 1 TANK BDE | MAJ GEN | GOC 2 ARMD DIV 1940-41 (HOME)<br>KIA JAN 41, NORTH AFRICA |

| NAME | BEF/ NWEF | COMMAND 1940 | HIGHEST RANK WW2 | POST 1940 SERVICE (THEATRE) |
|---|---|---|---|---|
| UTTERSON-KELSO | BEF | 131 BDE | MAJ GEN | GOC 47 DIV 1941-43 (HOME)<br>MAJ GEN, INF 1943 (HOME)<br>GOC 76 DIV 1944 (HOME)<br>GOC 47 DIV 1944 (HOME) |
| WATSON | BEF | BGS III CORPS | LT GEN | GOC 2 DIV 1940-41 (HOME)<br>DIR ARMY STAFF DUTIES 1941-42 (HOME)<br>ASST CIGS 1942 (HOME)<br>DEP ADJT-GEN 1942-44 (HOME)<br>GOC W CMD 1944-46 (HOME) |
| WEST | BEF | ASST MIL SEC | MAJ GEN | BGS HOME FORCES 1940-41 (HOME)<br>BGS UK DEL TO NZ FORCES 1941-42<br>MAJ GEN GEN STAFF HOME FORCES, ATT COSSAC 1943-44<br>MAJ GEN GEN STAFF ATT SHAEF 1944-45 |
| WHITAKER | BEF | 7 GDS BDE | MAJ GEN | BGS HOME FORCES 1940-42 (HOME)<br>COS, W CMD 1942 (HOME)<br>DMT 1942-45 (HOME) |
| WILSON | BEF | 3 BDE | MAJ GEN | BGS HOME FORCES 1940-42 (HOME)<br>CMDT SCH OF INF 1942-43 (HOME)<br>DIR, INF 1943-46 (HOME) |
| WOOLNER | BEF | 8 BDE | MAJ GEN | GOC SIERRA LEONE & GAMBIA 1941<br>GOC 82 DIV 1943-44 (FE)<br>CDG W MIDLANDS DIST 1944-45 (HOME) |
| WOOTTEN | NWEF | CHF ADMIN STAFF OFF | MAJ GEN | DEP QMG TO US FORCES IN UK 1942 (HOME)<br>CDG N MIDLANDS DIST 1944-46 |

**Table 4.9 Officers Taught by Brooke and Montgomery at Camberley, Quetta and The Imperial Defence College**

| NAME | AGE | FORCE | ROLE 1940 | STAFF COLL | IDC |
|---|---|---|---|---|---|
| BARRY | 50 | BEF | CRA 5 DIV | Y 1924 | |
| **IRWIN** | **47** | **BEF** | **6 BDE (TO 20 MAY)** | **Y 1924** | Y 1936 |
| **POPE** | **49** | **BEF** | **BGS II CORPS** | **Y 1924** | **Y 1934** |
| **WATSON** | **51** | **BEF** | **BGS III CORPS** | **Y 1924** | |
| **BOND** | **49** | **BEF** | **C/ENG CRE I CORPS** | **Y 1925** | **Y 1933** |
| **MORGAN** | **49** | **BEF** | **BGS 1 CORPS** | **Y 1925** | |
| **SWAYNE** | **49** | **BEF** | **BGS BEF** | **Y 1925** | **Y 1933** |
| MANSERGH | 47 | BEF | DA&QMG II CORPS | Y 1926 | |
| **CLARK** | **47** | **BEF** | **12 BDE** | **Y 1926** | |
| DUNCAN | 50 | BEF | CRA III CORPS | Y 1926 | |
| **GALE, H** | **49** | **BEF** | **DA&QMG III CORPS** | **Y 1926** | |
| GREENSLADE | 48 | BEF | DQMG DIR QTRG BEF | Y 1926 | |
| **HUDSON VC** | **48** | **BEF** | **2 BDE** | **Y 1926** | |
| **NORMAN** | **49** | **BEF** | **1 LT ARMD RECCE BDE** | **Y 1926** | |
| **WHITAKER** | **43** | **BEF** | **7 GDS BDE** | **Y 1926** | |
| **ANDERSON** | **48** | **BEF** | **11 BDE** | **Y 1927** | |
| **BARKER** | **45** | **BEF** | **10 BDE** | **Y 1927** | |
| **HAWKESWORTH** | **47** | **BEF** | **12 BDE** | **Y 1927** | |
| **LEESE** | **45** | **BEF** | **DCGS HQ BEF** | **Y 1927** | |
| **WEST** | **47** | **BEF** | **ASST MIL SEC** | **Y 1927** | Y 1936 |
| **WOOLNER** | **46** | **BEF** | **8 BDE** | **Y 1927** | |
| **MCCREERY** | **42** | **BEF** | **2 ARMD BDE** | **Y 1928** | |
| NICHOLSON | 41 | BEF | 30 BDE | Y 1929 | |
| **RITCHIE** | **42** | **BEF** | **BGS II CORPS** | **Y 1929** | |
| VALLENTIN | 44 | BEF | CRA 1 ARMD DIV | Y 1929 | |
| **DEMPSEY** | **43** | **BEF** | **13 BDE** | **Y 1930** | |
| FURLONG | 42 | BEF | 6 BDE (FROM 20 MAY) | Y 1930 | |
| **STEELE** | **45** | **BEF** | **132 BDE** | **Y 1930** | |

(Officers highlighted in bold are those who advanced in rank after 1940)

Twenty-nine officers from the 1940 group who were Staff College graduates attended during the periods when Brooke and Montgomery were members of the directing staff there. All were graduates from Camberley; none of the 1940 group attended Quetta during Montgomery's time as an instructor. Twenty-two of the combined group would advance to major general or above during the course of the war. Although being taught by either Montgomery or Brooke should not be overemphasised as a single factor, with 22 out of 29 reaching the rank of major general, this 75 percent 'success rate' would indicate that assertions elsewhere[104] that both senior officers 'talent spotted' during their respective tenures has some merit. Of the 22, Irwin, Watson, Morgan, Swayne, Gale, Anderson, Barker, Hawkesworth, Leese, McCreery, Ritchie and Dempsey would also progress further to lieutenant general during the war, 12 of 22, or 54 percent, of the advancing group, or 41 percent of the whole group. These 12 held senior administrative, corps, and army level commands before its end.

This factor alone did not in and of itself indicate a constant state of approval or continuously positive career management by their patrons, and Brooke in particular. For example, although Noel Irwin, a Staff College pupil in 1924, performed well in France after temporarily taking over a division and would end the war as a substantive lieutenant general, an unfortunate tendency to a short temper and being 'difficult'[105] with colleagues would cause Brooke much anguish. In 1941, as Corps Commander of XI Corps, Irwin almost instantly clashed severely with his immediate superior, Lieutenant General Laurence Carr, GOC Eastern Command, proclaiming no faith in his abilities, leaving Brooke minded to dismiss both officers. Yet Brooke wanted to find alternative employment for Irwin,[106] noting that Carr 'did not have the right qualities for this command.'[107] Carr would see out the war in a dead-end job as Senior Military Assistant to the Ministry of Supply whereas Irwin would be sent to command VI (Indian) Corps, and the Eastern Army in the Far East.[108] Brooke's faith and reprieve were not repaid; his handling of the Arakan Offensive of 1942–43 was a failure. HQ staff remarked on his 'egocentric and dictatorial temperament,'[109] a tendency to drive his personnel excessively hard and to apportion blame to others. Although it may have been motivated as much by a long-standing personal animus affected by a perceived personal and professional slight to one of Irwin's friends,[110] Irwin's attempt to sack 'Bill' Slim from command of his Corps was a step too far. He was recalled home and temporarily demoted. His fall from grace was compounded by bemoaning his fate on return, which left Brooke unwilling to use him further, and he remained unemployed for the remainder of the war.[111]

Nick Smart considers Brooke as 'using his powers of patronage to the full', and that he was 'more than selectively generous'.[112] He adds further, 'It is a reasonable generalisa-

104 For example, D. French 'An Extensive Use of Weedkiller' in D. French & B. Holden Reid, (Eds.), *The British General Staff – Reform & Innovation, 1890–1939* (London: Frank Cass, 2002), pp.132–45.
105 Mead, The Last Great Cavalryman…, p.221.
106 A. Danchev and D. Todman (eds), *War Diaries 1939–1945: Field Marshal Lord Alanbrooke* (London: Weidenfeld and Nicholson, 2001), p.148.
107 D. French, 'Colonel Blimp and the British Army: British Divisional Commanders in the War against Germany, 1939–1945' in *The English Historical Review*, Vol. 111 (444) (1996), p.1195.
108 VI Indian Corps.
109 L. Allen, *Burma: The Longest War 1941–45'* (London: Phoenix Publishing, 2000), p.94.
110 R. Mead, *Churchill's Lions – A Biographical Guide to the key British Generals of World War II* (Stroud: Spellmount, 2007), p.221.
111 Danchev and Todman, *War Diaries…*, p.510.
112 Smart, Biographical Dictionary…, p.44.

tion to say that those British Generals who, by 1945 could be said to have had a 'good war' tended to be those senior (and not so 'senior') officers who had served under Brooke in II Corps with the BEF.'[113] While this was not true of most of his subordinate major generals, except of course Montgomery, that all of his brigadiers, plus his Chief of Staff, Neil Ritchie, achieved promotion lends this assertion weight.

## Another Patron?

On the surface, the starred career of Sir John Dill before, during and after the First World War would suggest that encouragement and patronage from such an officer would be as potentially enhancing to a junior officer's prospects as that of Brooke or Montgomery proved to be. A veteran of the Boer War, Dill graduated from the Staff College in 1911 and by 1918 was a 38-year old brigadier general. His second connection to Camberley came as its Chief Instructor in 1919. He was on the original Directing Staff of the Imperial Defence College on its opening in 1927, and where Brooke was a student on the first course. He was Commandant at Camberley from 1931 to 1934. Furthermore, while renowned for his commitment and self-discipline towards his profession Dill also impressed contemporaries and subordinates, in the words of Major General Sir John Kennedy with his '...great courtesy, warmth of heart.... [and] obvious sincerity.'[114]

When Chief Instructor, Dill trained 'Becky' Beckwith-Smith, James Gammell, Colin Jardine and Eric Miles from those officers who progressed, as all graduated from Camberley in 1922.[115] As noted earlier in this study, no officers who progressed beyond brigadier graduated from Camberley after 1932, therefore limiting Dill's direct influence when Commandant. Brian Horrocks and James Steele, who were both to end the war as lieutenant generals, were students under Dill, even though Horrocks was only in his first year of attendance when Dill departed Camberley. None of the non-progressing officers were students at Camberley during his tenure as Commandant.

Although Dill replaced Ironside as CIGS in May 1940, despite being 'universally respected' and considered that he 'held the confidence of the army'[116] his cautionary advice to Churchill, and the latter's confrontational personal approach led to his counsel being discounted and labelled, pejoratively, as 'Dilly-Dally'.[117] By 1941, he had lost Churchill's confidence, but would serve invaluably as head of the British Military

113 Smart, Biographical Dictionary...
114 Quoted in Mead, *The Last Great Cavalryman...*, p.121 Kennedy served under Dill as his GSO2 when he was Director of Military Operations & Intelligence in 1934.
115 He would also have trained 12 officers who did not progress after 1940, among them Jack Churchill, Archibald Beauman, Henry Currey and Gerald Roupell VC.
116 Smart, *Biographical Dictionary...*, p.86; also A. Danchev, 'John Dill' in John Keegan (ed.) *Churchill's Generals* (London: Abacus, 1991) p.65.
117 Ibid. and A. Danchev, 'Sir John Greer Dill' in the DNB, www.oxforddnb.com accessed 27 February 2020

Mission to Washington DC until his untimely death in November 1944. Although three brigadiers from the 1940 group ultimately followed Dill to the United States, two arrived when he was already seriously ill, and the other, Douglas Pratt, had no obvious connections to Dill.[118] For all the esteem, indeed deep affection, with which he was held within the army, Dill cannot be considered as having generated a patronage network of any measure of influence.

## The 'Coat Tails Effect'

Although this study has focussed on brigade command, in this section the intention is to see whether the divisional commanders under whom brigadiers in fighting formations served had any effect on the careers of those who advanced after 1940. In certain divisions, all the brigadiers advanced; in others, none. In the following divisions, no officer who served as a brigadier advanced in rank during the course of the war; 12th,[119] 23rd,[120] 46th, and 48th. However, in others all of the brigadiers were promoted: 3rd, 4th, 5th and 1st Armoured. That the divisions lacking any progressing officers were Territorial Army based ones, and those with a perfect record were from the pre-war Regular Army indicates that service with the latter was also an advantage.

It might be expected, as the Division went into captivity after its capture at St Valery-en-Caux on 12 June 1940, that no brigadiers from the original 51st (Highland) Division would progress. However, Brigadier Herbert Stewart, commanding 152 Brigade, had been wounded and evacuated to the UK before the surrender. After spending two years as an Aide-de-Camp to the King (reverting to colonel) in 1941–43,[121] he would serve briefly (January 1943-July 1944) as the Commander, South-Western Area of Southern Command. As Major General Fortune spent the war in captivity, and Stewart did not graduate from Staff College, access to patronage networks as discussed here is limited.

In the 2nd Division, as Irwin was temporarily promoted to take over his division in France, he cannot therefore coat tail himself. He and Gerald Gartlan were both graduates of the Staff and Imperial Defence Colleges, being overlapping contemporaries at the

118 Frank Davidson, the former Director of Military Intelligence and Alec Lee, who had been BGS II Corps briefly in 1940

119 12th Division was disbanded on 11 July 1940 following its return from France and its units dispersed. Joslen, *Orders of Battle*, vol. 1, p.56

120 23rd Division was broken up on its return to the UK on 30 June 1940 and its units dispersed. Joslen, *Orders of Battle*, vol. 1, p.62

121 *HYAL*, January 1942 p.69; *Army List* February 1944, column 205c. Other officers who served as ADCs to the King were Gerald Blunt (1937–1938), Jack Churchill (1938–1943), Charles Findlay (1938–1939), Thomas Grainger-Stewart (1943–1952), Ian Grant (1944), Fendall Pratt (1944–1946), Douglas Pratt (1944–1946), James Steele (1951), Frank Witts (1938–1941, the date of his death) and Richard Wootten (1938). Of these 11, none would advance to major general, eliminating it as a factor in patronage or promotion.

former (graduating in 1924 and 1925) but not the latter (graduates of the 1937 and 1936 courses respectively) but they did not serve together during the rest of the war.

It is noteworthy that all eight[122] of the brigadiers serving in Brooke's II Corps (3rd, 4th and 5th Divisions) progressed to major general or above after 1940. However, serving under Montgomery while he commanded the senior division in the Corps in the BEF did not lend any particular advantage to his subordinate brigadiers. 'Jack' Whitaker (7 Guards Brigade), despite being a Baronet, an Eton-educated Guardsman, younger than the average (43 in 1940) and taught by Brooke (he graduated from Camberley in 1926) spent the rest of the war in the United Kingdom[123] in staff positions. This included as the Director of Military Training from 1942–1945. However, his recurring connection to Brooke came from their mutual enthusiasm for ornithology.[124]

'Kit' Woolner of 8 Brigade graduated from Staff College in 1927 and would have been present when Brooke was on the directing staff. He made little impression on either his divisional or Corps commanders in France and thereafter, despite having been a highly decorated sapper in the First World War and both an instructor at Woolwich in the 1920s and Deputy Commandant of the School of Military Engineering in 1939.[125] Most of the rest of his war was spent in West Africa, as a district and divisional commander.

William Robb, of 9 Brigade, who on his return from France spent nine months as Commandant of the Senior Officers' School at Sheerness, then commanded the defences of South Wales for two years as a temporary major general before being reconnected with his senior commander in France, Lord Gort, as commander of the Malta Garrison from 1943–1945 when the latter served as Governor. He was not a Staff College graduate and did not attract much attention from Brooke or Montgomery.

Although Major General Dudley Johnson, GOC 4th Division, was a highly decorated veteran of the First World War[126] and had held a brigade command in India between the wars, he was quickly replaced and side-lined after the fall of France.[127] He was briefly commander at Aldershot and the last Inspector of Infantry before the post was abolished and redesignated as Director of Infantry in 1944. His influence on the progress of his brigadiers was therefore limited. However, his three subordinates, Evelyn Barker (10 Brigade), Kenneth Anderson (11 Brigade) and John Hawkesworth (12 Brigade) would all progress to the rank of lieutenant general during the course of

122 The 5th Division, originally commanded by Major General H. E. Franklyn, had only two infantry brigades during the Battle of France, whereas 3rd and 4th Divisions had the standard three. Joslen, *Orders of Battle,* vol. 1, pp.43, 45 & 47.

123 Except for a fact finding mission to the Far East in the summer of 1945; A. Danchev and D. Todman (eds), *War Diaries 1939–1945: Field Marshal Lord Alanbrooke* (London: Weidenfeld and Nicholson, 2001), p.719.

124 Danchev & Todman, *War Diaries…*, p.683.

125 *HYAL* January 1940, p.114.

126 He held the Victoria Cross, two DSOs and a Military Cross.

127 Brooke had wished to replace him, fearful that his health would not withstand combat operations, but the German assault came before he could do so. French in French & Holden Reid, (Eds.), *The British General Staff…*, p.145.

the war. All were direct Staff College contemporaries taught by Montgomery. Anderson and Hawkesworth would serve in North Africa and the Middle East, but Anderson, commanding First Army in Tunisia, was not favoured by Montgomery, who considered him over promoted, unsuitable for Army command and 'a divisional commander at best'.[128] Although such criticism was typical of Montgomery, being pointed, direct and more than unfair, it influenced Brooke. He removed Anderson from command of Second Army, to which he had been appointed on return from Tunisia, in favour of Dempsey. This was a choice more palatable to Montgomery, even though his own preference had been to bring Oliver Leese back from the Mediterranean, where he had been commanding XXX Corps.

Barker spent most of the period from 1940–1944 in the UK training troops, but was picked by Montgomery for Operation Overlord, to command 49th Division. Hawkesworth was described as 'a master of infantry tactics' in Tunisia and Italy,[129] but remained in the Mediterranean for the remainder of the war.[130] Barker performed solidly enough to replace O'Connor as commander of VIII Corps in North-West Europe from among a more experienced field and established a reputation as a popular commander with a keen eye for physical fitness in his men.

The brigadiers of 5th Division, initially commanded by Harold Franklyn, were Miles Dempsey and 'Monty' Stopford. Neither was taught by Montgomery or Brooke (graduating from Camberley in 1930 and 1924 respectively, before Brooke's arrival). As Franklyn, despite a creditable performance in France, especially during the Arras counter-attack on 21 May, was restricted to home commands on grounds of his age, his influence over previous subordinates was, again, of limited value to them. Dempsey, however, was marked out by Montgomery for command and he 'demanded' him for XIII Corps in Eighth Army.[131] As noted above, while Dempsey was not Montgomery's first pick to command British Second Army, he was a candidate acceptable to both Brooke and Montgomery, even if, by the end of the war the former felt Dempsey to have 'a swollen head'.[132]

His fellow brigade commander, Stopford, handled his brigade well in France, particularly on the Ypres-Comines Canal Line. On his return to England, he served as GOC 56th Division. This was a formation which proved a launchpad to high command as Douglas Graham, Gerald Templer and Lewis Lyne also commanded it between 1941–1943.[133] Stopford also survived Montgomery's ruthless weeding of XII Corps in 1940–1941 and may have impressed him; in early 1941 he was appointed Commandant of the

128 Montgomery to Alexander, quoted in Mead, *Churchill's Lions…*, p.51.
129 G. Blaxland, *Alexander's Generals* (London, William Kimber, 1979), p.228.
130 Recalled home on grounds of ill-health, he died of a heart attack on the troopship home at Gibraltar in May 1945. Smart, *Biographical Dictionary…*, p.145.
131 A. Danchev and D. Todman (eds), *War Diaries 1939–1945: Field Marshal Lord Alanbrooke* (London: Weidenfeld and Nicholson, 2001), p.323.
132 Danchev and Todman, *War Diaries…*, p.702.
133 Joslen, *Orders of Battle*, vol. 1, p.37.

Staff College, charged with consolidating the lessons learned from operations into the truncated wartime course. After a brief return to the desert, from 1943 Stopford saw out the war in the Far East, effectively and successfully fighting the Japanese.

The only brigadier from Giffard Martel's 50th Division to progress was William Ramsden. Despite divisional (50th) and corps command (XXX) in the Western Desert, he was an infantryman and had little further connection to his former commander, a pioneer in armoured warfare. Martel spent much of the war thereafter as Director, Royal Armoured Corps and later as the Head of the Military Mission to the Soviet Union. Martel and Ramsden did not cross paths directly again. Ramsden, who did not attend Staff College, fell foul of Montgomery in the autumn of 1942 on the latter's assumption of command of Eighth Army, and was described as 'a dull .... pedestrian infantryman .... who inspired none of us.'[134] Rapidly posted to command of the Sudan area, he saw out the war there.

Although there were plans for a III Corps to be formed in France, under the command of Sir Ronald Adam (later the Adjutant General and a close comrade and confidant of Brooke), the offensive in the West shifted its role towards the maintenance of the defensive perimeter around Dunkirk and the safe gathering in of retreating units and troops. Purely on paper, the senior divisional commander within the corps, William Holmes (42nd Division), looks to be a future prospect for supporting the advancement of his subordinates from France. He was the youngest divisional commander in France at 48; he was first to be promoted lieutenant general on his return and was given a corps command. However, poor performance in the Western Desert under Ritchie and Auchinleck during the retreat to Egypt in the spring of 1942 led to his removal and side-lining.

Two of Adam's brigadiers advanced after 1940; Eric Miles of 126 Brigade and 'Jackie' Smyth of 127 Brigade. Miles, a graduate of Camberley in 1922 and the IDC in 1934, being taught there by Brooke, later succeeded to command of 42nd Division and thence to 56th Division, commanding both in the Middle East and Tunisia. Being wounded in the later stages of the Tunisian campaign led to his evacuation home. Smyth, despite having been an instructor at Camberley from 1931–1934 and a VC, was from an Indian Army background and was returned to India in 1941 to a divisional command. However, ill-health – which he sought to conceal – during the retreat in Burma in February 1942 led to a poor command decision at the Sittang Bridge [135] which destroyed his command and hastened the Japanese advance on Rangoon. He was hospitalised and medically retired in late 1942.

Edward 'Sigs' Osborne of 44th Division had made a bad impression on Brooke in France as he had 'grown very fat'.[136] However, he was promoted to corps command in

134 R. M. P. Carver, *Out of Step: Memoirs of a Field Marshal* (London, Hutchison 1989) p.70.
135 Smyth ordered the bridge demolished prematurely which trapped the majority of his Division on the wrong side of the river. Although Sir William Slim took a sympathetic view of the decision in *Defeat Into Victory* (London, Cassell, 1956), p.17, stating that it was easy to criticise the decision but hard to make it, he stopped short of endorsing Smyth's actions.
136 A. Danchev and D. Todman (eds), *War Diaries 1939–1945: Field Marshal Lord Alanbrooke* (London: Weidenfeld and Nicholson, 2001), p.58.

the UK, spending 1940–1941 on anti-invasion planning and training. While there, Osborne had a severe personality clash with Charles Hudson VC, commanding one of his divisions, leading to the latter's dismissal and demotion. Brooke's occasional visits to Osborne's area (including a visit to 46th Division, by then commanded by Miles Dempsey, but showing in Brooke's words 'positive hallmarks' of Kenneth Anderson, his predecessor)[137] left him determined to remove Osborne, among others, in, as he wrote in his diary after the event 'a pretty drastic clearing which ought to make way for younger material' in November 1941.[138] Osborne, who was 56, retired at the same time.

Two of Osborne's 1940 brigadiers advanced. 'Jack' Utterson-Kelso (131 Brigade), despite his being a highly decorated (two DSOs, two MCs, five MiDs and five wounds) First World War veteran, was not a Staff College graduate. Notwithstanding a key role in advancing modern training by being the first divisional commander to incorporate a Battle School in 1941, he did not advance past major general. This was despite sufficiently impressing Bernard Paget when he was GOC Home Forces to have him appointed 'Major General, Infantry' and to establish the GHQ Battle School. Thereafter he only commanded training divisions at home. James 'Daddy' Steele (132 Brigade) was an Ulsterman who had added a DSO for Dunkirk to his First World War MC. Having spent much of the interwar period in staff appointments, after France he served in senior staff appointments in the Middle East, before becoming Director of Staff Duties at the War Office from 1943–1945. For such a capable staff officer (he would become Adjutant General in 1947 and retired as a full general), he barely features in either Montgomery's or Brooke's diaries and memoirs and does not appear to have benefitted from patronage.

Major General Roger Evans' ill-starred command of the 1st Armoured Division in France led to his rapid removal before the end of 1940. He took the move with bad grace; this further reduced his currency in Brooke's estimation, who had formed a poor opinion of him as 'depressing' and 'not cutting much ice …. no-one listens to him…' as early as January 1940.[139] He was quickly side-lined to command of Aldershot, which was a regular resort for those Brooke wished to remove, and retirement. Hence, his standing as a patron would not be of much value.

Nonetheless, all Evans' brigadiers advanced to senior, significant command, lieutenant general's rank and eminence. 'Dick' McCreery of 2 Armoured Brigade was a pupil of Montgomery at Camberley in 1928–1929, but his career after France would be guided more by impressing both Brooke, through his being a cavalryman who embraced mechanisation and, above all, Alexander. Brooke's diaries make frequent favourable comment on him during the Middle East campaign, especially in the difficult period in late 1942 after Auchinleck's dismissal. Montgomery, however, was less supportive, considering McCreery 'out of touch …. with the practical side of battle.'[140] John Crocker

137 Danchev and Todman, *War Diaries…*, p.167.
138 Danchev and Todman, *War Diaries…*, p.197.
139 Danchev and Todman, *War Diaries…*, p.101.
140 Montgomery to Alanbrooke, Alanbrooke Papers 6/2/22, Liddle Hart Centre for Military Archives.

of 3 Armoured Brigade graduated from Quetta before Montgomery's arrival there, but despite a torrid experience in France, he had come to the attention of both Brooke and Alexander and continued to impress them in the Middle East. Despite a reputation for taciturnity and occasional temper, his ability impressed the critical triumvirate of Brooke, Montgomery and Alexander.

Frederick Morgan (1 Armoured Support Group) had not encountered Montgomery or Brooke prior to the war, having served in staff appointments in India. In France, the cheeseparing of his innovative formation, a mix of artillery, infantry, engineers and other support arms to make up deficiencies elsewhere made it impossible for him to function in a coherent command. This was a trend – commanding under-resourced formations – which followed him until his appointment in 1943 as head of the Chief of Staff Supreme Allied Commander (COSSAC) organisation, in charge of planning the Allied invasion of France. However, the antipathy towards the organisation coming from both Brooke and Montgomery placed Morgan in an unenviable position, in a post Brooke considered no real job and that others, Montgomery pre-eminent among them, felt too inclined towards the Americans. Montgomery spared no effort to discredit Morgan to colleagues. Brooke's diary entries, although are few on the matter, are universally dismissive of Morgan and his difficulties. Under these conditions, patronage from these seniors can be considered nonexistent.

James Drew, GOC 52nd Lowland Division, was one of the oldest divisional commanders in France at 57 (even though his command's stay in France was short and piecemeal, covering the withdrawal of the '2nd BEF' from Cherbourg in June 1940). It was unsurprising that he was removed quickly from divisional command and thereafter was Director of Training for Combined Operations from 1941 to 1944. As a member of the first post-war Staff College course in 1919, he did not interact directly with Brooke or Montgomery and did not initially particularly impress the former with his training methods at Combined Operations, who thought them 'too stereotypical'.[141] The only brigadier from Drew's division to advance was Sir John Laurie Bt (157 Brigade), whose only remarkable contribution to the war effort was to leapfrog his former commander and become Commandant of the Combined Operations Training Centre in 1941. Neither could be described as benefitting from patronage from a senior officer.

141 Danchev and Todman, *War Diaries*,

**Table 4.10 'The Coat Tails Effect' Divisional Commanders in France and Advancing Brigadiers**

| | |
|---|---|
| I CORPS | Lieutenant-General M. G. H. Barker |
| **2nd Division** | Major-General H. C. Loyd (to 16th May) |
| | **Brigadier F. H. N. Davidson** (16-20 May) |
| | Major-General N. M. S. Irwin (from 20th May) |
| 4th Brigade | Brigadier E. G. Warren |
| 5th Brigade | **Brigadier G. I. Gartlan** |
| 6th Brigade | **Brigadier N. M. S. Irwin** (to 20th May) |
| | Brigadier D. W. Furlong (from 20th May) |
| **48th Division** | Major-General A. F. A. N. Thorne |
| 143rd Brigade | Brigadier J. Muirhead |
| 144th Brigade | Brigadier J. M. Hamilton |
| 145th Brigade | Brigadier A. C. Hughes (to 15th May) |
| | Brigadier The Hon. N. F. Somerset (from 15 May) |
| II CORPS | Lieutenant-General A. F. Brooke |
| **3rd Division** | Major-General B. L. Montgomery |
| 7th Guards Brigade | **Brigadier J. A. C. Whitaker** |
| 8th Brigade | **Brigadier C. G. Woolner** |
| 9th Brigade | **Brigadier W. Robb** |
| **4th Division** | Major-General D. G. Johnson |
| 10th Brigade | **Brigadier E. H. Barker** |
| 11th Brigade | **Brigadier K. A. N. Anderson** |
| 12th Brigade | **Brigadier J. L. I. Hawkesworth** |
| **5th Division** | Major-General H. E. Franklyn |
| 13th Brigade | **Brigadier M. C. Dempsey** |
| 17th Brigade | **Brigadier M. G. N. Stopford** |
| **50th Division** | Major-General G. le Q. Martel |
| 150th Brigade | Brigadier C. W. Haydon |
| 151st Brigade | Brigadier J. A. Churchill |
| 25th Brigade | **Brigadier W. H. C. Ramsden** |
| III CORPS | Lieutenant-General Sir R. F. Adam, Bt. |
| **42nd Division** | Major-General W. G. Holmes |
| 125th Brigade | Brigadier G. W. Sutton |
| 126th Brigade | **Brigadier E. G. Miles** |
| 127th Brigade | **Brigadier J. G. Smyth** |
| **44th Division** | Major-General E. A. Osborne |
| 131st Brigade | **Brigadier J. E. Utterson-Kelso** |
| 132nd Brigade | **Brigadier J. S. Steele** |
| 133rd Brigade | Brigadier N. I. Whitty |
| **12th Division** | Major-General R. L. Petre |
| 35th Brigade | Lieutenant-Colonel A. F. F. Young (10th–12 May) |
| | Brigadier V. L. de Cordova (from 13th May) |

| | |
|---|---|
| 36th Brigade | Brigadier G. R. P. Roupell |
| 37th Brigade | Brigadier R. J. P. Wyatt |
| **23rd Division** | Major-General A. E. Herbert |
| 69th Brigade | Brigadier The Viscount Downe |
| 70th Brigade | Brigadier P. Kirkup |
| **46th Division** | Major-General H. O. Curtis |
| 137th Brigade | Brigadier J. B. Gawthorpe |
| 138th Brigade | Brigadier E. J. Ginling |
| 139th Brigade | Brigadier H. A. F. Crewdson (to 22nd May) |
| | Brigadier R. C. Chichester-Constable (from 22 May) |
| **51st Division** | Major-General V. M. Fortune |
| 152nd Brigade | **Brigadier H. M. V. Stewart** |
| 153rd Brigade | Brigadier G. T. Burney |
| 154th Brigade | Brigadier A. C. L. Stanley-Clarke |
| **1st Armoured Division** | Major-General R. Evans |
| 2nd Armoured Brigade | **Brigadier R. L. McCreery** |
| 3rd Armoured Brigade | **Brigadier J. H. Crocker** |
| 1st Support Group | **Brigadier F. E. Morgan** |
| **52nd Division** | Major-General J. S. Drew |
| 155th Brigade | Brigadier T. Grainger-Stewart |
| 156th Brigade | Brigadier J. S. N. Fitzgerald |
| 157th Brigade | **Brigadier Sir J. E. Laurie, Bt.** |

(Names highlighted in bold are those officers who advanced in the course of the war)

## Conclusions

Of the original group of 156 officers who were serving as brigadiers in 1940, 58 of them were promoted to the rank of major general or above, over a third of the group. While a minority of the whole, this is still a considerable proportion when not all officers could expect to advance to such a rank. This also disproves any contention that service in France or Norway at this level of command, or responsibility in the case of staff appointments, was definitively detrimental to the promotion prospects of these officers. Twenty-one officers would be further promoted to lieutenant general, over a third of the group of officers promoted, and while this represents less than one in seven of the whole France and Norway group, it further reinforces the idea that service in France or Norway was not automatically career limiting.

The dominance of the public schools in producing army officers was sustained among this group, with 54 of the 58 being products of the public schools. When the number of schools producing more than one officer who was advanced to major general is taken further into account, a smaller group of certain public schools retains its dominance in the production of successful officers, with the seven 'great' schools of the Clarendon Group generating 48 percent of the list, although some other schools with traditionally strong army connections, such as Lancing, had 100 percent success (even if it only produced two generals).

Although direct contemporaneousness at school among the 58 was limited at only six, the number of connections broadens significantly when close – arriving within a year – or near – arriving within two years – attendance at schools is considered, involving 14 of the 18 schools in the group which produced general officers from brigadiers in this 1940 group. Only four schools had no contemporary pupil networks.

Although the infantry dominates in the group, with 31 of the 58 officers being from county or line regiments at first commissioning, no particular single regiment predominates in the list of officers successful in gaining promotion. Although all three Guards officers from the 1940 group reaching major general were from the Coldstream Guards, on balance this is more likely to be coincidence than design. If there is a 'regimental group', it could be argued that this was from the Royal Tank Corps/Regiment, as four officers who progressed would transfer to it from their original regiments or corps in the interwar period.

Regarding previous war or active service, the majority of the 58 were veterans of the Western Front, with only four officers spending all of the First World War away from this theatre. This indicates the significance of the Western Front, as the primary theatre, as a route of experience towards promotion for officers in the post-war period. Some secondary theatres produced groupings of officers with common experience, such as Gallipoli and Egypt, where five officers' service overlapped in various periods from 1915–1917, creating a group with common experience and knowledge. However, the largest single group was of those officers who served in India on operations between 1919–1937, with 12. This demonstrates the predominance of India as the main interwar theatre in which to gain operational experience in the group. Other areas, such as Iraq or Persia, did not generate connected networks of officers.

Attendance at Staff College, either at Camberley or Quetta, retained its significance as a route both to promotion and as a generator of networks between officers. 40 of the 58 – over two-thirds – were graduates of Staff College. Camberley, with 36, was dominant. With no officers from the group graduating before 1922 or after 1932, the core years for developing groups of contemporaries were from 1924 to 1928, when 25 of the group passed through Camberley and generated overlapping contemporary networks. Quetta was less significant in generating networks due to the low number of graduates from it (four) and the space between attendance. All nine of the officers in the whole 1940 group who attended the Imperial Defence College between 1933–1939 were promoted to major general or above; six of them were contemporaries at the College with two each in 1933–1935, producing further close networks.

The possession of an award for gallantry or distinguished service, be it in the First World War, interwar campaigns or indeed for service in 1940, does appear to have had some impact on whether an officer was advanced between the wars or after 1940. Over three-quarters of the officers in the 1940 group had one or more decorations prior to 1939; 73 officers in the overall group received distinctions and/or decorations for service in France or Norway, receiving a total of 82 awards (when multiple awards to individuals are accounted for). Although the group of officers who did not progress gained more awards (44 to 38), the officers promoted generally received higher awards; seven out of eight officers who received the Companion of the Order of the Bath for 1940 would be promoted; 6 of the 10 first awards of the Distinguished Service Order, an award for gallantry or leadership were to officers who were promoted.

Networks among the advancing group can therefore be found based on certain schools, successful, overlapping attendance at Staff College and the Imperial Defence College, and commonality of operational service away from the Western Front and in India. Receipt of decorations or distinctions, while not a 'network' can also be argued to have been a promotion enhancing factor in comparison with those who did not receive them or received recognition of lower grade (such as a MiD alone).

Existence of patronage networks among those promoted is present, but not completely obvious. The single most significant figure is Brooke, as on paper all the brigadiers in his corps progressed to major general or above after 1940, even if few of the divisional commanders in II Corps (with the signal exception of Montgomery) advanced themselves or were put aside into less significant commands. Being taught by Brooke or Montgomery, and more particularly the former, was an influence in a number of cases, but not to the extent that it was a critically decisive factor in an officer's promotion. Also, Brooke's favour was not permanent; results mattered and his support, however intangible, could soon disappear,

# 5

# British Brigadiers in the Battle of Normandy

> When pressure mounts and strain increases everyone begins to show the weaknesses in his makeup. It is up to the Commander to conceal his: above all to conceal doubt, fear, and distrust.
>
> General Dwight D. Eisenhower, Supreme Allied Commander,
> (letter to his wife. 30 December 1942)
> Quoted in Ambrose *Letters to Mamie*[1]

By the spring of 1944, with the invasion of the European Continent imminent, the British Army had been at war for four and a half years. Having recently defeated the Axis powers in the Middle East, and despite ongoing operations in the Mediterranean, there was a larger pool of officers with recent combat experience from which to draw for senior command postings than existed in 1939–1940. This chapter applies the methodology employed with the brigadiers of 1940 to brigadiers who were serving on D-Day, 6 June 1944, and in the initial stages of the Battle of Normandy in June and July. The aim is to make comparisons between the careers of this latter group serving in British Second Army in 1944 and those in the primary group, the 1940 British Expeditionary Force and North-West Expeditionary Force.

From this point, the intention is to determine any changes in the patterns of recruitment, education, promotion and service between officers serving in the initial period of the Second World War and the beginning of the campaign in North-West Europe. This will compare whether the army of 1944 showed patterns of networking comparable to or different from those of 1940 and to highlight any changes in between those dates, whether or not they may have come into effect due to the experience of war.

This chapter seeks to examine and test a number of assumptions, assembled by this author which arose from the examination of the earlier group, for purposes of comparison. First, that the average age of the Normandy group would be lower, and therefore

1 J. Eisenhower (ed.) *Letters to Mamie* (New York, Doubleday, 1978) quoted in S. Ambrose, *Eisenhower: Soldier and President* (New York, Simon & Schuster, revised edition 1992), p.88.

they would be younger, than its 1940 counterpart. Second, that previous battle experience between 1939 and 1944 would have contributed to accelerated promotion at an earlier age and whether possession of gallantry decorations and other honours also contributed to this process of appointment. Third, that a Staff College qualification was still a prerequisite, or advantageous, in advancement to brigade command. Fourth, that schools attended, regiments served in, and previous active service created networks as with, and in comparison to, the 1940 group and whether conditions existing in 1939–1940, such as no officer who were Territorials at the outbreak of war holding a field command at this level, were still applicable.

Due to the size of British Second Army in June 1944 the restriction of officers to those holding fighting commands, namely infantry, armoured, commando and airborne brigades and independent brigade groups; brigadiers in staff positions, such as BGS' at divisional level and above or specialists in role. Brigadiers, Royal Artillery (BRA) and medical officers (among others) have been omitted in this case for reasons of space; a full examination of all the officers holding field commands and staff appointments at brigadier level merits a separate study of its own. The selection is restricted, to the divisions of British Second Army and officers who replaced brigadiers in France by the end of June 1944. There are 45 officers in the group.[2]

In 1939–1940, to recapitulate, officers serving in a brigadier's appointment were predominantly pre-war, Regular Army officers with First World War service.[3] Of the 32 brigadiers serving in non-combat staff roles at GHQ BEF in 1940, nine were officers aged 55 or older (two of them were aged over 60)[4] recalled from retirement to fill skill gaps in specialist roles. In some fighting brigades, Regular Army officers replaced Territorial Army officers commanding Territorial Army brigade equivalents due, in a few proven specific cases, to a prejudice against the latter by the former when in command of Territorial Army divisions. (No Territorial Army divisions in France or Norway in 1940 were commanded by officers whose careers had been in the Territorial Army and all divisional commanders were Regular Army officers).

By 1944, 25 of the brigadiers, had not seen active service in the First World War, almost entirely for having been too young to see active service in that war.[5] Additionally,

2 The brigadier commanding 4 (Special Service) Brigade, Brigadier Bernard 'Jumbo' Leicester, had originally been commissioned into the Royal Marines and his brigade was made up of Royal Marine Commando units. Due to the Royal Marines being under the control of the Royal Navy, he is not considered further in this chapter.

3 Of the 154 officers in the 1940 group, 122 of them (79.2 percent) had received at least one decoration for gallantry or distinguished service between 1914 and 1919; two brigadiers in 1940 were too young to have served in the First World War (q.v. Downe and Young) and one, though old enough in 1918, did not serve overseas (Nicholson) making lack of First World War service an exception.

4 Brigadier Gervase Thorpe, Base Commandant Cherbourg, was 63 in May 1940 and Brigadier the Honourable Hubert Clementi-Smith, the Signal Officer in Chief, was 61.

5 Eight of the group, born in 1899–1900, would have been old enough to serve overseas, but did not; Gwatkin, the first of the Normandy group to serve, was commissioned into the

three officers in the Normandy group came from a pre-war Territorial Army background and had not served in the Regular Army.[6] Two of these officers had commanded Territorial battalions and other formations, usually brigades, in North Africa, Tunisia and Italy. This suggests that the prejudice towards Territorial officers holding operational command above battalion level had, in part. been overcome by mid-1944. By this point in time, with more opportunities for active service, and the expansion of the army providing a greater supply of new officers to fill junior posts, brigadiers in general had more experience both of battle and of command of troops either in training, on active service or both.

Although as originally constituted 21st Army Group was made up of subordinate units which had seen little or no active service since 1940, Montgomery was fully aware that he needed to leaven the untried with the experienced and pressed the higher command both for the recall of battle-hardened divisions from the Mediterranean (50th, 51st Highland and 7th Armoured) and appointment of his preferred officers in key roles. For example, he wanted Oliver Leese and Miles Dempsey to command Second British and First Canadian Armies respectively, regardless of any previous selections and Allied sensitivities.[7] (Both Leese and Dempsey had served as brigadiers in the BEF).[8] He 'lost little time'[9] in replacing those individual officers he deemed either too inexperienced or experienced but in his view incompetent, even as far down as brigade majors, with veterans of the desert and Mediterranean. His choices were not universally accepted, especially by Brooke as CIGS and not all of them would prove successful in post (which, in fairness, Montgomery would later concede in part, especially over the appointments of Bucknall to XXX Corps and retaining Erskine at 7th Armoured).[10]

Not all brigade commanders landing in France had combat experience prior to the Second World War. As noted above, over half had not served in the First World War and for most, their interwar active service, if at all, was predominantly on Imperial policing duties. The latter included operations on the North-West Frontier of India or pacifying risings in the Near and Middle East. Although service overseas away from the regiment in the interwar period provided opportunities to broaden experience, it does not appear to have been of a particular advantage for progression. Eight officers served

Coldstream Guards in December 1918.

6 Colin Barber, commanding officer 46 Brigade in 15th Division, who later transferred to the Regular Army; James Oliver, commanding officer 154 Brigade in 51st Division and 'Ronnie' Senior, commanding officer 151 Brigade in 50th Division.

7 See D. French, 'Invading Europe: The British Army and its preparations for the Normandy Campaign, 1942–44' in E. Goldstein and B. J. C. McKercher, B. J. C., *Power and Stability: British Foreign Policy 1865–1965* (London: Cassell, 2003), pp.271–94.

8 Leese had originally gone to France to take up the post of BGS III Corps under Adam but served at GHQ BEF when that Corps was diverted to establish and sustain the Dunkirk perimeter. Dempsey commanded 13 Brigade in Franklyn's 5th Division. Joslen, *Orders of Battle*, vol. 1, p.251.

9 French, 'Invading Europe….' in Goldstein and McKercher, p.287.

10 French, 'Invading Europe…' in Goldstein and McKercher, p.288.

on campaign in India at various points in the 1920s and 1930s; four served in staff positions there, three of whom did not see any fighting.[11] Three officers served on attachment in Africa, but also saw no action. Three officers in the group served during the Arab Revolt in Palestine, 1936 to 1939.[12] It cannot be asserted that active service overseas from 1919–1939 was therefore a major contributor to advancement by 1944.

The tables below indicate, first, the initial assault divisions and their subordinate brigades and second, those formations which followed up to the end of June 1944. These tables show the arrival dates of the units, the ages of their commanders and whether individuals were public school educated and/or graduates of the Staff College, and the percentage of officers in the latter two categories in the divisions on landing.

**Table 5.1 Normandy: Divisions and Brigades Landing On D-Day**

| UNITS | CDR | ARRIVAL | AGE D-DAY | PUBLIC SCHOOL | p.s.c.[13] |
|---|---|---|---|---|---|
| 3rd Division | | | | 75% | 50% |
| Maj Gen | T.G. Rennie | | 44 | Y | Y |
| 8 Bde | E.E. Cass | 6 June | 46 | Y | N |
| 9 Bde | J.C. Cunningham | 6 June | 50 | Y | N |
| 185 Bde | E.P. Smith | 6 June | 45 | unk | Y |
| 50th (Northumbrian) Division | | 6 June | | 100% | 50% |
| Maj Gen | D.A.H Graham | | 51 | Y | Y |
| 69 Bde | F.Y.C. Knox | 6 June | 45 | Y | Y |
| 151 Bde | R.H. Senior | 6 June | 39 | Y | N |
| 231 Bde | A.G.B. Stanier Bt. | 6 June | 45 | Y | N |
| 7th Armoured Division | | | | 66% | 66% |
| Maj Gen | G. Erskine | 6 June | 44 | Y | Y |
| 22 Armd | W.R.N. Hinde | 7 June | 43 | Y | N |
| 131 Bde | M.S. Ekins | 8 June | 45 | N | Y |

11 Cass, commander of 8 Brigade, 3rd Division was Chief Instructor at the Small Arms School (India) from 1935–1939; Ekins, commander 131 (Infantry) Brigade, 7th Armoured Division, served at GHQ India 1936–1938 and as a brigade major in the Indian Army, 1938–1939; Mole commander 129 Brigade, 43rd Division served briefly with the Royal West African Frontier Force before spending 1923–1933 in staff appointments in India. Stanley Jones, commander 158 Brigade in 53rd Division, spent most of the 1920s in India, but saw active service twice before 1925.

12 Elrington, commander 177 Brigade of 59th Division; Johnson, commander 32 Guards Brigade of Guards Armoured and Mackintosh-Walker, commander 227 Brigade of 15th Division. Elrington received a DSO for his service in Palestine, a rare distinction (*London Gazette*, 22 December 1939), p.8529.

13 In both tables, Officers attaining the p.s.c. qualification from Camberley or Quetta prior to 1944 (Based on the April 1944 Army List) "Staff Qualified" only – indicated by *s.* next to an officer's name in the Army List – is excluded.

| UNITS | CDR | ARRIVAL | AGE D-DAY | PUBLIC SCHOOL | p.s.c.[13] |
|---|---|---|---|---|---|
| 51st (Highland) Division | | 6 June (Part) | | 25% | 75% |
| Maj Gen | D.C. Bullen-Smith | | 45 | unk | Y |
| 152 Bde | D.H. Haugh | 8 June | 46 | unk | Y |
| 153 Bde | H. Murray | 7 June | 41 | N | Y |
| 154 Bde | J.A. Oliver | 10 June | 38 | Y | N |
| 6th (Airborne) Division | | 6 June | | 100% | 50% |
| Maj Gen | R.M. Gale | | 47 | Y | Y |
| 3 Para | J. Hill | 6 June | 33 | Y | N |
| 4 Para | N. Poett | 6 June | 36 | Y | Y |
| 6 Airland | Hon. H. Kindersley | 6 June | 45 | Y | N |
| 79th (Armoured) Division | | 6 June | | 100% | 100% |
| Maj Gen | P.C.S. Hobart | | 59 | Y | Y |
| 30 Armd Bde | N.W. Duncan | 22 June | 44 | Y | Y |
| Independent Brigades | | | | 75% | 50% |
| 1 Sp Svc Bde | Lord Lovat | 6 June | 32 | Y | N |
| 8 Armd | B. Cracroft | 6 June | 38 | Y | Y |
| 27 Armd | G.E. Prior-Palmer | 6 June | 41 | Y | N |
| 56 Bde[14] | E.C. Pepper | 6 June | 44 | unk | Y |

**Table 5.2 Normandy: Divisions and Brigades, Follow-On Divisions to the End of June**

| UNITS | CDR | ARRIVAL | AGE ON D-DAY | PUBLIC SCHOOL | p.s.c. |
|---|---|---|---|---|---|
| 49th (West Riding) Division | | 13 June | | 100% | 25% |
| Maj Gen | E.H. Barker | | 49 | Y | Y |
| 146 Bde | A. Dunlop | 10 June | 37 | Y | N |
| 147 Bde | E.R. Mahony | 12 June | 45 | Y | N |
| 70 Bde | E.C. Cooke-Collis | 14 June | 41 | Y | N |
| 11th Armoured Division | | 13 June | | 100% | 0% |
| Maj Gen | G.P.B. Roberts | | 37 | Y | N |
| 29 Armd | C.B.C.R. Harvey | 15 June | 43 | Y | N |
| 159 Bde | J.G. Sandie | 15 June | 46 | Y | N |
| 15th (Scottish) Division | | 14 June | | 100% | 50% |
| Maj Gen | G.H.A. Macmillan | | 46 | Y | Y |
| 44 Bde | H.D.K Money | 17 June | 47 | Y | N |
| 46 Bde | C.M. Barber | 17 June | 46 | Y | Y |
| 227 Bde | J.R. Mackintosh-Walker | 18 June | 46 | Y | N |
| 43rd (Wessex) Division | | 24 June | | 75% | 50% |

14 Attached to 50th (Northumbrian) Division for the landings; Joslen (1960) Vol.1, p. 196.

| UNITS | CDR | ARRIVAL | AGE ON D-DAY | PUBLIC SCHOOL | p.s.c. |
|---|---|---|---|---|---|
| Maj Gen | G.I. Thomas | | 50 | Y | Y |
| 129 Bde | G.H.L. Mole | 24 June | 47 | Y | N |
| 130 Bde | N.D. Leslie | 24 June | 34 | Y | N |
| 214 Bde | H. Essame | 24 June | 47 | N | Y |
| 53rd (Welsh) Division | | 27 June | | 75% | 50% |
| Maj Gen | R.H.K. Ross | | 51 | Y | N |
| 71 Bde | V. Blomfield | 25 June | 45 | Y | Y |
| 158 Bde | S.O. Jones | 23 June | 48 | Unk | Y |
| 160 Bde | L.G. Whistler | 28 June | 45 | Y | N |
| 59th (Staffordshire) Division | | 27 June | | 75% | 50% |
| Maj Gen | L.O. Lyne | | 45 | Y | Y |
| 176 Bde | R.W.H Fryer | 29 June | 44 | Y | N |
| 177 Bde | M.S. Ekins | 27 June | 45 | N | Y |
| 197 Bde | J. Lingham | 29 June | 46 | Y | N |
| Guards Armoured Division | | 28 June | | 100% | 33% |
| Maj Gen | A.H.S. Adair | | 46 | Y | N |
| 5 Gds Armd | N.W. Gwatkin | 30 June | 44 | Y | N |
| 32 Gds | G.F. Johnson | 25 June | 41 | Y | Y |

The divisions earmarked to lead the invasion of Europe on the two British landing beaches of Sword and Gold were a mixture of the veteran and the inexperienced, a trend which continued as the follow-on divisions arrived throughout June. The records of their commanders also reflected this. The assault division on Sword, 3rd Division, commanded by Major General Tom Rennie, was a Regular Army formation but had seen no active service since Dunkirk. Rennie had escaped from German captivity shortly after 51st (Highland) Division's surrender at St Valery in June 1940; after a staff appointment and battalion command at El Alamein, he commanded 154 Brigade of 51st (Highland) Division during the invasion of Sicily where he was wounded and impressed Montgomery with his abilities. Its counterpart on Gold Beach, 50th (Northumbrian) Division, still notionally a Territorial Army formation, had been constantly on operations in France, the Middle East and the Mediterranean since the outbreak of war.

Rennie's brigade commanders in 3rd Division also had a mixture of active service up to this point. Edward 'Copper' Cass, in command of the initial assault brigade, 8, was a very experienced officer. In 1936, he was also the Officer Champion Shot of the Army.[15] A multiple gallantry recipient in the First World War[16] he received a bar to the DSO for command of his battalion, 1st Battalion the King's Own Yorkshire Light Infantry

15 Dix, Noonan, Webb (Auctioneers), Orders, Medals and Decorations sale 25 March 2014; Lot 1106 'Orders, Medals and Decorations of Brigadier EEE Cass', catalogue notes.

16 DSO, MC and Mentioned in Dispatches.

(1/KOYLI), in Norway in 1940.[17] His service in Tunisia and Sicily, commanding 11 Brigade of 78th Division, added a CBE and an American Silver Star, the latter showing that he was an experienced field commander capable of operating successfully with allies. The follow-on brigade, 9, was under the command of James 'Jim' Cunningham, who, apart from 18 months in command of the Shetland Defences earlier in the war and of his D-Day brigade from 1942, had no notable combat experience in the war to this point. He had spent much of the interwar period on the North-West Frontier of India. The final brigadier, 185 Brigade's Kenneth Smith,[18] had had an exotic interwar career in parts of Russia during the intervention there in 1919, in Africa and India. He had also been 'effectively dismissed' by Montgomery from command of an infantry brigade on Malta during the siege there of 1941–1942.[19] Rennie and Smith were Staff College graduates, Rennie from Camberley in 1934, Smith from Quetta in 1935. All four were public school alumni; Rennie from Loretto, Cass from St Bees, Cunningham from Malvern and Smith from Eton. On D-Day, Rennie was 44, Cass 46, Cunningham 50 and Smith was 45, a rare case of the divisional commander being younger than his subordinate brigadiers.

The commander of 50th Division, Major General Douglas Graham, a Lowlander among Highlanders,[20] had left France before the German invasion in May 1940. His battalion served in Miles Dempsey's brigade, the latter ultimately commanding British Second Army in Normandy. Graham was posted home to command 153 Brigade, part of 9th (Scottish) Division. (9th Division was used as the basis from which to reconstitute 51st (Highland) Division after its surrender at St Valery and was subsequently redesignated as such). Graham led the Brigade at El Alamein. He then served under the command of the then Major General Neil Ritchie, who would command XII Corps in Normandy. Despite being a Lowlander, he was retained when Douglas 'Tartan Tam' Wimberley strove aggressively to keep the division exclusively Highland in nature; a measure of his effectiveness. Graham was personally selected by Montgomery to assume command of 56th (London) Division in Tunisia, remaining with it for the Sicily and Italy campaigns. He was seriously injured in a jeep accident in Italy in October 1943 and evacuated to the UK. However, he was deemed sufficiently recovered by January 1944

17 1/KOYLI was part of 15 Brigade in SICKLEFORCE, under Major General Bernard Paget; Cass served alongside Arthur Kent-Lemon, then commanding 1/Y&L in Norway, before taking command of the Brigade when Herbert Smyth was wounded; Kent-Lemon was the only senior officer to serve both there and in France in 1940.

18 He styled himself 'Pearce-Smith' in documents and his later autobiography *Adventures of an Ancient Warrior in War, Peace and Revolution* (Milford on Sea, Stone's Printers, 1984) but the Army List lists him simply as 'K. P. Smith'.

19 See Pearce-Smith, *Adventure…*, p.94 and A. Stewart, *Caen Controversy: The Battle for Sword Beach*' (Solihull, Helion & Co., 2014), pp.110–11.

20 He had originally been commissioned into the Cameronians (The Scottish Rifles), *HYAL* 1938.

to take over 50th Division for the invasion of France. Graham was considered 'a Monty favourite', widely respected and 'a pure fighting soldier'.[21]

Graham was a student at Camberley in 1924–1925. His contemporaries included 23 other officers who would rise to general officer rank during the Second World War, among them Archibald 'Archie' Nye (Vice Chief of the General Staff) and Humfrey Gale (Chief Administrative Officer at SHAEF). Several others would also command divisions, such as Ivor Thomas (43rd (Wessex) Division), a fellow commander in Normandy.[22] His D-Day brigadiers were Fergus Knox (69 Brigade), Ronald Senior (151 Brigade) and Sir Alexander Stanier (231 Brigade).

Although Knox, who was 45 on D-Day, had received a DSO for his effective command of 2nd Battalion Royal Ulster Rifles at Dunkirk (including personally leading a bayonet charge at the enemy) he had no other active service after 1940, remaining in the UK throughout.[23] Allan Converse, however, described Knox as 'a Monty man' who upset his battalion commanders who thought him 'too old and unused to modern methods'.[24]

'Ronnie' Senior, a month short of his fortieth birthday on D-Day, was a pre-war Territorial officer who had been awarded a DSO for command of a company of the Territorial 1st/7th Battalion The Queen's (Royal West Surrey) Regiment in France in 1940. He commanded 5th Battalion, the Royal West Kent Regiment (also Territorial) and 1st/7th Battalion The Queen's at El Alamein, returning from the former to the latter when its CO was wounded. A Bar to the DSO followed, as did appointment to take over 151 Brigade in Tunisia when his predecessor was sacked.[25] Although Senior was thought to be a good brigade commander by veterans, his relationship with his battalion commanders was sometimes as antagonistic as Knox's either through regular emphasis of his connections to the Queen's Regiment or an alleged disregard of the experience of his subordinates.[26] Converse, however, described him as 'a popular and effective Brigadier'.[27]

Sir Alexander 'Sammy' Stanier was a Baronet, a Welsh Guardsman and was personally selected by Montgomery for this command. He had distinguished himself during the defence of Boulogne in May 1940 and was thought 'tough, courageous, unflappable and a good planner.'[28] His war service since Dunkirk had been in home defence roles; while he was the same age as Knox, this did not attract the same criticism from within the brigade.

21 Smart, *Biographical Dictionary…*, p.120.
22 *The Army List* (London: HMSO, January 1925), p.920.
23 A. Converse, *Armies of Empire: The 9th Australian and 50th British Divisions in Battle 1939–1945* (Australian Army History Series)' (Melbourne; Cambridge University Press Australia, 2011), p.185.
24 Converse, *Armies of Empire…* p.185.
25 Brigadier Daniel Beak VC DSO MC*; Daniel Rolf suggests Beak's sacking after Medenine in March 1943 was unfair and motivated by Montgomery's intent to advance favourites, particularly Kirkman. D. Rolf, *The Bloody Road to Tunis* (London, Greenhill,2001).
26 Watson, Lieutenant Colonel William Innes commanding 6/DLI; IWM Oral History Recording 10420 (1988). Imperial War Museum.
27 Converse, *Armies of Empire…* p.64.
28 Converse, *Armies of Empire…* p.185.

Graham, who was 51 on D-Day, went to an independent school[29] and, as noted, was a Staff College graduate. Knox, 45, was a grammar school pupil; did not attend Staff College but was annotated 's.' in the Army List (staff qualified) from the short wartime course. Senior, 39, came from a public school, Cheltenham, and as a Territorial officer did not attend Staff College, even after a limited number of vacancies were made available to them in the late 1930s. Stanier, also 45, was educated at Eton and was not a Staff College graduate.

Among the follow-on forces (listed in order of their initial arrival in France), 51st (Highland) Division, arrived between 6 and 10 June commanded by Major General Charles Bullen-Smith. The Division had been reconstituted from 9th (Scottish) Division in 1940–41 and saw action in the Middle East and Mediterranean. Although Bullen-Smith had fought in France in 1940, his time since then had been spent training troops in the UK, where he gained a strong reputation for doing so. He had also replaced Wimberley in command and faced resentment from within the division both for this and for being, despite a career spent in a Highland regiment, an Englishman.[30]

7th Armoured Division, which landed on Juno, the Canadian assault beach, on 7 June[31] are the 'Desert Rats' of popular repute, having fought in the Western Desert and Italy; its commander after January 1943 was Major General George 'Bobby' Erskine, 45 years old, educated at Charterhouse and commissioned into the King's Royal Rifle Corps in 1918. Although he did see active service on the Western Front in WW1, he spent much of the interwar years in India or in staff postings in the UK. He graduated from Camberley in 1930; two of his contemporaries were Herbert Lumsden and Neil Ritchie, both of whom would become general officers in the Second World War. He served in North Africa as an infantry battalion commander and then as the BGS to Brian Horrocks when the latter commanded XII Corps in the Middle East.

Erskine's brigadiers landing in Normandy were Robert 'Looney' Hinde (22 Armoured Brigade) and Maurice Ekins (131 Brigade). Hinde, educated at Wellington, was a cavalryman and too young to have served in the First World War. He had spent much of the interwar years in India, reportedly obsessed with playing polo; he did not attend Staff College. He earned his first DSO after taking command of his regiment, 15th/19th Hussars, in France in 1940 when the commanding officer was killed. Hinde commanded the same brigade in the Western Desert from 1942, earning both a second DSO and his unfortunate soubriquet for his fearless command style, riding around the battlefield alone on a motorcycle to reach his units. Maurice Ekins, also 45 on D-Day, was from an unclear educational background; initially educated at Aldershot County Secondary School, in the 1911 Census he is shown as a 'student' lodging at an address in Whitley Bay with his parents.[32] A Royal Fusilier, he was wounded in action in late 1918 and

29 The Glasgow Academy.
30 Smart, *Biographical Dictionary…*, p.51; French, 'Invading Europe….' in Goldstein and McKercher, p.288.
31 Other divisional elements followed up to 12 June.
32 1911 Census of England and Wales, RG14PN30815.

spent his whole interwar career in staff postings in Turkey, the Rhine Army and India. He attended the Staff College in 1933–34 alongside Tom Rennie; from 1935–1939 he served in staff posts in India. His war service up to 1942 is not apparent; from August 1942-January 1944 he commanded 177 Brigade in 59th (Staffordshire) Division.

11th Armoured Division, which came ashore on 13 June, was a new formation. Its commander, Major General George 'Pip' Roberts, was the youngest general in the British Army at the time, and was 37 on D-Day.[33] He already had considerable combat experience both in command and in staff posts in the Western Desert and Tunisia, despite his comparative youth.[34] Of his brigadiers, Charles 'Roscoe' Harvey (commanding 29 Armoured Brigade) was a professional interwar cavalryman and international polo player who had help form one of the war-raised cavalry units in the United Kingdom, the 23rd Hussars. He then commanded it in 1941–1942, before briefly taking over 4 Armoured Brigade in the later stages of the Libyan campaign in 1942–43. John Sandie of the divisional Infantry brigade, 159 Brigade, was a 46-year-old infantryman with First World War experience and had earned a DSO in France in 1940 commanding his battalion (where he remained until 1942) but had spent the rest of the war so far in the UK. All the senior formation commanders in 11 Armoured were public school educated, but none had attended Staff College. Although this is mitigated by an armoured division lacking one brigade by comparison to an infantry division, 11 Armoured was unique at this point among its contemporary formations in having no Staff College graduates in fighting command positions. (Second was Guards Armoured, having only one p.s.c. among its commanders – George Johnson of 32 Guards Brigade. Neither the divisional commander, Alan Adair, nor the armoured brigade commander, Norman Gwatkin, had been educated at Staff College.)

49th (West Riding) Division, had had some battle experience as two of its brigades had been sent to Norway in 1940, but thereafter had spent two years garrisoning Iceland and training in the UK. Major General Evelyn 'Bubbles' Barker, 49, had taken command in November 1943;[35] a brigade commander at Dunkirk he was credited with inspiring and toughening up the division prior to D-Day. Barker's brigadiers included Andrew Dunlop (146 Brigade), a 37-year-old Argyll and Sutherland Highlander who had spent most of the 1930s attached to the King's African Rifles or as an Adjutant in a Territorial battalion; no combat experience is recorded for him prior to 1944. Edmond (known in some circles as 'Tim') Mahony, 45, was an Irish Guardsman who had been Assistant Military Attaché in Paris from 1937 to 1939, only rising to command 1st Battalion Irish Guards in 1941, followed by a period on the staff of the Senior Officers' School at

33 Smart, *Biographical Dictionary...*, p.274. He had served on the staffs of 4th Armoured Brigade, 7th Armoured Division and XXX Corps before commanding, in 1942–1943 alone, 22nd Armoured Brigade, 26th Armoured Brigade and 30th Armoured Brigade; he assumed command of 11th Armoured Division in December 1943.

34 Smart, *Biographical Dictionary...*, p.274.

35 Lieutenant Colonel H. F. Joslen, *Orders of Battle*, vols 1 & 2, History of the Second World War, United Kingdom Military Series (London: HMSO, 1960), volume. 1, p.79.

Sheerness before taking over 147 Brigade in 1943. Edward Cooke-Collis of 70 Brigade, known as 'Red Ted', both for his colouring and forthright politics,[36] was an experienced Green Howard who was 'a veteran of high reputation in 50th Division'[37] even though he was only 41 on D-Day. He had commanded a Territorial battalion and 69 Brigade in the Middle East; he already possessed two DSOs and two MiDs before landing in France. In 49th Division, all the formation commanders were public school alumni, but only Barker had graduated from Camberley.

Another untested division was 15th (Scottish), under Major General Gordon MacMillan; it had spent the whole of the war so far in the United Kingdom, training. Macmillan had served as a BGS in the Middle East, culminating in command of a brigade in Sicily before being appointed to his division in August 1943.[38] His subordinates were Henry Money, 47, (44 Brigade) a First World War veteran of the Mesopotamia campaign who, after service in the Indian Army, commanded a battalion of the Royal Scots in France in 1940 and Colin Barber of 46 Brigade. Barber started his commissioned career in the First World War as a Territorial but served as a regular in India in the 1920s, followed by postings in Scotland and Southern Command in the 1930s. Also a battalion commander in the BEF, he was one of the few to avoid capture at St Valery; between 1941 and 1944 he commanded the same brigade in the UK that he took to Normandy.[39] John Mackintosh-Walker, 46 on D-Day, had been wounded three times and decorated three times (three Military Crosses) as an officer of the Seaforth Highlanders during the First World War; he was Mentioned in Dispatches for service in Palestine in 1937 and escaped from German hands with Tom Rennie in France in 1940; he had commanded 227 Brigade since 1942. All four were public school alumni, but only Macmillan and Mackintosh-Walker were graduates of the Staff College.

43rd (Wessex) Division, another formation based initially on Territorial Army units, had been intended to go to France in 1940, but the pace of the German invasion and the subsequent evacuation of the BEF precluded this. Major General Ivor Thomas' longevity in command of his division before and ultimately after D-Day was unusual amongst the Normandy divisions; he had been appointed in March 1942.[40] (His lengthy tenure was ascribed to his 'energetic and ruthless methods, demanding the highest standards.'[41]) Thomas, originally a gunner, had had no actual combat experience in the war thus far, having held senior staff positions at the War Office, including a period as Director of

36 Converse, *Armies of Empire…*, p.6.
37 A. Converse, *Armies of Empire…* p.6.
38 N. Smart, *Biographical Dictionary of British Generals of the Second World War* (Barnsley: Pen & Sword Military, 2005), p.203.
39 Smart, *Biographical Dictionary…*, p.20; Smart suggests that he commanded 54th (East Anglian) Division, a home defence formation, from 1941–43 (when it was disbanded and broken up), making his reversion to a brigade for Normandy puzzling, but this is possibly a misreading for Evelyn Barker. However, as Joslen identifies the divisional commander as 'E. H. Barber' (Vol.1 p.89) – most likely a misprint – the misunderstanding is comprehensible.
40 Joslen, *Orders of Battle*, vol. 1, p.69.
41 Mead, *The Last Great Cavalryman…*, pp.384–335; Smart, *Biographical Dictionary…*, p.308.

Organisation. His brigadiers were Gerald Mole (129 Brigade), Norman Leslie (130 Brigade), and Hubert Essame (214 Brigade). Mole, 47, had served on the Western Front and in Russia in 1918/1919 and earned a Military Cross; however, he spent four years overseas with the Royal West African Frontier Force and did not attend Staff College. Leslie, young for the post at 34 on D-Day, had commanded a Territorial battalion of The Queen's Regiment in Tunisia and came to Thomas' division after a period as a GSO 1 in 51st (Highland) Division. Essame, 47, had spent a long period in India in the 1920s and 1930s in regimental and staff posts; he served in the War Office and then the BEF as a GSO 2, before commanding of an infantry battalion in the UK in 1941–1942. He assumed the post at 214 Brigade in September 1942.[42] Thomas, Mole and Leslie were public school alumni,[43] but only Thomas and Essame were Staff College graduates; Thomas from Camberley in 1925 and Essame from Quetta in 1930.

53rd (Welsh) Division had both no previous combat experience during the war and a divisional commander who had not seen action in it, Major General Robert 'Bobby' Ross. Although Ross had served in Palestine during the Arab Uprising of 1936–1939, he had seen no active service since the end of the First World War. He was promoted to command of the division in September 1942[44] via one of its subordinate brigades, 160 Brigade, which he had led since 1940. (It is possible, but not confirmed, that both Ross and Douglas Graham may have encountered and impressed Montgomery in Palestine in 1938–1939, when the latter briefly took command of the re-activated 8th Division there).[45] Ross' brigadiers, Valentine Blomfield (47, 71 Brigade) Stanley Jones (48, 158 Brigade) and Lashmer 'Bolo' Whistler (45, 160 Brigade), had varying degrees of active service experience. Blomfield was a veteran of the First World War and of operations on the North-West Frontier in the 1920s; he had been Mentioned in Dispatches in 1940 as a major. Jones was also a veteran of the First World War and post-war operations in India, but also had experience on the staff in the 1920s and 30s, including two years in the War Office. He temporarily commanded 6 Brigade but was then Commandant of the Senior Officers' School across the middle of the war. Whistler, who had been held prisoner in the First World War, had extensive combat experience in the war so far, having been awarded a DSO for France, commanding a Territorial battalion; he was present at Alam Halfa and El Alamein in 1942 in command of the infantry brigade of 7th (Armoured) Division and served in Tunisia. He returned home with that division, transferring to 53rd (Welsh) Division in January 1944.[46]

42 Joslen, *Orders of Battle*, vol. 1.

43 Mole was educated in India; Essame attended Nottingham High School now, but not then, a member of the HMC; Leslie was a Rugbiean.

44 Joslen, *Orders of Battle*, vol. 1, p.87.

45 P. McCarty, 'Dangerously Overexposed?' – Divisional Operations on the flanks of MARKET GARDEN September to December 1944' in J. Buckley & P. Preston-Hough, *Operation Market Garden: The Campaign for the Low Countries, Autumn 1944: Seventy Years On* (Solihull: Helion & Co., 2016).

46 Brigadier Sir J. Smyth, *Bolo Whistler: The Life of General Sir Lashmer Whistler GCB KBE DSO DL; A Study in Leadership* (London: Muller, 1967).

Although Ross and Whistler were both educated at public schools (Ross at Cheltenham College, Whistler at Harrow) neither attended either Camberley or Quetta; Blomfield was both a public school product (Rugby) and a Camberley graduate; Jones' educational establishment has not been traced, but he did attend Staff College.

59th (Staffordshire) Division, a war-raised unit, had originally been intended as a Motor Division carrying lorry mounted infantry to exploit 'break-ins to breakthroughs' in support of armoured divisions, but when this concept was abandoned after Dunkirk it reverted to being a conventional infantry division. Predominantly engaged in home defence duties for much of the war, despite impressing Brooke with its training progress in 1942–1943,[47] the arrival of Montgomery as commander of 21st Army Group led to its commander and two of its brigadiers being replaced by more experienced officers. The new GOC was Major General Lewis 'Lou' Lyne, who had gone from a lieutenant colonel commanding an infantry battalion in 1940 to commanding a division in under three years, aged 43. This is even more surprising for the fact that his frontline experience only began in the spring of 1942. But he served under Graham in his previous posting as GOC 56th (London) Division in the Mediterranean where both had impressed Montgomery.

His brigadiers were Reginald Fryer (44; 176 Brigade), Maurice Ekins (45, 131 Brigade) and John Lingham (46, 197 Brigade). Lyne was therefore equal to or younger than his brigadiers, which as noted in Chapter 1, was a touchstone for Blaxland concerning Harold Alexander's early promotion to divisional command by dint of being a Guardsman. Fryer had received a Military Cross in the First World War and served in Iraq in the 1920s; Ekins spent most of his interwar career in staff postings in Germany, and after Camberley in 1933–1934, in India; for 18 months in 1941–1942 he had commanded 177 Brigade in the UK before transferring to 131 Brigade.[48] Lingham had served in France, Egypt and Mesopotamia in the First World War, been wounded and awarded a Military Cross in 1918. From 1940–1942 he commanded a Territorial battalion of the Northamptonshire Regiment before moving to the brigade he arrived in Normandy with. Lyne, Fryer and Lingham were public school educated;[49] Lyne and Ekins were Staff College graduates.

The last division fully to arrive, on 28 June 1944, was Guards Armoured, under Major General Sir Allan Adair. He had been a founding member of the division in September 1941 as commander of 6th Guards Armoured Brigade. Adair, who had returned from France in early 1940 to become Chief Instructor at No.1 Infantry Officer Cadet Unit – the Royal Military College, Sandhurst was rapidly recalled after the German invasion to command his battalion of the Grenadier Guards, who had an 'eventful' campaign.[50] After command of a Guards infantry brigade, and his tenure at 6th Guards Armoured, he took over the division in 1942 from another Grenadier, Oliver Leese – also a Dunkirk

47 A. Danchev and D. Todman (eds), *War Diaries 1939–1945: Field Marshal Lord Alanbrooke* (London: Weidenfeld and Nicholson, 2001), p.166.
48 Joslen, *Orders of Battle*, vol. 1, p.356.
49 At Haileybury, Wellington and City of London respectively.
50 R. Mead, *Churchill's Lions* (Stroud: Spellmount, 2007), pp.35–37.

veteran. Despite lacking any frontline service after 1940, Adair inspired great loyalty and affection in his subordinates but unlike many other commanders lacking such experience was able to resist Montgomery's attempts to remove him from post – ostensibly for lacking 'drive'– 'due to the Guards looking after their own.'[51]

Adair's brigadiers were Norman Gwatkin (44, 5 Guards Armoured Brigade) and George Johnson (41, 32 Guards Brigade). As noted, Adair was a Grenadier; Gwatkin was a Coldstreamer and Johnson came from the Scots Guards. Gwatkin had missed service in the First World War but spent four years as the Adjutant of the RMC from 1931 to 1935 and then as Assistant Comptroller of the Lord Chamberlain's Office in the Royal Household.[52] North-West Europe was to be his first combat service in the war. Gwatkin was described as 'a man of high colour, a choleric expression, a loud and infectious laugh and beloved by all…'[53] Johnson was unusual amongst Guardsmen in that he had been commissioned into the Brigade of Guards[54] after having first been an officer in the Territorial Army, had served in Palestine in 1936–1937 as a staff officer and had also been a battalion commander in his regiment up to 1941. (His marriage to Lady Ida Ramsay, daughter of the 14th Earl of Dalhousie, in January 1938 would also have strengthened his social and regimental connections as his father in law had served with the Scots Guards in South Africa in 1901).[55] In June 1942 he was taken prisoner only three days after having taken over 201 Guards Motor Brigade Group; he would later escape from a prisoner of war camp in Italy and return to the UK, where he took over his Brigade in December 1943. All three were public school educated, but only Johnson had passed Staff College.[56]

The two specialist divisions remaining were 6th (Airborne) Division, commanded by Major General Richard 'Windy' Gale and 79th (Armoured) Division under Major General Percy 'Patrick' Hobart. 6th Airborne had been formed in the United Kingdom in May 1943 to provide a second airborne division (along with 1st Airborne) ahead of the invasion of France. Gale, 47 on D-Day, transferred from the latter's 1 Parachute Brigade to command the new formation, which was brought up to full establishment in September 1943.[57] Gale's interwar career, despite graduating from Quetta in 1931, reflected the stagnation of an officer corps overstaffed and with a lack of promotion opportunity; by 1940 he was only a lieutenant colonel commanding a Territorial

51 Mead, *The Last Great Cavalryman…*, p.37; Smart, *Biographical Dictionary…*, p.2. Adair also discussed this point in his own memoir, *A Guards' General: the Memoirs of Major General Sir Allan Adair, Bt, GCVO, CB, DSO, MC, JP, DL* (London, Hamish Hamilton, 1986), p.150

52 *HYAL* January 1940, p.424; from the 'TA General List'.

53 Sir D. Fraser, Wars and Shadows: The Memoirs of General Sir David Fraser (London: Penguin, 2003), p.112

54 From the 'TA General List' to be 2nd Lieutenant Scots Guards, 12 September 1925, *HYAL* January 1940. p.697.

55 Charles Mosley (ed.), *Burke's Peerage, Baronetage & Knightage*, 107th edition, 3 volumes (Wilmington: Burke's Peerage (Genealogical Books) Ltd, 2003) Vol. 1, p.1021.

56 *HYAL* January 1940, p.694.

57 Joslen, *Orders of Battle…*, vol. 1, p.106.

battalion[58] but the standard of his training impressed Brooke when the latter was GOC Home Forces. This led to Gale occupying senior staff posts developing Britain's airborne capability, including that of Deputy Director Staff Duties (Air). Gale formed and trained a completely new specialist formation, requiring much retraining from scratch which was declared ready for active service in under nine months. This left, however, only four months to complete the specific to task training for D-Day.

Gale's brigadiers were comparatively youthful, as is discussed below. James Hill (3 Parachute Brigade) was 33; Nigel Poett (4 Parachute Brigade) was 36. The Hon. Hugh Kindersley (6 Airlanding Brigade) was almost as old as Gale at 45 and had left the army in the 1920s after First World War service (where he was wounded and decorated) but remained on the reserve and rejoined the army on the outbreak of war. This pattern was duplicated in 1st Airborne Division, with comparatively youthful parachute brigade commanders, namely Lathbury, 1 Parachute Brigade aged 38; Hackett, 4 Parachute Brigade, aged 34 and Hicks, 1 Airlanding Brigade, aged 49.

Initially Kindersley was a member of Guards Armoured Division on its formation, but transferred to airborne forces in early 1943, completing parachute and glider pilot training at the age of 44. Hill was a regular officer before the war but resigned in 1936 to go into business. Rejoining the army in 1939, he served in France in staff posts at GHQ BEF in 1940, transferring to airborne forces and commanding 1st Parachute Battalion in Tunisia. He took over 3rd Parachute Brigade on the formation of 6th Airborne Division.[59] Poett had originally been commissioned into the Durham Light Infantry and served in India and the Sudan; at the outbreak of war he was serving in the War Office. He was briefly commanding officer of a DLI battalion on home service before being transferred to airborne forces. All four were educated at public school, but only Gale and Poett were p.s.c.

79th Armoured, intended to breach the complex array of beach defences facing the invasion force, was commanded by the pre-war armoured pioneer Major General Percy Hobart, an atypical 58 years old on D-Day. Hobart's vision, ability and intellect were not used to best advantage in a cash-strapped army, 'his successive superiors .... [were] unable to understand Hobart's theories of warfare or match his intellect .... [Hobart was] undoubtedly a difficult subordinate with scant regard for those who did not share his opinions.'[60] Immediately pre-war he had antagonised superior officers by disobeying direct instructions in favour of his own theories; his tenure as Director of Military Training, where he could have propagated his thinking to more effect, was unsuccessful and lasted under a year in 1937/1938. He also made enemies of powerful officers such as Henry Maitland, 'Jumbo' Wilson and Archibald 'Archie' Wavell; John Dill considered

58 N. Smart, *Biographical Dictionary of British Generals of the Second World War* (Barnsley: Pen & Sword Military, 2005), p.112; at the end of the First World War, aged 21, he had been an acting major.

59 'Extended biography of Brigadier James Hill – compiled from his own service notes.' *https://paradata.org.uk/articles/extended-biography-brig-james-hill* accessed 20 February 2018.

60 Mead, *The Last Great Cavalryman…*, p.203.

him 'impatient, hot-headed and intolerant.'[61] Dismissed, ostensibly on grounds of age, in 1940, his restoration to command of 11th (Armoured) Division in the UK also lasted under a year, when he was considered too old to take a division overseas. Due to the specialist nature of the division's role, it had only one 'conventional' armoured brigade on strength in North-West Europe, 30.[62] 30 Brigade's commander was a specialist tank officer, 44-year-old Nigel Duncan.

Duncan and Hobart were both products of the public schools and Camberley, Hobart in 1920 and Duncan in 1936. Duncan was a pioneering officer in armour, serving in armoured car companies in Egypt, Northern Ireland and India, as Adjutant at the Tank Corps depot at Bovington, and on exercises in the UK with Hobart. When the war broke out, he was a staff officer with 1 Army Tank Brigade.[63]

As noted, both the assault and follow-on divisions, even after Montgomery's 'stiffening' of the initial order of battle with combat experienced formations, would have a mixture of commanding officers with and without battlefield experience in the present war. Some officers in the Normandy group had served in France or Norway in 1940 as regimental officers but again, not all of them had seen action since returning from the European Continent.

It is immediately apparent that unlike in 1940, commanders of fighting brigades in 1944 came from service branches appropriate to the brigade's role, i.e. infantry brigades were commanded by infantry officers (including all Guards formations being commanded by Guards officers), and tank/armoured brigades by officers from cavalry regiments or the Royal Tank Regiment. Although this did not continue at divisional level – Thomas, a gunner, commanding an infantry division and Erskine, an infantryman commanding an armoured division – at the next level down it remained constant.

In 1940, two infantry brigades had been commanded by officers of the Royal Engineers; 143 Brigade of 48th (South Midland) Division, commanded by Brigadier James Muirhead[64] and 8 Brigade of 3rd Division, commanded by Brigadier Christopher Woolner.[65] (The Guards Armoured Division, Guards Armoured Brigade and Guards Infantry Brigade were commanded by officers of the Foot Guards. The former arguably being infantry officers temporarily converted to the armoured role).[66] The Guards therefore sustained a 'closed shop' of command of their own formations into the North-

61 Smart, *Biographical Dictionary…*, p.154.
62 Joslen, *Orders of Battle*, vol. 1 p.30
63 IWM Sound Archive; Maj. Gen. N.W. Duncan 1976-09-24 Cat. No. 829.
64 Lieutenant Colonel H. F. Joslen, *Orders of Battle: Second World War 1939–1945* (London: Her Majesty's Stationery Office, 1960), vol.1, p.328. Muirhead commanded the Brigade from September 1939 to June 1940.
65 Joslen, *Orders of Battle*, vol. 1, p.246. Woolner was in command from February November 1940.
66 For example, Brigadier Gerald Verney DSO* MVO, Irish Guards who landed in Normandy in command of 6th Guards Armoured Brigade and assumed command of 7th Armoured Division in August 1944 after its commander, Major General 'Bobby' Erskine was dismissed. Joslen, *Orders of Battle*, vol. 1, pp.19 & 187.

West Europe campaign. This overall placing of 'square pegs in square holes' – of an officers' specialisation reflecting the role of the brigade reflects perhaps two factors as the war had progressed; a readier supply of officers to fill command appointments, and the weakening of the requirement or expectation to be a Staff College graduate to hold operational command.

## Age Profile

The average age of the officers is considerably lower, at 42.37 years, than the 1940 sample of 49.02 years for the BEF and North-West Expeditionary Force combined. (The median is 43, compared with 46 in 1940; the mode is 46, compared to 49). Of the Normandy group, 12 were aged under 40. Parachute and commando formations contained comparatively youthful officers for their rank, such as Lord Lovat (1 Special Service Brigade) who was 32; James Hill (3 Parachute Brigade) who was 33 and Nigel Poett (4 Parachute Brigade) who was 36. As parachute and commando formations had not existed at the outbreak of war, all three were infantry officers with pre-war service; Lovat with the Scots Guards, Hill the Royal Fusiliers and Poett the Durham Light Infantry.[67] All three were originally Regular Army officers. However, despite being atypically young in post they were not completely exceptional – the youngest brigadier in Normandy was Michael Carver, then 29; Norman Leslie of 130 Brigade in 43rd Division was 34.

However, there were variations between the several divisions landing in Normandy. Of the D-Day arrivals, the average age in 3rd Division was 47, (the highest figure among both D-Day and the follow-on formations) – where all the brigadiers were older than the divisional commander. In Graham's 50th Division it was 43; in 51st Division it was considerably below at 41.6. In 6th Airborne, despite having the fourth oldest divisional commander in Gale, the average age was one of the lowest due to the comparative youth of its brigadiers, at 38. With only two brigadiers, 7th Armoured's average was 44, with its two brigadiers at 43 and 45 bracketing the 44-year-old divisional commander. The pattern was similar in the follow-on divisions; in 49th Division the average was 41; 11th Armoured and Guards Armoured (with two brigades each) 44.5 and 42.5 respectively. In the other infantry divisions, 15th (Scottish) was 46.3. 43rd Wessex 42.7, 53rd Welsh 46.0, and 59th Staffordshire 45.0. Despite Montgomery's 'leavening' of inexperienced formations, in some divisions (such as 53rd Welsh) older officers who retained their posts after 1942 and 1943 contributed to a higher average age in their formations.

Secondly, the replacement of battle casualties by junior subordinates commanding infantry battalions and armoured regiments could reduce the age profile of brigade

67 *The Army List*, December 1938.

commanders. The six armoured brigades[68] contained among them the youngest brigadier in the Normandy group, the highly exceptional Michael Carver.[69] He took over command of 4 Armoured Brigade on 27 June 1944 aged 29, following the death in action of Brigadier John Currie – who was more typically representative at 46 years old.[70] The next youngest commander of an armoured brigade was Bernard Cracroft (8 Armoured Brigade), who was 38. The other three armoured brigade commanders were all aged over 40.[71]

In the infantry brigades, most commanders were over 40 years old, although there were exceptions. Of the five commanders of infantry brigades who were under 40, coincidentally, two of them were Scots originally commissioned into Scottish regiments, even though not all their brigade commands were in Scottish divisions. Brigadier Ronald Senior, commanding 151 Brigade in 50th (Northumbrian) Division was doubly anomalous in being under 40, he was 39, and originally a Territorial. He had already commanded 152 Brigade of 51st (Highland) Division on its return to the UK from North Africa.[72] The two Scottish regiment brigadiers serving outside the Scottish regimental group were Andrew Dunlop, aged 37, originally commissioned into the Argyll and Sutherland Highlanders, commanding 146 Brigade in 49th (West Riding) Division, and Norman Leslie, aged 34, who began his service in the Cameron Highlanders and commanded 130 Brigade of the 43rd (Wessex) Division.[73]

However, command replacements due to casualties in June and July 1944 also left some infantry brigades with commanders aged under 40, due to battalion commanders or members of the brigade headquarters staff stepping in to fill the gap left by the loss of their senior officer. An example is Edward Colville. Aged 38, he assumed command of 227 Brigade, 15th (Scottish) Division, on 17 July,[74] following the death in action of Brigadier John Mackintosh-Walker; Colville had been commanding officer of 2nd Battalion, Gordon Highlanders in the Brigade. Mackintosh-Walker was of the more typical age of 46 years old when he became a casualty. The eldest brigadier to fight in the initial stages of the Normandy battles was the fifty-year-old James Cunningham, who landed on D-Day with his command, 9 Brigade of 3rd

68 4, 8, 22, 27, 5 Guards and 6 Guards.

69 Carver was also a regular officer, having been commissioned into the then Royal Tank Corps in 1935. *The London Gazette*, 1 February 1935, p.773.

70 *The Times*, London, issue 49999, November 24 1944, p.7; Joslen, *Orders of Battle*, vol. 1, p.153.

71 Hinde, (22 Armoured Brigade) was 43; Prior-Palmer (27 Armoured Brigade) was 41; Gwatkin (5 Guards) was 44, Verney (6 Guards) was 43.

72 Oliver, a solicitor before the Second World War, had commanded 7th Battalion, The Black Watch at El Alamein and been awarded the Distinguished Service Order for Tunisia. *London Gazette*, 31 December 1942, p.5055.

73 Leslie had already moved away from the Scottish regimental tribe by serving with the West African Frontier Force from 1936–38; he also commanded a Territorial battalion of The Queen's Regiment briefly in 1943.

74 Joslen, *Orders of Battle*, vol. 1 p.334.

Division.[75] Wounded around 1300hrs on 6 June by a mortar strike on his brigade headquarters near Hermanville-sur-Mer, Arthur Orr[76] (who was 43) replaced him.[77]

The Chart below illustrates the age distribution of the Normandy brigadiers. Two cumulative spikes appear; 12 officers aged 40 or under, over a quarter, 26 percent, of the whole group, whereas officers aged 45–46 are the same proportion – although the spread of 18 officers aged 41–45 is 40 percent, To compare with 1940 is inexact due to the disparity in the number of officers, but with only three officers under 40 (no officers were exactly 40), under 2 percent, 13, or 8 percent of the group being 45–46, and 33 or 21 percent, in the 41–46 bracket, an element of rejuvenation is apparent between 1940 and 1944. The largest clusters in 1940 were the 47–49 group (53, or 34 percent) and the 51–53 (30, or 19 percent) being over half of all officers.

**Chart 5.3 Normandy Fighting Brigadiers, Age Distribution**

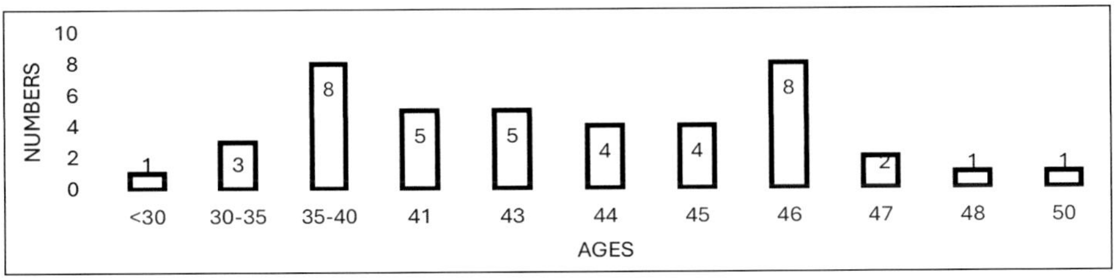


## Schooling and Education

With schooling, while eight of the 45 officers' place of secondary education was untraceable, among the remaining 37, products of the public schools were dominant again in the 1944 list with 36 officers educated at them. Although Eton was once more significant, with four Old Etonians, Wellington College overtook it, with eight in the list. Cheltenham produced three officers in this group, with Downside, Malvern, Marlborough and Rugby two officers apiece, a total of 23. 12 schools produced a single officer for the 1944 group, as follows:

75 Cunningham had originally been commissioned into the Argyll and Sutherland Highlanders.
76 Orr was originally commissioned into the Royal Scots Fusiliers in 1920. *HYAL* January 1940 p.610–613.
77 TNA WO171/616 9 Brigade War Diary.

**Table 5.4 1940/44 Comparison of Schools Attended, Normandy Brigadiers (Sole Attendee)**

| SCHOOL | 1940 | 1944 |
|---|---|---|
| Ampleforth | 0 | 1 |
| Clifton College | 4 | 1 |
| Coleraine College | 0 | 1 |
| Nottingham High School | 0 | 1 |
| Peter Symond's Winchester | 0 | 1 |
| Shrewsbury | 2 | 1 |
| St Bees | 1 | 1 |
| St Xavier's Calcutta | 0 | 1 |
| Stonyhurst | 1 | 1 |
| Trinity College Glenalmond | 1 | 1 |
| Uppingham | 3 | 1 |
| Winchester | 9 | 1 |

**Chart 5.4A Comparison of Schools Attended, Multiple Normandy Brigadiers**

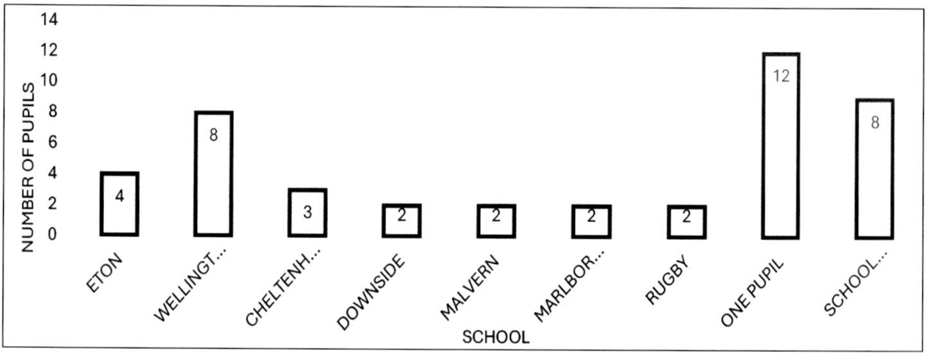


Therefore, except for Peter Symonds' College in Winchester (a boys' grammar school founded in 1897) and the eight untraceable officers, this Normandy group has 34 former pupils of schools in the Clarendon Group or the Headmasters' Conference, 80 percent of the total. Such dominance of a concentrated and specific group in a limited period therefore indicates that even after four and a half years of war, with an expanded army requiring more officers and a ready supply of replacements for casualties, the dominance of the public school as a source of officers remained and even increased compared with the larger 1940 group.

Examining which officers of the Normandy group were school contemporaries shows proportionally fewer than those of 1940. In the largest single grouping, Wellingtonians, there is a ten-year spread between the eight indicating that they were not all at the school contemporaneously. Six of them were in education at the College in the same period, albeit at opposite ends of the school experience in terms of time of admission, i.e. two arriving as two left the College. However, two were direct school contemporaries. Cyril

Coleman (160 Brigade, 53rd Welsh Division) and George Prior-Palmer (27 Armoured Brigade, independent GHQ formation) entered in the same year, 1917. Of the Old Etonians, all four were present at the school at the same time as there is only a four-year window, 1913–1917, for their dates of entry. The youngest, George Johnson (32 Guards Brigade, Guards Armoured Division) arrived in 1917, when Sir Alexander Stanier Bt[78] (231 Brigade, 50th Division) and the Honourable Hugh Kindersley (6 Airlanding Brigade, 6th Airborne Division) were leaving Eton. Gerald Verney (6 Guards Armoured Brigade) was a year behind Kindersley and Stanier, arriving in 1914 and leaving in 1918.

The three officers who attended Cheltenham College were present in a six-year bracket from 1912–1918. John Currie (4 Armoured Brigade, Independent GHQ formation) attended from 1912–1918; Edward Cooke-Collis (70 Brigade, 49th Division) from 1916–1920 and Ronald Senior (151 Brigade, 50th (Northumbrian) Division) from 1918–1922). They therefore did not coincide as a group, although Cooke-Collis and Henry were in the College at the same time albeit separated by two years.

Of the schools providing two officers to the group, the pair at Downside (Charles Harvey of 29 Armoured Brigade, 11th Armoured Division and Noel Poett of 5 Parachute Brigade, 6th Airborne Division) were separated by seven years and were therefore not contemporary; James Cunningham (9 Brigade, 3rd Infantry Division) and Hugh Cracroft (8 Armoured Brigade, Independent GHQ formation) had an even greater separation at Malvern, of 12 years. James Hill (3 Parachute Brigade, 6th Airborne Division) and Edward Colville (227 Brigade, 15th (Scottish) Division) were five years apart in their attendance at Marlborough, Hill being the junior, from 1925. At Rugby, Valentine Blomfield (71 Brigade, 53rd (Welsh) Division) and Norman Leslie (130 Brigade, 43rd (Wessex) Division) were separated in attendance by 11 years.

To compare 1940 and 1944 in respect of schools:

**Table 5.5 Comparison of Schools Attended 1940 & 1944**

| SCHOOL | 1940 NUMBER | PERCENTAGE OF GROUP (156) | 1944 NUMBER | PERCENTAGE OF GROUP (45) |
|---|---|---|---|---|
| ETON | 12 | 7.8 | 4 | 8.9 |
| WELLINGTON | 10 | 6.5 | 8 | 17.7 |
| CHELTENHAM | 9 | 5.8 | 3 | 6.7 |
| DOWNSIDE | 1 | 0.6 | 2 | 4.4 |
| MALVERN | 2 | 1.2 | 2 | 4.4 |
| MARLBOROUGH | 6 | 3.9 | 2 | 4.4 |

78 Stanier became the 2nd Baronet in 1921 on the death of his father, Sir Beville Stanier, for whom the Baronetcy was created in 1917 in recognition of his efforts in organising sugar beet production during the war. See Stanier in Charles Mosley (ed.), *Burke's Peerage and Baronetage*, 106th edition, 2 volumes. (Crans, Switzerland: Burke's Peerage (Genealogical Books) Ltd, 1999)

| SCHOOL | 1940 NUMBER | PERCENTAGE OF GROUP (156) | 1944 NUMBER | PERCENTAGE OF GROUP (45) |
|---|---|---|---|---|
| RUGBY | 8 | 5.2 | 2 | 4.4 |
| ONE PUPIL | 26[79] | 16.8 | 12 | 26.7 |
| **TOTALS** | **74** | **48.0** | **35** | **77.8** |

Although single products of one school predominate in both comparisons overall, there is a commonality between the 1940 and the 1944 groups of brigadiers amongst schools providing multiple officers to the group. A distinct group of schools, Eton, Wellington, Cheltenham, Rugby and Marlborough dominate. Therefore, across the two groups combined not only do the public schools as a whole provide a majority of all officers reaching the rank of brigadier – at least 109 of 199, or 54.8 percent – but a group of five schools produced 71 of the 109, or 65.1 percent of it. Five schools, therefore, provided over one-third of the whole group – 71 out of 199, or 35.7 percent. It can therefore be concluded that even after four and a half years of war, the public schools – and furthermore an even smaller group within them, increased their dominance considerably over the route of entry to the profession of any army officer who would rise to senior command.

**Table 5.6 Schools Combined 1940 & 1944**
**Associations of Schools and Regiments of First Commissioning, 1944 Group**

| 1940 SCHOOL | NUMBER | PERCENTAGE OF WHOLE GROUP (199) |
|---|---|---|
| ETON | 16 | 8.0 |
| WELLINGTON | 18 | 9.0 |
| CHELTENHAM | 12 | 6.0 |
| DOWNSIDE | 3 | 1.5 |
| MALVERN | 4 | 2.0 |
| MARLBOROUGH | 8 | 4.2 |
| RUGBY | 10 | 5.0 |
| ONE PUPIL | 38 | 19.1 |
| TOTALS | 109 | 54.8 |

The correlation of regiments to schools in the 1944 group is as follows, including only those educational institutions which produced two or more officers who attained the rank of brigadier before or during the initial stages of the Battle of Normandy.

79 Excluding Downside for 1940 calculations, as it is included as a line item above to allow comparison with the 1944 group.

**Table 5.7 Association of Schools and Regiments**

| School | No. | Arm | Regiment |
|---|---|---|---|
| CHELTENHAM | 1 | ARTILLERY | ROYAL HORSE ARTILLERY |
| | 2 | INFANTRY | GREEN HOWARDS QUEEN'S (TA) |
| ETON | 5 | INFANTRY | GUARDS (4) KING'S OWN YORKSHIRE LIGHT INFANTRY |
| DOWNSIDE | 1 | INFANTRY | DURHAM LIGHT INFANTRY |
| | 1 | CAVALRY | 10TH HUSSARS |
| MALVERN | 1 | INFANTRY | ARGYLL & SUTHERLAND HIGHLANDERS |
| | 1 | ARMOUR | ROYAL TANK CORPS |
| MARLBOROUGH | 2 | INFANTRY | ROYAL FUSILIERS<br>GORDON HIGHLANDERS |
| RUGBY | 2 | INFANTRY | CAMERON HIGHLANDERS<br>BORDER REGIMENT |
| WELLINGTON | 2 | CAVALRY | 9TH LANCERS<br>15TH/19TH KINGS HUSSARS |
| | 5 | INFANTRY | ROYAL NORTHUMBERLAND FUSILIERS<br>DUKE OF CORNWALL'S LIGHT INFANTRY<br>WELCH REGIMENT<br>ARGYLL & SUTHERLAND HIGHLANDERS<br>SEAFORTH HIGHLANDERS |
| | 1 | INDIAN ARMY | INDIAN ARMY UNATTACHED LIST |

Again, as highlighted in Chapter 2, the notion of 'Eton and the Guards' is sustained with all four officers from Eton College being initially commissioned into the Regiments of Foot Guards, even though Hugh Kindersley (originally an officer of the Scots Guards) was serving away from the Guards in command of 6 (Airlanding) Brigade on D-Day. Also, in common with the 1940 brigadiers, there is little – arguably, in this case no – correlation between the location of the school attended and the infantry regiment of first commissioning; for example, officers commissioned into Scottish regiments were not old boys of Scottish schools.

## Regimental and Pre-War Service

Unlike the practice in the First World War and in 1940, by 1944 fighting commands in all but one case were 'to arm appropriate', i.e. infantry officers commanded infantry brigades; Guards officers commanded Guards formations (both infantry and armoured) and cavalry/Royal Tank Regiment officers commanded armoured brigades. Officers originally of the Royal Artillery and Royal Engineers did not command fighting formations outside their own arm of service on D-Day, with the sole exception of Brigadier John Currie. Currie was originally commissioned into the Royal Horse Artillery, commanded 2nd Field Regiment, Royal Artillery in France in 1940 and 9 Armoured Brigade in

1942/43, after a successful campaign in the Western Desert.[80] Currie was killed in action on 26 June 1944 by an enemy artillery barrage while returning to his command tank.[81] As noted above, he was replaced in command by Michael Carver, originally commissioned into the 2nd Battalion, Royal Tank Corps on 1 February 1935.[82] As Carver's case illustrates, brigadiers who became casualties were quickly replaced from within by junior, sometimes younger, officers; major generals and above would be replaced often from without by other officers of level status, e.g. Verney's replacement of Erskine at 7th Armoured Division in August 1944 and Bucknall being replaced by Horrocks at XXX Corps also in August, although both were lieutenant generals. In 1940, the only replacements of brigadiers were those temporarily separated from their units in the retreat in France; only one was killed, in the final stages of the evacuation when the chain of command had been disrupted, so a direct comparison is not possible.

Among the 45 officers in this group, the regiment of first commissioning produced several smaller subgroupings as follows, which can be used to further define regimental connections:

**Table 5.8 Normandy Brigadiers, Regiment of First Commissioning**

| | |
|---|---|
| GUARDS | 7 |
| CAVALRY | 3 |
| ROYAL TANK CORPS/REGIMENT | 2 |
| INFANTRY | 33 |
| TOTAL | 45 |

A further division can be made into officers who served in the same regiments (albeit not at the same time) which shows:

**Table 5.9A Normandy Brigadiers: Regiment of First Commissioning: Guards and Cavalry**

| GUARDS | OFFICER | DATE OF COMMISSIONING |
|---|---|---|
| SCOTS GUARDS (3) | LOVAT[83] | AUGUST 1931 |
| | JOHNSON | NOVEMBER 1923 |
| | KINDERSLEY | AUGUST 1917 |
| ROYAL TANK CORPS/REGIMENT (2) | CARVER | JANUARY 1935 |
| | CRACROFT | JANUARY 1925 |

80 Currie, while a gunner. was awarded the Distinguished Service Order in February 1942 for the Middle East, with a bar awarded for the Battle of El Alamein in February 1943 and a second bar for command of 4 Armoured Brigade in Italy *http://www.hambo.org/hazelwood/view_man.php?id=114* accessed 19 May 2017.

81 http://www.cwgc.org/find-war-dead/casualty/2956014/CURRIE,%20JOHN%20CECIL Commonwealth War Graves Commission. accessed 19 May 2017.

82 *London Gazette*, 1 February 1935, p.773.

83 Simon Fraser (as he then was) had originally been commissioned as a Second Lieutenant in a Territorial regiment, The Lovat Scouts, in January 1930; however, he transferred to the Regular Army in August 1931. London Gazette, 2 September 1932, p. 5621.

## Guards and Cavalry

### *Scots Guards*

While Kindersley, Johnson and Lovat were all officers of the Scots Guards, their mutual connection pre-war beyond a common cap badge was slight. Despite being decorated with an MC in the First World War, Kindersley had resigned his commission in 1920 at age 21 and gone onto the Regular Army Reserve of Officers, from which he rejoined the regiment in November 1938. Lovat, after succeeding his father as the 15th Lord Lovat in 1932, also resigned his commission as a lieutenant in 1937 to be placed on the Supplementary Reserve of Officers; when he returned to the army from the reserve in 1939, it was to a commission in the family regiment, The Lovat Scouts, which was a Territorial Army unit. (The regiment was a 'family' one in the truest sense, having been formed by the 14th Lord Lovat to fight in the Second Boer War; although the 14th Lord Lovat, father of the 15th, was promoted during the First World War, the family connection remained strong and direct, as shown by the 15th Lord's return to command it). Johnson, commissioned in between them, was the only officer with uninterrupted interwar service, being promoted captain in March 1932; from 1936 to 1939 he served in staff appointments at home and overseas[84] before being appointed lieutenant colonel to command the war-raised 3rd Battalion of the regiment in 1940. Kindersley transferred to the Scots Guards battalion converting to armour in the newly raised Guards Armoured Division before being appointed to command the 6 (Airlanding) Brigade in 1943. It is therefore unlikely that the three served together before the war and the likelihood lessened further between 1940 and 1944.

### *Royal Tank Regiment*

Bernard Cracroft[85] was first commissioned into the Royal Tank Corps in January 1925, when Michael Carver was still at Winchester College. The latter was commissioned into the same corps almost exactly 11 years after Cracroft, in January 1936. By this stage Cracroft was an instructor at the Tank Gunnery School at Lulworth Cove in Dorset and had been since November 1933. From April 1930 to March 1931, he had participated in operations on the North-West Frontier of India, suppressing the 'Red Shirt'

84 He served as a General Staff Officer Grade 3 (GSO 3) in Palestine, September-December 1936; as the Brigade Major, London District March 1937-October 1938 and as a GSO 2 in the War Office, October 1938-December 1939 *HYAL*, January 1942, p.606.

85 His given names were Hugh John Bernard, (named after his father Colonel Hugh, Royal Army Service Corps), but he went by Bernard. His younger brother, Lieutenant Colonel Robert Cracroft MC RTR (born 1910) was killed in action in Normandy, commanding 158th (9th Bn Loyal Lancashire Regiment) Regiment, Royal Armoured Corps, on 13 August 1944. www.cwgc.org/find-wardead/casualty/2847858/CRACROFT,%20ROBERT%20GEORGE Commonwealth War Graves Commission 'Find War Dead', accessed 1 June 2017.

uprising of Afridi tribesmen.[86] It has not been possible to confirm definitively whether Cracroft instructed Carver (the former left the school in November 1936).[87] Both had field commands in North Africa in 1943, but by the time Carver had been appointed the commanding officer of 1st Battalion, Royal Tank Regiment (in April 1943), Cracroft was in a different brigade. On Cracroft's appointment briefly to command 4 Armoured Brigade in December 1943,[88] Carver was about to leave Italy with 1st Battalion, Royal Tank Regiment to prepare for Normandy with 22 Armoured Brigade and their paths did not directly cross.

## Infantry – English/Irish Regiments

**Table 5.9B Normandy Brigadiers: Regiment of First Commissioning: Same Regiment Infantry Regiments: English/Irish**

| | OFFICER | DATE OF COMMISSIONING |
|---|---|---|
| BORDER REGIMENT (2) | BLOMFIELD | APRIL 1916 |
| | ELRINGTON | SEPTEMBER 1917 |
| KING'S OWN YORKSHIRE LIGHT INFANTRY (2) | CASS | OCTOBER 1916 |
| | WALKER | DECEMBER 1920 |
| NORTHAMPTONSHIRE REGIMENT (2) | ESSAME | MARCH 1916 |
| | LINGHAM | SEPTEMBER 1915 |
| ROYAL FUSILIERS (2) | EKINS | DECEMBER 1917 |
| | HILL | 1931 |
| ROYAL ULSTER RIFLES (2) | MOLE | APRIL 1916 |
| | KNOX | JUNE 1917 |

As referred to above, infantry brigade commands in Normandy were 'to arm appropriate', in effect, commanded by officers who had been commissioned into the infantry as their original arm of service. This did not necessarily translate as being that officers commissioned into English country regiments automatically commanded infantry brigades in English divisions, or that officers originally commissioned into Scottish regiments commanded Scottish brigades in Scottish divisions. By 1944, manning demands meant that attempts to sustain regional characteristics in infantry brigades and divisions, especially in those units from the Territorial Army which had recruited from specific areas (such as 50th (Northumbrian) Division being made up of brigades, battalions and soldiers from the English North-East) had become unsustainable and largely artificial.

86 Service in this campaign was recognised by the award of the India General Service Medal 1908 with clasp 'North-West Frontier 1930–31'.

87 Cracroft, Hugh John Bernard in *HYAL* January 1942, p.691.

88 He moved to command 8 Armoured Brigade in March 1944, Joslen, *Orders of Battle*, vol. 1, p.160

For example, the 53rd (Welsh) Division was commanded by an Englishman and one of its subordinate formations was known as 'The International Brigade', as it contained at least notionally English, Scottish and Welsh infantry battalions.[89] The only brigade commander in the division originally commissioned into a Welsh infantry regiment[90] was Stanley Jones, late of the Royal Welch Fusiliers, in 158 Brigade. Although two brigadiers in the group had come from the same Northern Irish infantry regiment, the Royal Ulster Rifles, on D-Day both were commanding infantry brigades in English, originally Territorial Army, divisions.[91]

Valentine Blomfield (71 Brigade, 53rd (Welsh) Division) and Maxwell Elrington (177 Brigade, 59th (Staffordshire) Division) had both begun their careers in the Border Regiment, the former in April 1916, the latter in September 1917. Blomfield had served in the 1st Battalion[92] during the First World War; Elrington served less than a year as a regimental officer before spending the rest of the war as an aide-de-camp to a divisional commander in Italy from July 1918-February 1919, and his and Bloomfield's paths did not intersect. However, both officers served on operations in Waziristan from 1921–1924. Both were pre-war Staff College contemporaries, graduating in December 1935.[93]

Edward 'Copper' Cass of the King's Own Yorkshire Light Infantry (8 Brigade, 3rd Division) was commissioned into its 2nd Battalion in October 1916, serving exclusively on the Western Front, where he was wounded, Mentioned in Dispatches and awarded both a DSO and an MC, all before he was 21.[94] His sole active service between the wars was as an instructor at the Small Arms School, India from February 1935 to February 1939. Eton-educated John Walker (146 Brigade, 49th (West Riding) Division) was too young for First World War service, being commissioned in December 1920; he, however, served overseas putting down the Afridi 'Red Shirt' rebellion in 1930–1931 (as had Bernard Cracroft, passim).

Hubert Essame of 214 Brigade, 43rd (Wessex) Division and John Lingham of 197 Brigade, 59th (Staffordshire) Division, both served in the Northamptonshire Regiment and were near contemporaries. Essame was commissioned in March 1916, serving almost three years on the Western Front, he was wounded, mentioned in dispatches and awarded an MC. Lingham was commissioned in September 1915, was also wounded and received an MC, but ended his war in the Middle East serving with the Egyptian Expeditionary Force for most of 1918. Both officers attended the Staff College in the

89 C. N. Barclay, *The History of the 53rd (Welsh) Division in the Second World War* (London: Wm. Clowes & Sons, 1936)

90 The Royal Welch Fusiliers, The Welch Regiment, the South Wales Borderers and the Welsh Guards.

91 Brigadier Fergus Knox, commanding 69 Infantry Brigade in 50th (Northumbrian) Division and Brigadier Gerald Mole, commanding 129 Infantry Brigade in 43rd (Wessex) Division. Both had been commissioned into the Royal Irish Rifles in 1917 and 1916 respectively, although Mole spent most of the war until early 1919 attached to the Machine Gun Corps. *HYAL* December 1938, pp.456 & 480.

92 TNA WO/95/4311 War Diary, 1st Battalion Border Regiment January 1916.

93 *The Times*, London, issue 47297, 13 February 1936, p.9.

94 'Edward Earnshaw Eden Cass Private Papers', Imperial War Museum IWM Documents, 1471, 1987–2002.

interwar period, although Essame went to Quetta[95] and spent 1926 to 1934 in various staff appointments in India before returning to take up a GSO 3 posting at the War Office. Lingham specialised in staff appointments connected to weaponry in the early 1930s, including a period as an instructor at the Small Arms School at Netheravon before moving into conventional staff roles in Northern Command from 1937 to 1939. Lingham graduated from Staff College in December 1935.[96]

In professional terms, Maurice Ekins and James Hill were a generation apart, the former being 12 years older than the latter. Ekins was commissioned into the 2nd Battalion, Royal Fusiliers in December 1917, serving briefly on the Western Front, where he was wounded. Interwar he served as a staff officer (Allied Military Liaison Officer) in Turkey in 1923, and as a staff captain in the Rhine Army in 1928–1929, in Northern Command 1929–32 and then in India, from October 1936 to November 1938. Hill served as a platoon commander in the 2nd Battalion up to 1936, when he left the army to work in his family's business but rejoined the army on the outbreak of war in 1939; his path is therefore unlikely to have crossed with Ekins, even though they served in the same battalion of the same regiment.[97]

Gerald Mole and Herbert Knox were both Royal Ulster Rifles officers, close in age (46 and 45 on D-Day) and First World War veterans. Knox, known as 'Gandhi'[98] was a Staff College graduate, had been wounded twice on the Western Front and spent much of the interwar period as a staff officer in the UK, serving with Territorials, in a staff captain's post in Southern Command and as a brigade major in Western Command. (He would command the 2nd Battalion, Royal Ulster Rifles in France in 1940).

## Infantry – Scottish

**Table 5.9C Normandy Brigadiers, Regiment of First Commissioning: Same Regiment Infantry Regiments – Scottish**

| | OFFICER | DATE OF COMMISSIONING |
|---|---|---|
| ARGYLL & SUTHERLAND HIGHLANDERS (2) | CUNNINGHAM | AUGUST 1914 |
| | DUNLOP | AUGUST 1926 |
| CAMERON HIGHLANDERS (3) | BARBER | OCTOBER 1916 |
| | MURRAY[99] | AUGUST 1923 |
| | LESLIE | AUGUST 1930 |
| SEAFORTH HIGHLANDERS (2) | HAUGH | JULY 1917 |
| | MACKINTOSH-WALKER | APRIL 1916 |

95 He graduated in December 1930, a direct contemporary of Colin Barber; *The Times*, London, issue 45765, 7 March 1931, p.17.
96 *The Army List*, January 1935 'Staff College: Senior Division' Column 920 (London: HMSO, 1935).
97 *https://paradata.org.uk/articles/extended-biography-brig-james-hill* accessed 07 May 2017.
98 David Orr and David Truesdale, *The Rifles Are There: 1st and 2nd Battalions of the Royal Ulster Rifles* (London: Pen & Sword, 2005), p.52
99 Murray was originally commissioned into the Cameronians (Scottish Rifles).

James Cunningham, the eldest of the Normandy group, was a considerably experienced officer having been commissioned in August 1914, during the early days of the First World War; after brief service on the Western Front, much of his war was spent in the Balkans. He ended the war as a 26-year old temporary lieutenant colonel commanding a service battalion, having been wounded and receiving a Military Cross. Reverting to major, he spent the next three years as a brigade major in the Black Sea and Turkey occupation forces. He also saw active service in India in 1935–1936 during operations on the North-West Frontier. He did not attend the Staff College and did not regain the rank he had held in 1919 until 1941. Andrew Dunlop was only commissioned in 1926; he served overseas on attachment to the King's African Rifles from December 1933 to October 1936 and on return served as the Adjutant of a Territorial Army unit from 1937. However, he graduated from Staff College after 1940. Due to their various absences abroad, it is unlikely that Cunningham and Dunlop knew each other through common service.

The trio of Cameron Highlander officers are anomalous as although there was a fourteen-year bracket between the first (Colin Barber, 46 Brigade, 15th (Scottish) Division) and the last (Norman Leslie, 130 Brigade, 43rd Wessex Division) commissioned in 1916 and 1930 respectively; the officer in the middle of the three in terms of original commission date, Horatius Murray (153 Brigade, 51st (Highland)) Division actually joined the Cameronians in 1923, transferring to the Cameron Highlanders in 1935. Barber, who had graduated from the Staff College in Quetta in December 1930[100] was another veteran of Waziristan in the 1920s, being Mentioned in Dispatches in 1925 for his conduct there. After Quetta, he served in several staff posts in Scottish and Southern Commands in the UK from 1932–37. Norman Leslie, the youngest, spent his time on regimental service, reaching the rank of captain in August 1938 on the eighth anniversary of his commissioning; he spent two years on attached service to the Royal West African Frontier Force from 1936 to 1938. Horatius Murray spent 1936–1938 at the Staff College, Camberley and was then posted to a GSO 2 job at the War Office. The paths of Leslie and Murray may briefly have crossed paths regimentally around 1935.

David Haugh (152 Brigade, 51st (Highland) Division) and John Mackintosh-Walker (227 Brigade, 15th (Scottish) Division) were roughly contemporary in the Seaforth Highlanders, receiving commissions in July 1917 and April 1916 respectively. Haugh spent much of the rest of the war through to 1920 attached to the Machine Gun Corps on the Western Front, where he was twice wounded, mentioned in dispatches and received a Military Cross. He graduated from Quetta at the end of 1930,[101] and spent the next six years on active service on the North-West Frontier and in Burma. John (also known as 'Ronnie') 'Tosh' Mackintosh-Walker was posted to the 2nd Battalion on commissioning; he ended his First World War Service with a Military Cross and two bars and a Mention in Dispatches. He served as a Company Commander at the RMC

100 Staff College, Quetta. *The Times*, London, issue 45765, 7 March 1931, p.17.
101 Thus making him an exact contemporary of Hubert Essame, passim.

from 1929–33,[102] and saw active service on the North-West Frontier and in Palestine, where he was again Mentioned.[103] He did not attend Staff College.

## Staff College

For the purposes of this study, only officers who attended the full courses at the Staff Colleges at Camberley and Quetta and held the p.s.c. qualification have been considered.[104] Short war courses during either World War have been disregarded as reliable and comprehensive lists of attendees are not available and the length of the course – weeks, rather than years – was less likely to be a source of nascent networks.[105] Of the 45 officers in the group, 16 or 37 percent, were Staff College graduates – 13 from Camberley and 3 from Quetta.[106]

Into the 1930s, the number of applications to Staff College greatly exceeded the number of places available. This was due, in part, to a common realisation that in a system where promotion prospects had stagnated due to bottlenecks and a lack of incentives for officers to retire early, professional distinctions may put one ahead of the pack. Even officers with a conditional offer awaiting a vacancy after passing the competitive examination could not be certain of a guaranteed place.

Among the 16 are some direct contemporaries in the 1944 group. The Quetta officers, who all graduated in December 1930,[107] were Colin Muir, Hubert Essame and David Haugh, when the Commandant was Major General (later Lieutenant General Sir) Thomas Humphreys, a former Director of Military Operations and the Chief Instructor was Colonel C. J. E. Auchinleck, (later Field Marshal Sir). The group of four who left Camberley together at the end of 1935 were Valentine Blomfield, Maxwell Elrington, George Johnson and John Lingham, when the Commandant was Major General (later General Sir) Clement Armitage. Maurice Ekins was in his second year at Camberley as Armitage took over as Commandant and Blomfield, Elrington, Johnson and Lingham were joining the College.

Of the remaining officers of the Normandy group, Stanley Jones left Camberley in December 1932, when John Dill, later Chief of the Imperial General Staff, was

102 *The Times*. London, issue 45295, 30 August 1929, p.7.
103 Obituary, *The Times*, London, issue 49923, 1 August 1944, p.6.
104 No officers in the Normandy group attended the RAF or RN Staff colleges under the exchange arrangements.
105 Graduates of the Junior Staff Courses held in France between November 1916 and April 1917 or at Cambridge University between September 1917 and January 1919 were indicated in the Army List by the abbreviation (*s.c.*), or (*S.C.*) if graduates of the Senior Staff Courses held between the same dates. If the letters were unitalicised, it meant that the officer had attended an equivalent short war course after 1939.
106 If Bernard Leicester were included, the figure would be 17, as he was also a graduate of the Army Staff College.
107 *The Times*, London, 7 March 1931, issue 45765, p.17.

Commandant. Ernest Pepper arrived when Armitage held that post but graduated in December 1936, during the relatively brief tenure as Commandant of the future Viscount Gort (March 1936 to September 1937). The last of the Normandy group to graduate before the reorganisation of the Staff College course in 1939[108] were Horatius Murray in 1937 and Kenneth Smith in 1938.

The aim of the College reorganisation was to lower the age at which officers became eligible to join the restructured junior division, with an intention to favour officers aged under 30. The reformed senior division – for which there was no entrance examination – would be held at Minley Manor near Aldershot, aimed at older officers, typically in their mid-thirties, and perhaps already (but not essentially) graduates of the junior division. The goal of this division was to increase the supply of General Staff Officers Grade 1 (GSO 1), usually a lieutenant colonel's posting. However, the approach of war curtailed this reform and the 1939 Camberley course intake was terminated after only seven months to provide officers to serve on operations; the Chief Instructor on the outbreak of war, Colonel Brian Horrocks, went to France to command an infantry brigade. In January 1940, the course was restructured to run for 17 weeks and focussed on the essentials of divisional staff work.[109] John Churcher, Bernard Cracroft, Nigel Poett and Gerald Verney were graduates of the curtailed course.

In terms of 'talent spotting' and being beneficiaries of patronage, those who arrived at Camberley in the second half of the 1930s were perhaps less fortunate than their forebears of a decade before, when the likes of Alan Brooke, Bernard Montgomery and Bernard Paget were serving as instructors. Although Lord Gort, Ronald Adam[110] and Bernard Paget[111] held the post of Commandant of the Staff College in quick succession from 1936 to 1939, their relatively brief tenures due to promotion away to posts vital to the coming war effort lessened their impact as the instigators of their own networks. It should be noted, however, that those at Camberley in the mid-1930s were taught by such significant figures as Archibald 'Archie' Nye (Vice Chief of the Imperial General Staff 1941–44), who instructed from 1932 to 1935; 'Bill' Slim (Commander, XIV Army, Burma) and Humfrey Gale (later Chief Administrative Officer, SHAEF) from 1934 to 1937.

## Accelerated Promotion?

The officers serving as brigadiers in 1944 had occupied a range of ranks in 1940, from lieutenant to lieutenant colonel. The step from lieutenant colonel to brigade command (bypassing a posting as a full colonel in a staff posting) was not unusual or atypical. In

108 OUR SPECIAL CORRESPONDENT, 'New Army Staff Course.' *The Times*, 24 January 1939, p.9.
109 E. Smalley, 'Qualified, but unprepared: Training for War at the Staff College in the 1930s' in *British Journal of Military History*, vol. 2, issue 1 (November 2015), pp.55–71.
110 Adjutant General of the Army, 1941–1945.
111 GOC Home Forces, 1941–1944, et cetera

1940, six of the Normandy group were lieutenant colonels, a further four were majors, acting lieutenant colonels. Twenty-five were majors (one of whom was temporarily in command of his battalion as a major, not as a temporary or acting lieutenant colonel).[112] There were two acting majors, eight captains and a lieutenant – the latter being the, again most atypical, Michael Carver. Active service can, therefore, in the cases of the Majors and below, be credited as a promotion enhancer; under peacetime conditions to rise from major to brigadier in four years would be most unlikely. Of the majors and below, 15 were Staff College graduates (the precocious Carver did not attend Camberley until 1950), indicating that the qualification was desirable, and an aid to faster advancement. Although again, the factor that the need to fill vacancies outstripped the supply of pre-war p.s.c. should not be discounted.

## Decorations for Previous Service

Of the 46 officers holding brigade commands on or after D-Day, a considerable proportion had been decorated for services in connection with the war to this point; others received awards in addition to those granted for service in the First World War. The intention in this section is to correlate the possession of gallantry awards and appointment to brigade command in this specific context.

As noted above, 16 of the 45 officers were Staff College graduates, some 37 percent. However, the number of officers in the group who had earned decorations prior to D-Day came to 37 – 82 percent of the total. 13 officers carried decorations earned in the First World War: one DSO,[113] 12 MCs, two with bars to the MC (second award) and one with a second bar (third award) to the MC.[114] There were seven awards of Mentions in Dispatches (MiD) for the First World War to the group. Rewards for interwar service were comparatively scarce; two MiDs and one DSO for operations in Palestine in 1936–37.[115] Prior to 1939, 16 officers had been decorated at least once during their career (including one for service to the Royal Family),[116] eight were recipients of multiple awards prior to 1939, six added Second World War decorations to their holdings.

112 Colin Barber, commanding 4/Cameron Highlanders.
113 Awarded to Lieutenant Edward Cass, then 2nd Battalion King's Own Yorkshire Light Infantry.
114 The MC and two bars were awarded to John Mackintosh-Walker: MC 1917, the first bar to MC in 1918, the second bar to MC in 1919. He was further Mentioned in Dispatches in 1937 for operations on Palestine. He would receive a posthumous Distinguished Service Order in October 1944 for his command of 227 Infantry Brigade, backdated to date of death, 15 July 1944, *London Gazette*, 19 October 1944, p.4785.
115 The DSO and one of the MiDs were to the same officer; Maxwell Elrington of the Border Regiment.
116 Gerald Verney was appointed Member of the Royal Victorian Order, 5th Class in 1937, while still serving with the Grenadier Guards, for services to the Monarch.

Of the 16 Staff College graduates in the Normandy list, 12 had received decorations, 5 prior to the Second World War and seven during it. The combination of an award and a p.s.c. qualification being therefore 26 percent of the group. Additional factors cannot be overlooked for officers not achieving a Staff College qualification. These included not taking the competitive exams for Staff College, not receiving a recommendation from a commanding officer, failing the competitive exam, or even being successful in the examination but insufficiently high in the pass list to gain entry from the limited number of places available. As shown, there is a statistical argument that a decoration was as influential an element for an officer's advancing to senior command as a staff qualification. However, two p.s.c. brigadiers in field commands in Normandy had no decorations or distinctions of any kind prior to 1944 – Maurice Ekins of 131 Brigade, and Nigel Poett of 5 Parachute Brigade.[117]

## Conclusions

The working assumptions for this chapter again, were to make a comparison with the 1940 group of officers; firstly, that the average age of the Normandy group of brigadiers would be lower than its 1940 counterpart. By the spring of 1944, the average age of brigadiers in fighting formations intended to operate during the invasion of France had dropped appreciably compared with their 1940 counterparts. However, this is explained in part by the creation after 1940 of new, special forces units such as parachute, airborne and commando formations which attracted officers who were younger and more ambitious than the norm. In conventional formations such as infantry and some armoured brigades, there had not been much change in the average since 1940 – with officers in command typically being in their mid-forties. Another factor in lowering the average age was the casualty rate for some brigadiers. In France in 1940 only one brigadier had been killed in action and this was during the evacuation, so he was not immediately replaced.[118] In Normandy, two brigadiers were killed in action in July and one wounded on D-Day itself; a fourth, Sandie, was sacked. In these cases, they were replaced by younger subordinates either from staff positions within or from component units of the brigade.

117 Poett would, however, end the war with two Distinguished Service Orders to his name: a late award for Normandy (*London Gazette* 29 March 1945, p.1709) and a bar for the Rhine Crossing, (*London Gazette*, 21 June 1945, p.3231). Maurice Ekins died of wounds on 7 November 1944 in conditions still considered as contentious. See A. Holborn, *The 56th Infantry Brigade and D-Day: An Independent Infantry Brigade and the campaign in North-West Europe 1944–45* (London, Continuum, 2010) pp.182–183.

118 No brigadiers were fatal casualties in Norway. The casualty was Brigadier Geoffrey Mansergh, the DA & QMG of II Corps who died of wounds received during the evacuation in hospital in the UK.

The average age of the officers is considerably lower in 1944, at 42.4 years overall, than the 1940 group – 49.02 years for the BEF and NWEF combined. (The median is 43, compared with 46 in 1940; the mode is 46, compared to 49). 16 officers in the Normandy group, nearly a third of them, were too young to have served in the First World War. In the Normandy group overall, 11 officers were under 40 on 6 June 1944. Seven of these were serving in armoured[119] and infantry brigades[120] and the fall in the average cannot, therefore, be purely ascribed to the emergence of those war-raised special forces after 1940.

The second factor considered, was whether previous battle experience between 1939 and 1944 contributed to accelerated promotion at an earlier age and whether possession of gallantry decorations and other honours contributed to this process of appointment. Thirty-seven of the 45 were in possession of decorations, of whom 13 had received them in the First World War; interwar decorations were scarce, indicating that awards in the course of the present war were an advantage for advancement. The combination of a Staff College qualification and a gallantry award was equally marked; of the 16 graduates of Camberley or Quetta, 12 had at least one, representing the single largest grouping among the officers. By peacetime standards, the progression of over half the group from major to brigadier in just under four years indicates that active service was a factor in accelerated advancement among this group.

In January 1940, 23 of the Normandy brigadiers were serving as majors; of these, 10 were Staff College graduates. There were five substantive lieutenant colonels, of whom none were Staff College graduates and of whom four had combat experience in the war thus far – two in France only: two in France and the Middle East and/or Mediterranean. Of the five acting lieutenant colonels, four had commanded battalions in 1940 – three in France and one in Norway; three were decorated in 1940, with one receiving a bar to a First World War DSO. Seven officers had started the war as captains, of whom only two were Staff College alumni; three of the seven were decorated for service in France in 1940 and five of them served in the Middle East and Mediterranean. The most marked advancement among the Normandy group was again the exceptional Michael Carver – a 'mere' lieutenant in 1940, but with extensive staff and combat experience in the North African and Mediterranean campaigns before 1944.

Additionally, unlike 1940, officers who had come up through the Territorial Army had risen to command both Territorial Army battalions and brigades in action. Territorials who had distinguished themselves in North Africa in 1941–1942, Tunisia and Italy in 1943 were not debarred from leading brigades in North-West Europe, although officers who had the accidental misfortune to command formations in Ken Anderson's First Army were less likely, regardless of their abilities, to serve in British Second Army due to Montgomery's preference to recall veterans of his – not Auchinleck's – Eighth Army.

119 Carver (4 Armoured Brigade) and Cracroft (8 Armoured Brigade).
120 Leslie (130 Brigade), Dunlop (146 Brigade), Colville (227 Brigade), Churcher (159 Brigade) and Senior (151 Brigade).

Ronald Senior and James Oliver, both part-time officers before the war, distinguished themselves in command of their battalions and later brigades and retained command in North-West Europe, indicating that the reluctance to promote pre-war Territorials to operational commands had been overcome by 1944.

The third factor was whether a pre-war Staff College qualification was still a prerequisite, or advantageous, in advancement to brigade command. With 37 percent of the group being in possession of a p.s.c. qualification the statistic is not decisive in and of itself alone.

The educational background of the 1944 group showed no deviation from 1940; former pupils of the public schools still dominated, and, in fact, increased as a proportion of the whole. A distinct group of schools, Eton, Wellington, Cheltenham, Rugby and Marlborough retained their dominance, although in 1944 Wellington had replaced Eton as the single largest provider of officers (and all the Guards Brigadiers). Over half, or 54.8 percent, of all the 109 officers reaching the rank of brigadier across the two groups were public school educated, but that group of five schools produced 71 of the 109, or 65.1 percent of it. 34 of the 45 in the Normandy group, an even higher proportion at 77 percent were public school educated. It can therefore be concluded that even after four and a half years of war, the public schools – and furthermore an even smaller group within them – remained the dominant means of entry to the profession of any army officer who would rise to senior operational command. From these figures, it also emerges that even though Territorial officers did rise to this level, a public school education was of advantage to them.

No regiments dominate among the group with only the Scots Guards and the Cameron Highlanders producing more than two officers, both contributing three; however, one of the Scots Guards officers, Lord Lovat, is a moot point in this regard, as he had resigned his regular commission and transferred to the Territorial Army before 1940. Of the seven regiments providing two officers to the group,[121] only four produced officers who could be considered close contemporaries at point of entry into the army, and only by disregarding further distinctions such as the specific battalion of a regiment.

A Staff College qualification was not an automatic route to brigade command, with just over a third of the Normandy group being pre-war or early war graduates of Camberley or Quetta, before the emphasis in the College's training shifted to producing as many officers qualified to operate as divisional staffs as possible in as short a time as possible to meet demand. Experience in France in 1940, highlighted in the Bartholomew Report, had noted deficiencies in staff training and capability. Combat experience, and other indicators of front line ability such as decorations, could therefore act as a route to command as much as, if not more than, the formal qualifications sought and preferred in peacetime.

121 The Border Regiment, The King's Own Yorkshire Light Infantry, The Northamptonshire Regiment, the Royal Fusiliers, the Royal Ulster Rifles, the Argyll and Sutherland Highlanders and the Seaforth Highlanders.

When divisional commanders are included in the comparison, only one division among either the initial assault or follow-on formations had a commander and his brigade commanding subordinates where all were public school educated and Staff College graduates, the 79th Armoured Division, but this was an atypical case as there was only one brigadier subordinate to the commander. Three out of six of the assault divisions commands were fully public school educated down to brigade level; in the follow-on divisions it was four out of seven. (In the other three, it was uniformly 75 percent, or three out of four). The fighting command groups of four of the seven follow-on divisions were 100 percent public school educated, with the other three being 75 percent so staffed; although one division had no Staff College graduates in its fighting command group, four of the others were 50 percent p.s.c.

There is no single paradigm for an officer who would be in place commanding a brigade in Normandy in June 1944. From these findings he would be aged between 43–46, educated at public school and preferably from a select group of schools, preferably but not necessarily with First World War experience, and again preferably a Staff College qualification and to be in possession of one or more gallantry awards before landing in France 1944. There was no preference or dominance of a particular regiment, except, perhaps for the Royal Tank Regiment in armoured commands. He would also be from a background appropriate to his command, i.e. infantry for infantry, airborne and commando and armour or cavalry for armoured formations. The era of sappers and gunners commanding infantry formations had, by 1944, passed on.

# 6

# Conclusions

As the summer of 1940 began, attention shifted from the catastrophic defeats in France and Norway towards the possibility of invasion from now occupied France. Although lessons clearly needed to be identified and changes made to how the army fought and, perhaps, was structured, in the face of impending danger radical change could not be imposed too swiftly as the army rebuilt. The Bartholomew Committee's final report on the defeat in France avoided direct criticism of individuals; its further recommendations were watered down as it passed around the army's senior commanders. Of most immediate application to this study was one that the brigade should be the fundamental operational fighting unit in preference to the division; this recommendation was not adopted.

The army which began the Second World War, especially at this level of command, continued to reflect the social and educational makeup of the army of the 1920s and 1930s, reaching back further to the First World War. Changes in the societal makeup of the officer corps between 1914 and 1918 did not much endure. Although the army underwent processes of evolution and change from 1940 to 1944 in officer selection, these did not impact greatly at this level of operation and command. Attempts at reform to clear promotion log jams prior to the outbreak of war came too little and too late to affect brigadiers in 1940, as did changes to personnel and officer selection during the war itself.

In the course of compiling this study – which it should be emphasised is not presented as or claiming to offer a paradigm for all senior officer advancement in the course of the Second World War, simply an examination of two specific groups based on rank, comparing a point of defeat, and another proceeding to victory – a number of factors proved to be of no preferential impact on an officers' advancement after 1940. Although public schools predominate in the educational backgrounds of all the officers, and counter-intuitively increased as a proportion in the 1944 group, no particular school dominates over others. No particular regiment figures greatly to the disadvantage of others; although the Royal Artillery is the most numerous single regiment, its officers in 1940 were in specialist gunner or senior staff posts, and in 1944 all officers were commanding brigades reflecting their background – infantry for infantry, cavalry/Royal Tank Regiment for armour. There is no lobby based on particular school or regiment.

Equally, there are no evident 'rings' among the officers, based either on places served, or officers served with or under. There is some evidence of patronage, notably from Alanbrooke and Montgomery, but this was occasionally overlapping and sometimes removed.

Notwithstanding the scale of the defeats in Europe in 1940, the charge that service in a brigadier's posting in either Battle of France or the Norwegian campaign in 1940 led to the automatic end of an officer's career is readily refuted. A brigadier's posting could be a temporary expedient to fulfil an operational need, and some officers in the 1940 group did revert to their substantive ranks, e.g. colonel, and did not progress further in the course of the war. However, a sufficient number of the group did advance in rank at least one step beyond brigadier – to major general or beyond, even if only temporarily, before 1945 and the end of the Second World War – to disprove the simplistic assertion that mere participation in either campaign was enough to stall, or end, a military career.

An officer holding a brigadier's position in France and Norway in 1940 was, with a few exceptions occasioned by operational circumstances (such as the commander becoming a casualty) a pre-war, professional Regular Army officer who had served throughout. By 1944, more officers who had progressed up the promotion chain came from a Territorial background, but regular soldiers retained their predominance in command positions. The majority of the officers in the group received their commissions before or in 1914; the immediate outbreak of the First World War produced a spike in the number of commissions reflecting the immediate need to expand the army in the summer of 1914, but few of the officers in the group were commissioned after 1915. Indeed, the highest single number of commissions among the group overall came in 1914.

At this time, officers who fitted pre-war social profiles of suitability through the advantages of birth and education had an edge; although the school and university OTC system had been established in 1908, a significant number of the 1940 brigadiers, nearly 20 percent of them, had been commissioned before then. A public school education, while not a mandated requirement for access to a commission, was sufficiently prevalent to be a distinct preference before 1916, when pure demand loosened this system. The 1940 brigadiers were, however, almost completely products of the public school system. They attended 35 different public schools at varying times. No single school absolutely dominates the group, although Eton with 12 former pupils and Cheltenham, Wellington and Winchester – all traditional sources of supply – with 9 each, figure prominently. The assertion by Bowman and Connelly that the Edwardian officer corps was dominated by the products of six great schools is not borne out among this group of officers, although over half did come from schools of the Clarendon Group and the Headmasters' Conference.

Although products of the grammar schools became acceptable officer candidates as the First World War progressed, after 1919 and the rapid demobilisation of a mass army, officers who stayed in the army and progressed were predominantly public school alumni.

University graduates are a minority in the group, albeit a significant one, represented at a significantly higher rate than in the wider population. The most represented universities were Oxford and Cambridge; although the Oxford graduates formed three loose groupings by virtue of their overlapping attendance, all attended different colleges of the university. As part of an elite within a set, firstly of public schoolboys and secondly, in an even smaller group, university graduates, those officers who both survived the First World War and progressed did so against not insignificant statistical odds against doing so, a factor which also applies to all the other officers of the group.

With the exceptions of Eton – with 5 of 12 officers heading to Guards Regiments and arguably Fettes, as a Scottish school sending both its alumni to Scottish regiments – there is no correlation between schools and specific county or line infantry regiments. This shows there is no direct network connection of school to regiment, such as a particular school directing its pupils to specific regiments. Nor is there any strong correlation between the school's geographical location and the local county regiment.

Almost none of the officers could be described as having emerged from working, or lower class, backgrounds with one notable exception who was commissioned from the ranks. However, neither do they comfortably fit a stereotype of the officer corps as being dominated by the aristocratic or land-owning classes. In this sense, they defy the Barnett and Williamson archetype that the aristocratic and upper classes dominated and were still the main source of supply to the British officer corps up to, into and beyond the First World War. Otley's assertion of weakening social dominance by those social strata is supported by Frost's analysis of certain 1944 commanders, and both of these analyses are borne out by the 1940 brigadiers in this study. This shows that the trend was maintained into the Second World War, although by D-Day, at least at the brigadier level there had been some reassertion of the social background of the 'officer type', with an increase in percentage terms of public school alumni, including the Territorial officers.

This study has shown that Sheffield's assertion that even 'temporary gentlemen' could be inculcated with the system of values to fit in when the post-war social norms began to reassert themselves stands in respect of the officers studied, whether they progressed or not. Among the 1940 officers, an additional advantage was lent by the earning of decorations for gallantry or distinguished service. Having 'proved' themselves in action this lent them an additional means to stand out against other candidates. Contrary to expectation, where Adam's reforms of personnel selection sought to better reflect the 'people's army' being formed and the ability to choose officer candidates based on testing and field experience, the proportion of public school educated officers, even with the higher number of Territorials occupying brigade level commands, actually increased. While Adam's reforms came into effect after the outbreak of war and cannot be expected to have influenced the selection of officers for this level of command – as all the 1940 and 1944 groups were already serving, either as Regulars or Territorials in 1939 – the presence of a bigger and socially wider pool from which to select officers for promotion may have been thought to broaden the paradigm, but this was not the case. Although the resistance to appointing officers who had come up through the Territorial Army was to some extent overcome in front line commands by 1944, those who did were generally sent to formations which had originated in the Territorial system, even if by 1944 the distinction had become increasingly blurred and nominally 'Territorial' formations became mixed.

Another sub-group, the officers who had served as GSOs during the First World War, is significant as nearly a third of the whole group did so. The number of those who already were, or subsequently were, graduates from the Staff College is also statistically significant, as it represented a quarter of the whole. The fact that the majority of those who did (19 from 22) advanced in rank during the Second World War suggests its status as something proffering distinction and advantage over other potential candidates, representing nearly a third of all the officers who progressed in rank.

Otley's assertion about the decline of scions of the upper classes making up the British officer corps in the interwar period has some applicability to the 1940 group, but its influence endured as the senior officers of the time reflected the social make up of their group a generation or two before, when they actually joined the army. Following from this, the largest single professional group of relatives of the officers is indeed that of an army officer, with just over a fifth of the whole group being the sons of professional officers. Other professional groups, with the possible exception of clergy, did not feature sufficiently to be an influential factor, however indirectly, in an officer's advancement. However, all of the officers who were set to inherit Baronetcies from their fathers did progress beyond brigadier.

With the return of peace and demobilisation, attitudes towards the profession of soldiering quickly reverted to pre-war norms and prejudices. This attitude was particularly visible in the area of professional education, where prejudices and custom would reassert themselves as the army returned to 'normal'. The continued existence of the Senior Officers' School was a focus for this among some officers, despite its commendable intent to prepare officers both for battalion command and to inculcate a wider world view in its students. Some commanding officers, to whom the role of training and preparing their subordinate officers for command had traditionally devolved, opposed the very existence of the Senior Officers' School (whether or not their juniors later gained entry to the Staff College). Furthermore, graduating or having been directing staff thereof did not proffer any particular advantage to officers in terms of advancement or the generation of networks. As most of its commandants were late in their careers who retired thereafter their ability to influence the careers of former subordinates was limited.

Officers who served as GSOs during the First World War, and especially those who subsequently graduated from Staff College had an edge over those who had not, but not decisively so as several officers who had not done so but did graduate from Camberley and Quetta did progress after 1940. Attendance at the Imperial Defence College after 1927, when it was founded, was influential, as all who attended it from the group were promoted to higher command during the war, and it also generated small, but close groupings of officers as minor networks, in once case reinforced by the officers being contemporaries both at Camberley and Buckingham Gate.

The single most influential path for advancement, whatever the actual value of the education offered there, remained the successful completion of Staff College at Camberley or Quetta. The assessment that Brooke and Montgomery used their times there as directing staff in later years to 'talent spot' is well-founded, but other officers such as John Dill also identified pupils they would later act as patrons for. Camberley also produced clusters of officers who would reach general's rank during the war. An officer who was public school educated, a Staff College graduate and who had served overseas between 1919–1939, was therefore possessed of advantages ahead of his contemporaries.

Of the original group of 156 officers who were serving as brigadiers in 1940, 58 of them were promoted to the rank of major general or above, over a third of the group. While a minority of the whole, this is still a considerable proportion when not all officers could expect to advance to such a rank. This also disproves any contention that service in France or Norway at this level of command (or responsibility in the case of staff appointments) was definitively detrimental to the promotion prospects of these officers. Twenty-one officers would be further promoted to lieutenant general, over a third of the group of officers promoted, and while this represents less than one in seven of the whole France and Norway group, it further reinforces the idea that service in France or Norway was not automatically career limiting.

The dominance of the public schools in producing army officers was sustained among this group, with 54 of the 58 being products of the public schools. When the number of schools producing more than one officer who was advanced to major general is taken further into account, a smaller group of certain public schools retains its dominance in the production of successful officers, with the seven 'great' schools of the Clarendon Group generating 48 percent of the list, although some other schools with traditionally strong army connections, such as Lancing, had 100 percent success (even if it only produced two generals). Although direct contemporaneousness at school among the 58 was limited at only six officers, the number of connections broaden significantly when close – arriving within a year – or near – arriving within two years – attendance at schools is considered, involving 14 of the 18 schools in the group which produced general officers from brigadiers in this 1940 group. Only four schools had no contemporary pupil networks.

Across both groups of brigadiers, 1940 and 1944, a distinct group of schools, Eton, Wellington, Cheltenham, Rugby and Marlborough retained their dominance, although in 1944 Wellington had replaced Eton as the single largest provider of officers (and all the Guards Brigadiers). Over half of all the officers who reached the rank of Brigadier across the two groups were public school-educated, but the five schools produced the majority of these officers. Again, the schools identified by Bowman and Connelly are not the predominant ones in the 1944 group, suggesting that their influence as a source had weakened by the Second World War, while it had not completely declined.

Although the infantry dominates in the 1940 group, with 31 of the 58 officers being from county or line regiments at first commissioning, no particular single regiment predominates in the list of officers successful in gaining promotion. While all three Guards officers from the 1940 group reaching the rank of major general were from the Coldstream Guards on balance this is more likely to be coincidence than design. If there is a 'regimental group', it could be argued that this was from the Royal Tank Corps/Regiment, as four officers would transfer to it in the interwar period.

Regarding previous war or active service, the majority of the 58 were veterans of the Western Front, with only four officers spending all of the First World War away from this theatre. This indicates the significance of the Western Front, as the primary theatre, as a root of experience towards promotion for officers in the post-war period. Some secondary theatres produced groupings of officers with common experience, such as Gallipoli and Egypt, where five officers' service overlapped in various periods from 1915–1917, creating a group with common experience and knowledge. However, the largest single group was of those officers who served in India on operations between 1919 and 1937, with 12. This demonstrates the predominance of India as the main interwar theatre in which to gain operational experience in the group. Other areas, such as Iraq or Persia, did not generate connected networks of officers.

Attendance at Staff College, either at Camberley or Quetta, retained its significance as a route both to promotion and as a generator of networks between officers. Forty of the 58, over two-thirds, were graduates of Staff College and Camberley, with 36, was dominant. With no officers from the group graduating before 1922 or after 1932, the core years for developing groups of contemporaries were from 1924–1928, when 25 of the group passed through Camberley and generated overlapping contemporary networks. Quetta was less significant in generating networks, firstly due to the low number of graduates from it, four, and secondly the space between attendance. All nine of the officers in the whole 1940 group who attended the Imperial Defence College between 1933 and 1939 were promoted to major general or above; six of them were contemporaries at the College with two each in 1933–1935, producing further close networks.

The possession of an award for gallantry or distinguished service, be it in the First World War, interwar campaigns or indeed for service in 1940, did have impact on whether an officer was advanced after 1940. Over three-quarters of the officers in the 1940 group had one or more decorations prior to 1939; 73 officers in the overall group received distinctions and/or decorations for service in France or Norway, receiving a total of 82 awards (when multiple awards to individuals are accounted for). Although the group of officers who did not progress gained more awards (44 to 38), when the seniority of the award is taken into consideration, the officers promoted are more significant; seven out of eight officers who received the Companion of the Order of the Bath for 1940 would be promoted, indicating its significance as a marker of approval. Six of the ten first awards of the Distinguished Service Order, an award for gallantry or leadership were to officers who were promoted.

Networks among the advancing group can therefore be found based on certain schools, successful, overlapping attendance at Staff College and the Imperial Defence College and commonality of operational service away from the Western Front and in India. Receipt of decorations or distinctions, while not a 'network' can also be argued to have been a promotion enhancing factor.

Existence of patronage networks among those promoted is present, but not completely obvious. The single most significant figure is Brooke, as on paper all the brigadiers in his corps progressed to major general and above after 1940, even if few of the divisional commanders in II Corps (with the signal exception of Montgomery) advanced themselves or were put aside into less significant commands. Being taught by Brooke or Montgomery, and more particularly the former, was an influence in a number of cases, but not to the extent that it was a critically decisive factor in promotion. Additionally, Brooke's favour was not permanent; results mattered and his support, however indirect, could soon disappear.

This study shows that the social networks existing within the British Army between 1919 and 1939 fell between those on a formal basis (such as fellow Staff College graduates) and informal ones, based on initial education, such as where the future officers attended the same schools, albeit at different periods, a loose connection as alumni and 'old boys'. Also, given the wide range of regiments represented among the group, there is no real influencing network based on any particular regiment, although there was an expectation that officers of line and county regiments felt that they could call upon the career advice of former officers – whether they knew them personally or not – who had risen to high rank.

Yet there is no strong evidence that officers who did exercise patronage to a greater or lesser extent were influenced by their previous cap badge – the Royal Artillery for Brooke, the Royal Warwickshire Regiment for Montgomery; Dill's regiment of first commissioning, the Leinster Regiment, had been disbanded in 1922 on the formation of the Irish Free State but there is no indication that he preferred officers of Irish regiments. For Brooke, the breadth of the Royal Regiment of Artillery and its branches made it difficult to specify individual types of gunners. For Montgomery, the virtual absence of officers from the Royal Warwicks in commands either in 1940 or 1944 points towards the other direction – to an avoidance of selecting them.

Equally, external influencing networks are weak; the professions of an officer's parents and grandparents do not provide firm linkages; of the 13 officers whose parent or grandparent was a senior officer, only six had forbears who rose above the rank of colonel. The sole candidate who was the son and a grandson of a general, Clifford 'Joe' Beckett, spent much of the war on Malta, eventually becoming a major general but was neither a GSO nor a Staff College graduate. Although not a real 'network' except a perceived one, all four officers who were the heirs to Baronetcies advanced to major general with two proceeding to lieutenant general.

With regard to patronage from senior officers, this work upholds French's findings on the status of Brooke and Montgomery as patrons and 'talent spotters', primarily when both were instructors at Camberley. None of the 1940 officers were students at Quetta under Montgomery. Twenty-nine officers passed through Camberley during their overlapping tenures as instructors; 22 of these became major generals of whom 12 would further progress to lieutenant general There is, therefore, cause to identify attendees at Camberley between 1923 and 1927 as a network of successful officers. Commandants of the Staff College are less successful as 'talent spotters' with respect to the 1940 group, not least due to their early retirements, with the exception of Sir John Dill, who promoted the career of Arthur Percival.

This work has also shown that there was no strong case to indicate that the majority of brigadiers in 1940 owed their advancement to the 'coat tails' of the major generals and lieutenant generals that they served under in France or Norway. Five divisions in France produced no major generals or above, whereas in four others all the brigadiers advanced (including all of those who had served under Montgomery in 3rd Division, two of whom had been students of his at Staff College) – and all eight who served under Brooke's Corps command did so. A general's failure in France was also not necessarily a block on advancement as all three brigadiers subordinate to Major General Roger Evans did so, even though their commander had performed badly and attracted the opprobrium both of Brooke and Montgomery.

As nearly all the officers in the group saw active service in the First World War, it is of lesser value in determining the enhancement of the career prospects of those who were promoted against those who were not. While the majority served on the Western Front, experience on other fronts was not of itself a bar to advancement, and small networks were created of officers who served in Gallipoli and Egypt, who progressed, although most of these served on the Western Front as well. Although, as has been shown, the award of one, or more, awards for gallantry during that war did have an impact on promotion prospects up to and after 1940, accelerated promotion during the war did not, as in the case of Archibald Beauman, who took 15 years to return to the temporary rank he had held in 1919. Only four of the officers promoted beyond brigadier after 1940 saw no service on the Western Front from 1914–1919.

Attendance at the Staff College – predominantly at Camberley, less so at Quetta – was influential in advancement; as noted above, there are grounds to support French's contention on Brooke and Montgomery 'talent spotting'; 21 from 36 officers who were promoted later in the war had been pupils under them between 1923–1927. The largest envelope of connected officers was between 1924–1926, with a total of 24 officers overlapping between their times in junior and senior years, although similar, smaller groups were created and similarly formed from 1927–1929; the numbers declined after 1929, but Ritchie and Dempsey were contemporaries albeit in separate divisions in 1931, while Dempsey and Horrocks were also in 1932. Attendance at the Imperial Defence College, in respect to the 1940 group, would prove in retrospect to be a guarantee of promotion beyond brigadier as all nine in the 1940 group carried on to major general or beyond. It produced three pairs of direct contemporaries also. Brooke would feature again, training four of the nine when an instructor from 1932 to 1934.

Overseas service between the world wars attached to other Commonwealth armies or to staff postings provided opportunities for officers to distinguish themselves when compared with their contemporaries. This was especially so when promotion prospects at home were log jammed by the combination of a lack of promotion prospects engendered by the seniority system, and a general lack of opportunities for active service. In the interwar period, over half the officers in the 1940 group as a whole served overseas at some point, with several serving in multiple areas. The single largest group served in India, both in staff postings and on active service on the North-West Frontier. However, the very size of India and the variety of posts and locations these officers served in during the period does not make it a decisive generator of an advantage for post-1940 promotion. Yet it did produce a number of groups of contemporaries whose service overlapped in respect of time spent in India, if not in precisely similar locations. In purely percentage terms, the most 'successful' area in which to serve was Palestine after 1936, with five out of the seven officers present there advancing in rank. All of these officers served in staff postings. Palestine was a rare example of active service due to the pre-war Arab Revolt of 1936–1939; it was also an opportunity to come to the attention of Montgomery and Dill, who held senior field commands in the region. However, in other areas, such as Iraq, China and Malaya, there were few informal networks and fewer opportunities to be seen by senior officers who could exert positive influence on their post-1940 careers.

Although some officers with overseas postings who were subsequently promoted after 1940 did not attend Staff College, the majority of them were graduates of Camberley or Quetta, making this a significant combination. Serving in multiple overseas postings from 1919–1939 was not decisive as a network or to enhance promotion prospects with the disparity of regions served in and less than half of the officers who did so advancing.

Of the 58 officers of the 1940 group who progressed in the course of the Second World War, 21, or 38 percent of the whole group, reached the rank of lieutenant general before 1945. The average age among this group in 1940, was 46.8 years, below the overall average of both the whole group which stood at 49.2 years, and of the overall advancing group, at 47.8. Of these 21 officers, only two had not attended Staff College (none of whom attended Quetta). Four had been contemporaries graduating in 1924; three in 1925 and two in 1928. Eight had been taught at Staff College by Brooke or Montgomery. Three were contemporary graduates of the IDC in 1935. All were products of the public schools. Only one of the 21 had not been decorated for gallantry in the First World War. Fifteen of the 21 would be decorated again for their services in 1940. Twelve saw overseas service in the period between 1919–1939.

With the 37 major generals, their average age in 1940 of 48.3 was higher than that of lieutenant generals: just below the whole group but higher than the average for the whole group of progressing officers. Fifteen of them did not graduate from Staff College; of the 22 who did, four attended Quetta. Three of the Camberley graduates did so in 1922; three in 1924; two in 1925 and two in 1927, making seven taught by Montgomery or Brooke. Two were contemporaries at Quetta in 1927. Two graduated from the IDC in 1934, with three passing out there in 1935. Only two of the group of 37 had not been educated at public school. 35 of the 37 had been decorated before 1939. 16 would receive further awards for their service in 1940, more in total, but fewer in proportion to the size of the sub-group. 30 of the 37 had seen overseas service between 1919–1939.

By 1944, veterans of the First World War were much less well represented among the brigadiers in fighting commands in the initial stages of the Battle of Normandy than among their 1940 counterparts. Over half of the 45 officers involved had not seen service between 1914–1918, mostly on the grounds of age, although some had been commissioned before the end of the First World War but did not see action. This meant that the average age of brigadiers in 1944 fell to 42.4; a contribution to this drop was made by the existence of war-raised specialist formations, such as airborne and commando brigades, which had attracted younger, more dynamic candidates. However, the rejuvenation was not completely due to the drop in average age; the replacement of battlefield casualties – a phenomenon less marked in 1940 – by younger, junior subordinates also contributed to this. The process was not universal; two brigade commanders, one infantry, one armoured, were under 40 years old on D-Day itself. Conversely, the eldest brigadier to land on D-Day was 50 years old – 6 years older than his divisional commander. In the distribution of ages of Normandy brigadiers, however, the number aged 46 on 6 June 1944 (thus born in 1898, and notionally old enough to have served in the First World War) equals that of officers aged 35 to 40. This indicates that rejuvenation of officers at this level was not a uniform phenomenon and, taken as a whole, brigade commanders in 1944 were in their mid-forties – not greatly distant from their 1940 counterparts.

Not all the brigade commanders landing in France had combat experience prior to the Second World War. This was either through being too young to serve in the First World War or through not having had the opportunity to serve either as attached service or on Imperial policing duties, such as on the North-West Frontier of India or pacifying risings in the Near and Middle East. Eight officers served on campaign in India at various points in the 1920s and 30s; four served in staff positions there, three of whom did not see fighting. Three officers served on attachment in Africa, but also saw no action. Three officers in the group served during the Arab Revolt in Palestine, 1936–1939. It cannot be asserted that active service overseas from 1919–1939 was therefore a major contributor to advancement by 1944.

An examination of the number of Normandy brigadiers also indicates that even though shorter wartime courses were instituted after 1939 to train officers in staff duties, the number of fully qualified p.s.c. officers among the brigade commanders was markedly reduced, with less than a third of the group being so. Some divisions landing on D-Day had only half of their fighting commanders so qualified, whereas one division landing in the follow-on forces, 11th Armoured had no p.s.c. officers at all in its fighting commanders. Another, 49th (West Riding) Division – had only its commander, Evelyn Barker – who had served in France in 1940, with those post-nominals. The officers who did attend Camberley or Quetta were less fortunate in their connection to officers who may have been patrons later in their careers than those who served when Montgomery and Brooke were instructing.

The aversion evident towards Territorial officers in brigade command was overcome to a degree by 1944; three officers in the Normandy group came from a Territorial Army background, two of whom had commanded battalions and other formations, usually brigades, which had an at least notionally Territorial lineage and composition in North Africa, Tunisia and Italy. (The influx of conscripts of all ranks during the course of the war meant that formations coming from the Territorial tradition were often Territorial in name only.) This suggests that the prejudice towards Territorial officers holding operational command above battalion level had, in part, been overcome by mid-1944. None, however, commanded Regular Army formations.

As to education and schooling, while a smaller group than both the 1940 grouping as a whole and the smaller group of officers advancing, the proportion of alumni of public schools actually increased. Although the educational background of 8 of the 45 could not be definitively identified, 35 of the remaining 37, came from public schools. There was some change among the schools represented, with five schools which produced no 1940 brigadiers (such as Ampleforth) generating at least one Normandy officer. Additionally, Eton was not the single highest producer officers this time; it was overtaken by Wellington College, with 8 of the 45. However, there is some commonality among the schools which produced the most officers in both the 1940 and 1944 groups, with Eton, Wellington, Cheltenham, Rugby and Marlborough dominant. This further indicates the weakening, across the Second World War, of the Bowman/Connelly dominance of a group of public schools before the First World War. There is also a weakening in the degree of contemporaneousness between those attending the same schools, with fewer officers being direct contemporaries.

Also, in 1944 there is no predominance of schools supplying to particular regiments, even though four of Eton's five officers were initially commissioned into Guards Regiments, thereby sustaining the label of 'Eton and the Guards' even if some officers transferred to other, war-raised units in the course of the war. Additionally, in Normandy, officers were 'to arm appropriate' – infantry commanding infantry, armour commanding armour – unlike 1940 when some officers originally commissioned as gunners or sappers held commands outside their speciality.

The 1944 group also demonstrates that accelerated promotion by virtue of active service was a genuine phenomenon; while most of the group were majors (either acting or substantive) in 1940, and therefore advanced four ranks in four years – one noteworthy officer went from lieutenant to brigadier. The possession of a decoration for gallantry or distinguished service was again an influencing factor in advancement; 37 of the 45 possessed them. 16 of these 37 were also Staff College graduates.

In summation, the variation in the notional paradigm of a brigade commander in the British Army both at the beginning of the Second World War who would advance in rank before its end, and those in 1944 commanding fighting formations in the advance to victory in North-West Europe is not as great as may be popularly assumed. He would be an alumnus of a public school in the Clarendon Group or Headmasters' Conference; in his mid-forties, preferably a graduate of the Staff College, in possession of one or more decorations for gallantry and/or distinguished service and with some overseas experience – whether active or on the staff – between 1919 and 1939. Patronage, or identification, by a senior officer, most commonly Brooke or Montgomery but also Dill, was no hindrance to progression, but neither did it offer guarantees of it. Although the nature of an operational commander did alter during the Second World War, certain consistent threads from before it endured. Transformation of the officer corps between the period of defeat in 1940 and the beginning of the road to victory in the spring of 1944 did occur, but not as radically as might be presumed.

# Bibliography

## Archives

**The National Archives, Kew**
*Record Classes*
CAB 101
CAB 106
FO 371
PMG 4
PMG 74
WO 32
WO 95
WO 166
WO 167
WO 168
WO 171
WO 197
WO 198
WO 106
WO 107
WO 208
WO 256
WO 277
WO 279

**British Library, India Office Records**
IOR/L/MIL/17/5/4073-5

**Liddell Hart Centre for Military Archives, King's College London**
*Personal Papers*
Anderson, K. A. N. Correspondence with Liddell Hart
Barker, E. H. Correspondence with Liddell Hart
Beauman, A. B. Correspondence with Liddell Hart

Beckwith-Smith, M. B. Correspondence with Liddell Hart
Bissett, F. W. L. Correspondence with Liddell Hart
Davidson, F. H. N. Diaries and Papers, 1935–1944
Fraser, The Hon. W. Papers (Selective)
Gale, H. M. Papers (Selective)
Greenslade, C. 1940 document in Lindsell Papers
Irwin, N. M. S. Correspondence with Liddell Hart
Norman, C. W. Papers 1914–65

**Imperial War Museum**
Banks, D. Papers
Beauman, A. B. WW1 papers
Cass, E. E. Papers
Fox-Pitt, W. A. F. L. Photograph album
Halstead, J. G. Papers
Hudson. C. E. Draft unpublished memoir
Laurie, Sir John WW1 papers
Morgan, W. D. Sound interview
Roupell, G. R. P. Papers
Shepherd, J. O. WW1 papers
Stopford, M. G. N. Diary, 1932–1935
Whitehead, The Hon J. G. N. Papers

**National Army Museum**
Woolner, C. G. Papers

**Nottinghamshire Record Office**
Whitaker, J. A. C. Papers

**University of Manchester John Rylands Library,**
Auchinleck, Field Marshal Sir C. J. E. Papers

**Government Publications and Legislation**
Army Order 160 of July 1908
Territorial and Reserve Forces Act 1907 (7 Edw. 7, c.9)
The London Gazette (Supplement) 9 July 1940, pp.4243–4269
The London Gazette (3rd Supplement to the edition of 23 July 1940), 26 July 1940, pp.4579–4586
War Office, *Staff College (Camberley) Regulations* (London: HMSO 1930)
War Office, *Field Service Regulations 1935 Operations*, Volume 2 (London: HMSO, 1935)

**Staff College, Camberley (Admission).**
Hansard HC Deb 16 February 1926 vol. 191 c1697

**Staff Colleges (Camberley and Quetta).**
HC Deb 10 March 1925 vol. 181 cc1104-5

## Published Books

'A.W.M.' (Ed.), *British Universities and the War: A Record and Its Meaning* (Boston: Houghton Mifflin Co,1917)
Aggett, W., *The Bloody Eleventh: The Devonshire Regiment*, Vol. III 1915–1969 (Exeter: Devon & Dorset Regiment, 1995)
Alexander, Field Marshal Lord, *The Alexander Memoirs 1949–1945*, (Barnsley: Frontline, 2010)
Alexander, M., *The Republic in Danger: General Maurice Gamelin and the Politics of French Defence 1933–1940* (Cambridge: CUP, 2003)
Allen, L., *Burma: The Longest War* (London: Dent & Sons, 1986)
Anonymous, *The Eton Register* vol. VII, 1899–1909 (Eton: Spottiswoode, Ballantyne and Co. 1922)
Anonymous, *University of London War List, containing names of Appointed and Recognised Teachers, Graduates and Matriculated Students who have served or who are serving in His Majesty's Armed Forces, 1914–1918* (London: University of London Press, 1918)
Anonymous, *Historical Records of the Queen's Own Cameron Highlanders*, volume V and volume VI, 1932–1948 (Edinburgh: Blackwood, 1952)
Astley, J. B. and Wilkinson, P., *Gubbins and SOE* (Barnsley: Pen and Sword, 2010)
Atkin, R. *Pillar of Fire: Dunkirk 1940* (London: Sidgwick and Jackson, 1990)
Badsey, S., *Doctrine and Reform in the British Cavalry, 1880–1918*, Wolverhampton Military Studies Series (Aldershot: Ashgate, 2008)
Barclay, Brigadier C. N., *On Their Shoulders – British Generalship in the Lean Years 1939–1942* (London: Faber & Faber, 1964)
Barnett, C., *The Desert Generals* (London: William Kimber, 1960)
Barnett, C., *Britain and Her Army 1509–1970: A Military, Political and Social Survey* (London: Allen Lane, 1970)
Baynes, J., *Forgotten Victor: The Life of Sir Richard O'Connor*, (London, Brassey's, 1989)
Beauman, A. B., *Then a Soldier* (London: Macmillan, 1960)
Belchem, Major General D., *All in the Day's March* (London: Collins, 1978)
Blackie, J., *Bradfield 1850–1975* (Bradfield: Bradfield College, 1976)
Blaxland, G., *Destination Dunkirk – The Story of Gort's Army* (London: William Kimber, 1973)
Blaxland, G., *The Plain Cook and the Great Showman* (London: William Kimber, 1977)
Blaxland, G., *Alexander's Generals* (London: William Kimber, 1979)

Blight, Brigadier G., *History of the Royal Berkshire Regiment 1920–47* (London: Staples Press, 1953)
Bond, B., *The Victorian Army and the Staff College, 1854–1914* (London: Methuen, 1972)
Bond, B. (Ed.), *Chief of Staff – The Diaries of Lt Gen Sir Henry Pownall*, Volume 1: 1933–1940 (Hamden Connecticut: Archon, 1973)
Bond, B., *British Military Policy Between the two World Wars* (Oxford: Clarendon, 1980)
Bond, B., *Britain, France & Belgium 1939–1945* (London: Brassey's, 2nd edition 1990)
Bond, B. (Ed.), *Fallen Stars – Eleven Studies of 20th Century Military Disasters* (London: Brassey's, 1991)
Bond, B. and Taylor, M., *France and Flanders: Sixty Years On* (Barnsley: Pen and Sword, 2001)
Bowman, T. & Connelly M., *The Edwardian Army – Recruiting, Training and Deploying the British Army 1902–14* (Oxford: OUP, 2012)
Brice, Christopher, *The Thinking Man's Soldier: The Life and Career of Sir Henry Brackenbury 1837–1914* (Solihull: Helion & Co, 2012)
Broad, R., *The Radical General – Sir Ronald Adam and Britain's New Model Army, 1941–46* (Stroud; Spellmount, 2013)
Brownrigg, General Sir D., *Unexpected (A Book of Memories)* (London, Hutchison, 1942)
Buckley, J., *Monty's Men* (London, Yale UP 2013)
Butler, E. and Selby-Bradford, J., *Keep the Memory Green: The Story of Dunkirk* (London, Hutchison, 2nd edition 1955)
Butler, E., *Mason-Mac: The Life of Sir Noel Mason-Macfarlane* (London: Macmillan, 1972)
Carey, G. V. (Ed.), *The War Roll of the University of Cambridge* (Cambridge: CUP, 1921)
Carton de Wiart, A., *Happy Odyssey* (Barnsley: Pen and Sword, 2007)
Clark, D., *Cede Nullis – A Personal History of the 1940 Normandy Campaign (*Bishop Auckland: Pentland Press, 2000)
Clayton, A., *The British Officer* (London: Routledge 2007)
Carver, R. M. P., *Out of Step: Memoirs of a Field Marshal* (London: Hutchison 1989)
Colville, J., *Gort: Man, of Valour* (London: Collins, 1972)
Connell, J., *Auchinleck* (London: Cassell, 1959)
Converse, A., *Armies of Empire: The 9th Australian and 50th British Divisions in Battle 1939–1945,* Australian Army History Series (Melbourne: CUP Australia, 2011)
Coulthard-Clark, C., *Duntroon: The Royal Military College of Australia, 1911–1986* (Sydney: Allen & Unwin, 1996)
Craig, E. S. and Gibson, W. M. (eds), *Oxford University Roll of Service* (Oxford, Clarendon Press, 1920)
Crang, J., *The British Army and People's War* (Manchester: Manchester UP, 2000)
Crowdy, T. and Bavin, S., *Donald Dean VC* (Barnsley: Pen and Sword, 2010)
Cunliffe, M., *History of the Royal Warwickshire Regiment 1919–1955* (London: Clowes & Sons 1956)
Danchev, A., *Very Special Relationship: Field Marshal Sir John Dill and the Anglo-American Alliance, 1941–44* (London: Brassey's 1986)

Danchev, A. & Todman, D. (Eds), *War Diaries 1939–1945: Field Marshal Lord Alanbrooke* (London: Weidenfeld & Nicholson, 2001)

Dawnay, Brigadier D., *The 10th Royal Hussars in the Second World War* (Aldershot: Gale & Polden 1948)

Dawson, Captain A., *Temporary Gentleman in France: Home Letters form an Officer at the Front* (London: George Putnam's 1916)

Dean, Captain C., *The Loyal Regiment* (North Lancashire) 1919–53 (RHQ: Preston 1955)

Delaney, D., *Corps Commanders – Five British and Canadian Generals at War 1939–1945* (Vancouver: UBC Press, 2011)

Derry, T. H., *The Campaign in Norway – Official History of the Second World War* (London: HMSO, 1952)

Doherty, R., Irish Generals – Irish Generals in the British Army of the Second World War (Belfast: Appletree Press, 1992)

Doherty, R., *British Armoured Divisions and their Commanders, 1939–1945* (Barnsley: Pen & Sword Military, 2013)

Ellis, Major L. F., *The Campaign in France & Flanders – Official History of the Second World War* (London: HMSO, 1953)

Farndale, General Sir M., *History of the Royal Regiment of Artillery – The Years of Defeat 1939–41* (London: Brassey's, 1996)

Fergusson, B., *The Black Watch and The King's Enemies* (London: Collins & Co., 1950)

Foster, Major R., *History of the Queen's Royal Regiment*, vol. VIII 1924–48 (Aldershot: Gale & Polden, 1953)

Fraser, Sir D., *Wars and Shadows: The Memoirs of General Sir David Fraser* (London: Penguin 2003)

French, D., *Raising Churchill's Army – The British Army & the war against Germany 1919–45* (Oxford: OUP, 2000)

French, D. & Holden Reid, B. (Eds.), *The British General Staff – Reform & Innovation 1890–1939* (London: Frank Cass, 2002)

French, D., *Military Identities – The Regimental System, the British Army & the British People c. 1870–2000* (Oxford: OUP, 2005)

Frost, J. D., *A Drop Too Many* (London: Cassell & Co., 1980)

Ferguson, N., *The Square and The Tower* (London: Allen Lane, 2017)

Godfrey, S., *British Army Communications in the Second World War* (London: Bloomsbury Academic, 2013)

Godwin-Austin, A. R., *The Staff & The Staff College* (London: Constable, 1927)

Gooch, J. (Ed.), *Decisive Campaigns of the Second World War* (Abingdon; Routledge, 1990)

Godfrey, S., *British Army Communications in the Second World War: Lifting the Fog of Battle* (Cambridge; CUP, 2013)

Gray, T. I. G., *The Imperial Defence College and Royal College of Defence Studies, 1927–1977* (Edinburgh: HMSO, 1977)

Greene, J. & Massignani, A., *Hitler Strikes North* (Barnsley: Frontline, 2013)

Hamilton, N., *Monty: The Making of a General* (London: Hamish Hamilton, 1981)
Hamilton, N., *Monty: Master of the Battlefield* (London: Hamish Hamilton, 1984)
Harman, N., *Dunkirk: The Necessary Myth* (London: Hodder & Stoughton, 1980)
Harris, J. P., *Men, Ideas and Tanks* (Manchester: MUP, 1996)
Harris, P., *The Men Who Planned the War: A Study of the Staff of the British Army on the Western Front 1914–1918* (London: Routledge 2017)
Horne, A., *To Lose A Battle* (London: Macmillan, 1969)
Hudson, C. and M., *Two Lives 1892–1992: The Memoirs of Charles Edward Hudson, VC, CB, DSO, MC* (Stroud: Spellmount,1992)
Jackson, B. & Bramall, E., *The Chiefs – The Story of the United Kingdom Chiefs of Staff* (London: Brassey's, 1992)
Jackson, J., *The Fall of France* (Oxford: OUP, 2003)
James, L., *Warrior Race: The British Experience of War from Roman Times to the Present* (London: Little, Brown, 2001)
Kadushin, C., *Introduction to Social Network Theory* (Oxford: OUP, 2004)
Kadushin, C., *Understanding Social Networks' Theories, Concepts and Findings* (Oxford: OUP, 2012)
Keegan, J. (ed.), *Churchill's Generals* (London: Abacus, 1991)
Kennedy, G. and Neilson, K., *Military Education, Past Present and Future* (Connecticut; Praeger, 2002)
Kersaudy, F., *Norway 1940* (London: Collins, 1990)
Kershaw, I., *Fateful Choices: Ten Decisions That Changed the World, 1940–1941* (London: Penguin Books, 2008)
Kinvig, C., *Percival of Singapore* (London: Brassey's, 1996)
Kirke, C., *Red Coat, Green Machine – Continuity and Change in the British Army 1700–2000* (London: Continuum, 2009)
Kynoch, J., *Norway 1940: the Forgotten Fiasco* (Shrewsbury: Airlife, 2002)
Lamb, R., *Churchill's Lions* (Stroud: Spellmount, 2007)
Langley, J. M., *Fight Another Day* (London: Jonathan Cape, 1973)
Leinster-Mackay, D. P., *The Educational World of Edward Thring: A Centenary Study* (London: Falmer Press, 1987)
Lewin, R., *Man of Armour: A Study of Lieut.-General Vyvian Pope* (London: Leo Cooper, 1976)
Lewin, R., *The Chief – Field Marshal Lord Wavell; C-in-C and Viceroy 1939–1947* (London: Hutchinson, 1980)
Lewis-Stempel, J., *Six Weeks: The Short and Gallant Life of the British Officer in the First World War* (London: Weidenfeld and Nicholson, 2010)
Liddell Hart, Captain B., *The Tanks: The History of the Royal Tank Regiment and its Antecedents*, vol. 1 1914–39 & vol. 2 1939–1945 (London: Cassell, 1959)
Longden, S., *Dunkirk: The Men They Left Behind* (London: Constable, 2008)
Lucas, M., *The Journey's End Battalion: The 9th East Surreys in the Great War* (Bradford: Pen & Sword, 2012)
Lukacs, J., *Five Days in London: May 1940* (New Haven: Yale UP, 1999)

Lynch, T., *Dunkirk 1940 – 'Whereabouts Unknown'* (Stroud: Spellmount, 2010)
Macleod, Colonel R. & Kelly, D. (eds), *Time Unguarded: The Ironside Diaries 1937–1940* (London: Constable, 1962)
McKay, S., *Dunkirk – From Disaster to Deliverance – Testimonies of The Last Survivors* (London: Aurum, 2014)
Mann, C., *British Policy & Strategy Towards Norway 1941–45* (Basingstoke: Palgrave Macmillan, 2012)
Marrinan, P., *Churchill & The Irish Marshals* (Belfast: Pretani Press, 1986)
Marshall-Cornwall Sir J., *Wars and Rumours of Wars* (London: Secker & Warburg, 1984)
Mead, R., *Churchill's Lions – A Biographical Guide to the key British Generals of World War II* (Stroud: Spellmount, 2007)
Mead, R., *The Last Great Cavalryman – the Life of Sir Richard McCreery* (Barnsley: Pen & Sword Military, 2012)
Messenger, C., *Call to Arms: The British Army 1914–1918* (London: Cassell, 2005)
Mills, Brig. G. & Nixon, Lt Col R., *Annals of the King's Royal Rifle Corps*, vol. 6, 1921–43 (London: Leo Cooper, 1971)
Montgomery, Viscount B., *Memoirs* (London: Collins, 1958)
Montgomery, Viscount B., *The Path to Leadership* (London: Collins, 1961)
Moore-Bick, C., *Playing the Game: The British Junior Officer on the Western Front 1914–1918* (Solihull: Helion & Co., 2011)
Moretz, J., *Towards a Wider War – British Strategic Decision-Making and Military Effectiveness in Scandinavia, 1939–40* (Solihull: Helion & Co., 2017)
Moretz, J., *Thinking Wisely, Planning Boldly: The Higher Education and Training of Royal Navy Officers, 1919–1939* (Solihull: Helion & Co., 2014)
More, C., *The Road to Dunkirk – The British Expeditionary Force & the battle of the Ypres-Comines Canal 1940* (Barnsley: Frontline, 2013)
Moyse-Bartlett, Lt. Col. J., *The King's African Rifles* (Aldershot: Gale & Polden, 1956)
Nalder, Major General R. W. H., *The Royal Corps of Signals: A History of its Antecedents and Development (circa 1800–1955)* (London: the Royal Signals Institution, 1958)
Nash, N. S., *Strafer Desert General – The Life & Killing of Lt Gen William Gott* (Barnsley: Pen & Sword Military, 2013)
Orr, D. and Truesdale, D., *The Rifles Are There: 1st and 2nd Battalions of the Royal Ulster Rifles* (London: Pen & Sword, 2005)
Paget, J., *The Crusading General: The Life of General Sir Bernard Paget* (Barnsley: Pen & Sword, 2008)
Panichas, G., *Promise of Greatness* (London: The John Day Company, 1968)
Parker, P., *The Old Lie: The Great War and The Public School Ethos* (London: Constable, 1987)
Pearce-Smith, K., *Adventures of an Ancient Warrior in War, Peace and Revolution* (Milford on Sea: Stone's Printers, 1984)
Prior, R., *When Britain Saved The West: The Story of 1940* (London: Yale University Press, 2015)
Richardson, General Sir C., *Flashback – A Soldier's Story* (London: William Kimber, 1985)

Rissik, D., *The DLI At War: History of the Durham Light Infantry 1939–1945* (Regimental Depot, Brancepeth Castle: the Regiment 1945)
Rolf, D., *The Bloody Road to Tunis* (London: Greenhill 2001)
Roy, R., *For Most Conspicuous Bravery: A Biography of Major-General George R. Pearkes, VC* (Vancouver: University of British Columbia Press, 2011)
Ryder, R., *Oliver Leese* (London: Hamish Hamilton, 1987)
Rhys-Jones, G., *Churchill and The Norway Campaign*
(Barnsley: Pen & Sword Military, 2008)
Robbins, S., *British Generalship during the Great War: The Military Career of Sir Henry Horne* (London: Routledge 2016)
Scott, J., *Social Network Analysis: A Handbook* (London: Sage Publishing, 3rd edition 2012)
Sebag-Montefiore, S., *Dunkirk: The Fight to the Last Man* (London: Penguin Viking, 2006)
Shrosbree, C., *Public Schools and Private Education: The Clarendon Commission, 1861–64, and the Public Schools Acts* (Manchester: MUP, 1988)
Sheffield, G., *Leadership in the Trenches: Officer-Man Relations on the Western Front* (London: Macmillan 2000)
Slim, General Sir W., *Defeat Into Victory* (London: Cassell, 1956)
Smalley, E., *The British Expeditionary Force 1939–40* (London: Palgrave Macmillan, 2015)
Smart, N., *British Strategy and Politics During the Phony War* (Westwood: Praeger, 2003)
Smart, N., *Biographical Dictionary of British Generals of the Second World War* (Barnsley: Pen & Sword Military, 2005)
Smith, C., *Singapore Burning: Heroism and Surrender in World War Two* (London: Penguin, 2006)
Smyth, Brigadier Sir J ., *Bolo Whistler: The Life of General Sir Lashmer Whistler GCB KBE DSO DL; A Study in Leadership* (London: Muller, 1967)
Spears, E., *Assignment to Catastrophe, volume 1: Prelude to Dunkirk* (New York: AA Wyn, 1955)
Spiers, E., *The Army & Society 1815–1914* (Harlow: Longman, 1980)
Spiers, E., *University Officers' Training Corps and the First World War* COMEC Occasional Paper No.4 (Council of Military Education Committees of the United Kingdom, University of Leeds, 2012)
Stewart, A., *Six of Monty's Men* (Barnsley: Pen & Sword Military, 2011)
Stewart, A., Caen Controversy: *The Battle for Sword Beach* (Solihull: Helion & Co., 2014)
Stewart, G., *Dunkirk & the fall of France* (Barnsley: Pen & Sword Military, 2008)
Stewart, Captain P., *The History of the XIIth Royal Lancers* (Oxford: OUP, 1950)
Takle, P., *The British Army in France after Dunkirk* (Barnsley: Pen & Sword Military, 2009)
Thompson, Major General J., *Dunkirk Retreat to Victory* (London: Pan, 2009)
Tombs, R. & Chabal, E. (eds), *Britain & France in Two World Wars Truth Myth & Memory* (London: Bloomsbury Academic, 2013)
Turner, E., *Gallant Gentlemen: A Portrait of the British Officer, 1660–1956* (London: Joseph 1956)

Vachell, H. A., The Hill: A Romance of Friendship (London: John Murray 1905)
Various (ed.), *Burke's Landed Gentry* (London: Burke's Ltd, various annual directories 1914–50)
Various (ed.), *Burke's Peerage* (London: Burke's Ltd, various annual directories 1914–50)
Various (ed.), *The Peerage of the United Kingdom of Great Britain and Ireland* (London: John Debrett Ltd. Various editions, 1812–2024)
Various (ed.), *Who's Who*, (Various editions. London: Baily Brothers Ltd,1849–1897. London: A. & C. Black Ltd,1897–2024)
Venn, J., *Alumni Cantabrigienses: A Biographical List of All Known Students, Graduates and Holders of Office at the University of Cambridge, from the Earliest Times to 1900*, volume 2 from 1752 to 1900 (Cambridge: CUP, 2011)
Warner, P., *Auchinleck: The Lonely Soldier* (London: Buchan and Enright, 1981)
Warner, P., *Horrocks: The General Who Led from The Front* (London: Hamish Hamilton 1984)
Wellington College, *Wellington College Register 1859–1984* (Wellington: The Old Wellingtonian, 1985)
Wilkinson, R *Gentlemanly Power: British Leadership and the Public School Tradition* (London: Oxford University Press, 1964)
Winton, H. R., *To Change an Army – Gen Sir John Burnett-Stuart and British Armoured Doctrine 1927–1938* (Lawrence: Kansas UP, 1988)
Young, Lieutenant Colonel F. W., *The Story of the Staff College 1858–1958* (Aldershot: Published for the Staff College by Gale and Polden Ltd, 1958)

## Chapters and Articles

Barnett, C., 'The Education of Military Elites' in *Journal of Contemporary History*, vol. 2(3) pp.15–35 (1967)
Bolton, P., 'Education: Historical Statistics' Standard Note SN/SG/4252, 27 November 2012 (London, House of Commons Library)
Bond, B., 'The Army Between The Two World Wars' in Bond, B., *From Liddell Hart to Joan Littlewood: Studies in British Military History* pp.84–92 (Solihull: Helion & Co., 2015)
Bond, B., 'Hore-Belisha at the War Office' in Bond, B., *From Liddell Hart to Joan Littlewood: Studies in British Military History*, pp.92–112 (Solihull: Helion & Co, 2015)
Bond, B., 'Britain's Field Force in France and Belgium 1939–40' in Bond, B., *From Liddell Hart to Joan Littlewood: Studies in British Military History*, pp.116–126 (Solihull: Helion & Co., 2015)
Bond, B., 'Hore-Belisha's Generals: Gort and Ironside' in Bond, B., *From Liddell Hart to Joan Littlewood: Studies in British Military History*, pp.128–158 (Solihull, Helion & Co., 2015)

Burrows, Lieutenant Colonel J., 'Junior Officers' Schools' in *Journal of the Royal United Services Institute*, vol. 73: No.490 (1928), pp.239–242

Caddick-Adams, P., 'Not a Popular Leader: General Sir Miles Dempsey' in *Journal of the Royal United Services Institute*, vol. 150 (5) (2005), pp.66–73

Caddick-Adams, P., 'Phoney war and Blitzkrieg: The Territorial Army in 1939–1940' in *Journal of the Royal United Services Institute*, vol. 143 (2) (1998), pp.67–74,

Connelly, M. and Miller, W. 'The BEF and the Issue of Surrender on the Western Front, 1940' in *War in History*, vol. 11 (4) (2004), pp.424–441

Delaney, D., 'A Quiet Man of Influence: General Sir John Crocker' in *Journal of the Society for Army Historical Research*, vol. 85 No.3 (2007), pp.185–207

French, D., 'Colonel Blimp and the British Army: British Divisional Commanders in the War against Germany, 1939–1945' in *The English Historical Review,* Vol. 111 (444) (1996), pp.1182–1201

French, D., "An extensive use of weedkiller': patterns of promotion in the senior ranks of the British Army 1919–1939' in French, D. and Holden Reid, B. (eds), *The British General Staff: Reform and Innovation, 1890–1939.* pp.159 – 174 (London: Frank Cass, 2002)

French, D., 'Officer Education and Training in the British Army, 1919–1939' in Kennedy, G. C. and Neilson, K. (eds), *Military Education. Past, Present and Future.* (Westport: Praeger, 2002), pp.105–128

French, D., 'Doctrine and Organization in the British Army, 1919–1932' in *The Historical Journal*, vol. 44 no.2 (2001), pp.497–515

French, D., 'Doctrine, Training and Organisation in the British Army, 1919–1940, Part 2' *Army Quarterly and Defence Journal*, vol. 127 (2) (1997), pp.195–201

French, D., 'Big Wars and Small Wars Between the Wars, 1919–1939' in: Strachan, H (ed.), *Big Wars and Small Wars. The British Army and the Lessons of War in the Twentieth Century* (Abingdon: Routledge & Co.,2006), pp.36–53

French, D., 'Invading Europe: The British Army and its Preparations for the Normandy Campaign, 1942–44' in Goldstein, E. and McKercher, B. J. C., *Power and Stability: British Foreign Policy 1865–1965* (London: Cassell & Co., 2003)

Frost, M., 'The British and Indian Army Staff Colleges in the Interwar Years' in Delaney, D., Engen, R. and Fitzpatrick, M. (eds), *Military Education in the British Empire, 1815–1949* (Vancouver, UBC Press, 2018), pp.156–157

Hamilton, N., 'Review of Sebag-Montefiore, Simon 'Dunkirk: Fight to The Last Man'' in *Journal of Military History*, vol. 71 issue 2 (2007), pp.557–559

Jackson, A., 'The Evolution of the Division in British Military History' in *Journal of the Royal United Services Institute*, vol. 152 no.6 (1997), pp.76–78

McCarty P., 'Dangerously Overexposed? – Divisional Operations on the flanks of MARKET GARDEN. September to December 1944' in Buckley, J. & Preston Hough, P., *Operation Market Garden: The Campaign for the Low Countries, Autumn 1944: Seventy Years On'* (Solihull: Helion & Co., 2014)

Murray, W., 'British Military Effectiveness 1919–1939' in Murray, W. and Millett, R. (eds), *Military Effectiveness, Vol.2: The Interwar Period* (Cambridge: CUP, 1988)

Otley, C. B., 'The Social Origins of British Army Officers' in *The Sociological Review*, vol. 18 no.2 (1970), pp.213–239

Otley, C. B., 'The Educational Background of British Army Officers' in *Sociology*, vol. 7 no.2 (1973), pp.191–209

Otley, C. B., 'Militarism and Militarization in the Public Schools, 1900–1972' in *The British Journal of Sociology*, vol. 29 no.3 (1978), pp.321–339

Percival, Major A. E., 'The West African Frontier Force' in *The Army Quarterly*, vol. XV no.1 (1927), pp.91–99

Prysor, G., 'The 'Fifth Column' and the British experience of retreat 1940' in *War in History*, vol. 12 no.4 (2005), pp.418–447

Pugsley, C., 'We Have Been Here Before; The evolution of decentralised command doctrine in the British Army 1905–89', Sandhurst Paper No.9, Royal Military Academy Sandhurst, 2011

Root, L., "Temporary Gentlemen' on the Western Front: Class Consciousness and the British Army Officer, 1914–1918', http://digitalcommons.unf.edu/ojii_volumes/72 (2006)

Sandilands, Colonel H. R., 'The Case for the Senior Officers' School' in *Journal of the Royal United Services Institute*, vol. 73 No.490 (1928), pp.235–238

Simpson, K., 'The Officers' in Beckett, I. and Simpson, K. (Eds.) *'A Nation in Arms'* (Manchester: Manchester UP), pp.85–96

Smalley, E., 'Qualified, but Unprepared: Training for War at the Staff College 1919–1939' in *The British Journal of Military History*, vol. 2, no.1 (2015), pp.55–72

Spiers, E. M., 'The Regular Army' in Beckett and Simpson (eds.), *A Nation in Arms* (Manchester, Manchester UP 1985), pp.36–61

Stevens, K., 'Duncan Force – the Shanghai Defence Force in 1927 & the Career of Captain Ronald Spear' in *Journal of the Royal Asiatic Society Hong Kong Branch*, vol. 48 (2008), pp.151–174

Summerfield, P., 'Dunkirk and the Popular Memory of Britain at War, 1940–58' in *Journal of Contemporary History*, vol. 45 no.4 (2010), pp.788–811

Wetherell, C., 'Historical Social Network Analysis' in *International Review of Social History*, vol. 43 no.2 (1998), pp.125–144

## Unpublished PhD Theses

Duncan, A. G., 'The Military Education of Junior Officers in the Edwardian Army' (University of Birmingham 2016)

Frost, M. R., 'Preparation is Key: The effect of the pre-war years on Senior Command in the British Army, 1944–45' (King's College London 2017)

Holborn, A., 'The Role of 56th (Independent) Infantry Brigade During the Normandy Campaign June-September 1944' (University of Plymouth 2009)

Peatty, J., 'British Army Manpower Crisis 1944' (King's College London, 2000)

Perry, F. W. P., 'Manpower and Organisational Problems in the Expansion of British and other Commonwealth Armies During the Two World Wars' (University of London, 1982)
Jones, A., 'Pinchbeck Regulars? The Role and Organisation of the Territorial Army, 1919–1940' (University of Oxford, 2016)
Newbold, D., 'British Planning and Preparations to Resist Invasion on Land, September 1939 – September 1940' (King's College London, 1988)

## Websites

www.findmypast.co.uk
https://www.forces-war-records.co.uk/
http://www.thepeerage.com/
www.debretts.co.uk
https://www.haileybury.com/explore/haileybury/heritage-archives/haileyburys-military-heritage
http://geneagraphie.com
http://venn.lib.cam.ac.uk/
http://www.oxforddnb.com
http://regiments.org
https://paradata.org.uk/

# Index

## Names

## Events and Places (including colleges, universities, schools, et cetera)

## *Wolverhampton Military Studies*

www.helion.co.uk/wolverhamptonmilitarystudies



### Submissions

The publishers would be pleased to receive submissions for this series. Please contact us via email (info@helion.co.uk), or in writing to Helion & Company Limited, Unit 8 Amherst Business Centre, Budbrooke Road, Warwick, CV34 5WE

### Titles

1 *Stemming the Tide. Officers and Leadership in the British Expeditionary Force 1914* Edited by Spencer Jones (ISBN 978-1-909384-45-3)

2 *'Theirs Not To Reason Why': Horsing the British Army 1875–1925* Graham Winton (ISBN 978-1-909384-48-4)

3 *A Military Transformed? Adaptation and Innovation in the British Military, 1792–1945* Edited by Michael LoCicero, Ross Mahoney and Stuart Mitchell (ISBN 978-1-909384-46-0)

4 *Get Tough Stay Tough. Shaping the Canadian Corps, 1914–1918* Kenneth Radley (ISBN 978-1-909982-86-4)

5 *A Moonlight Massacre: The Night Operation on the Passchendaele Ridge, 2 December 1917. The Forgotten Last Act of the Third Battle of Ypres* Michael LoCicero (ISBN 978-1-909982-92-5)

6 *Shellshocked Prophets. Former Anglican Army Chaplains in Interwar Britain* Linda Parker (ISBN 978-1-909982-25-3)

7 *Flight Plan Africa: Portuguese Airpower in Counterinsurgency, 1961–1974* John P. Cann (ISBN 978-1-909982-06-2)

8 *Mud, Blood and Determination. The History of the 46th (North Midland) Division in the Great War* Simon Peaple (ISBN 978 1 910294 66 6)

9 *Commanding Far Eastern Skies. A Critical Analysis of the Royal Air Force Superiority Campaign in India, Burma and Malaya 1941–1945* Peter Preston-Hough (ISBN 978 1 910294 44 4)

10 *Courage Without Glory. The British Army on the Western Front 1915* Edited by Spencer Jones (ISBN 978 1 910777 18 3)

11 *The Airborne Forces Experimental Establishment: The Development of British Airborne Technology 1940–1950* Tim Jenkins (ISBN 978-1-910777-06-0)

12 *Allies are a Tiresome Lot' – The British Army in Italy in the First World War* John Dillon (ISBN 978 1 910777 32 9)

13 *Monty's Functional Doctrine: Combined Arms Doctrine in British 21st Army Group in Northwest Europe, 1944–45* Charles Forrester (ISBN 978-1-910777-26-8)

14 *Early Modern Systems of Command: Queen Anne's Generals, Staff Officers and the Direction of Allied Warfare in the Low Countries and Germany, 1702–11* Stewart Stansfield (ISBN 978 1 910294 47 5)

15 *They Didn't Want To Die Virgins: Sex and Morale in the British Army on the Western Front 1914–1918* Bruce Cherry (ISBN 978-1-910777-70-1)

16 *From Tobruk to Tunis: The Impact of Terrain on British Operations and Doctrine in North Africa, 1940–1943* Neal Dando (ISBN 978-1-910294-00-0)

17 *Crossing No Man's Land: Experience and Learning with the Northumberland Fusiliers in the Great War* Tony Ball (ISBN 978-1-910777-73-2)

18 *"Everything worked like clockwork": The Mechanization of the British Cavalry between the Two World Wars* Roger E Salmon (ISBN 978-1-910777-96-1)

19 *Attack on the Somme: 1st Anzac Corps and the Battle of Poziéres Ridge, 1916* Meleah Hampton (ISBN 978-1-910777-65-7)

20 *Operation Market Garden: The Campaign for the Low Countries, Autumn 1944: Seventy Years On* Edited by John Buckley & Peter Preston Hough (ISBN 978 1 910777 15 2)

21 *Enduring the Whirlwind: The German Army and the Russo-German War 1941-1943* Gregory Liedtke (ISBN 978-1-910777-75-6)

22 *'Glum Heroes': Hardship, fear and death – Resilience and Coping in the British Army on the Western Front 1914–1918* Peter E. Hodgkinson (ISBN 978-1-910777-78-7)

23 *Much Embarrassed: Civil War Intelligence and the Gettysburg Campaign* George Donne (ISBN 978-1-910777-86-2)

24 *They Called It Shell Shock: Combat Stress in the First World War* Stefanie Linden (ISBN 978-1-911096-35-1)

25 *New Approaches to the Military History of the English Civil War. Proceedings of the First Helion & Company 'Century of the Soldier' Conference* Ismini Pells (editor) (ISBN 978-1-911096-44-3)

26 *Reconographers: Intelligence and Reconnaissance in British Tank Operations on the Western Front 1916-18* Colin Hardy (ISBN: 978-1-911096-28-3)

27 *Britain's Quest for Oil: The First World War and the Peace Conferences* Martin Gibson (ISBN: 978-1-911512-07-3)

28 *Unfailing Gallantry: 8th (Regular) Division in the Great War 1914–1919* Alun Thomas (ISBN: 978-1-910777-61-9)

29 *An Army of Brigadiers: British Brigade Commanders at the Battle of Arras 1917* Trevor Harvey (ISBN: 978-1-911512-00-4)

30 *At All Costs: The British Army on the Western Front 1916* Edited by Spencer Jones (ISBN 978-1-912174-88-1)

31 *The German Corpse Factory: A Study in First World War Propaganda* Stephen Badsey (ISBN 978-1-911628-27-9)

32 *Bull Run to Boer War: How the American Civil War Changed the Victorian British Army* Michael Somerville (ISBN 978-1-912866-25-0)

33 *Turret versus Broadside: An Anatomy of British Naval Prestige, Revolution and Disaster, 1860-1870* Howard J. Fuller (ISBN 978-1-913336-22-6)

34 *A Moonlight Massacre: The Night Operation on the Passchendaele Ridge, 2 December 1917. The Forgotten Last Act of the Third Battle of Ypres,* Second Edition, paperback Michael LoCicero (ISBN 978-1-911628-72-9)

35 *The Darkest Year: The British Army on the Western Front 1917* Spencer Jones (ISBN 978-1-914059-98-8)

36 *Ham & Jam. 6th Airborne Division in Normandy: Generating Combat Effectiveness, November 1942-September 1944* Andrew Wheale (ISBN 978-1-915070-85-2)

37 *Stemming the Tide. Officers and Leadership in the British Expeditionary Force 1914,* Revised Edition paperback edited by Spencer Jones (ISBN 978-1-91507-097-5)

38 *Kitchener and the Dardanelles Campaign: A Vindication* George Cassar (ISBN 978-1-915113-75-7)

39 *To Do the Work of Men: An Operational History of the 21st Division in the Great War* Derek Clayton (ISBN 978-1-804512-33-3)

40 *Botha, Smuts and the Great War* Antonio Garcia & Ian van der Wag (ISBN 9-78-19151137-7-1)

41 *Beyond the Great Silence: The Legacy of Shell Shock in Britain and Germany 1918- 1924* Stefanie Linden (ISBN 978-1-804514-30-6)

42 *The Best of All Appointments: The Evolution of Infantry Brigade Command in the British Army on the Western Front, 1915-1918* Roger Wood (ISBN 978-1-8045142-6-9)

43 *Point of Failure: British Army Brigadiers in The British Expeditionary Force and North Western Expeditionary Force, 1940. A Study of Advancement and Promotion* Philip McCarty (ISBN 978-1-804514-27-6